The IDG Books Advantage

We at IDG Books Worldwide created *MBONE: Multicasting Tomorrow's Internet* to meet your growing need for quick access to the most complete and accurate computer information available. Our books work the way you do: They focus on accomplishing specific tasks — not learning random functions. Our books are not long-winded manuals or dry reference tomes. In each book, expert authors tell you exactly what you can do with a network and how to do it. Easy to follow, step-by-step sections; comprehensive coverage; and convenient access in language and design — it's all here.

The authors of IDG books are uniquely qualified to give you expert advice as well as to provide insightful tips and techniques not found anywhere else. Our authors maintain close contact with end users through feedback from articles, training sessions, e-mail exchanges, user group participation, and consulting work. Because our authors know the realities of daily computer use and are directly tied to the reader, our books have a strategic advantage.

Our authors have the experience to approach a topic in the most efficient manner, and we know that you, the reader, will benefit from a "one-on-one" relationship with the author. Our research shows that readers make computer book purchases because they want expert advice. Because readers want to benefit from the author's experience, the author's voice is always present in an IDG book.

You will find what you need in this book whether you read it from cover to cover, section by section, or simply one topic at a time. As a computer user, you deserve a comprehensive resource of answers. We at IDG Books Worldwide are proud to deliver that resource with *MBONE: Multicasting Tomorrow's Internet*.

Brenda McLaughlin
Senior Vice President and Group Publisher

YouTellUs@idgbooks.com

MBONE: Multicasting Tomorrow's Internet

MBONE: Multicasting Tomorrow's Internet

Kevin Savetz, Neil Randall, and Yves Lepage

IDG Books WorldWide, Inc.

An International Data Group Company

Foster City, CA ✦ Chicago, IL ✦ Indianapolis, IN ✦ Braintree, MA ✦ Southlake, TX

MBONE: Multicasting Tomorrow's Internet

Published by
IDG Books Worldwide, Inc.
An International Data Group Company
919 E. Hillsdale Blvd.
Suite 400
Foster City, CA 94404

Library of Congress Catalog Card No.: 95-81949

ISBN: 1-56884-723-8

Printed in the United States of America

1B/ST/QS/ZW/IN

Distributed by Macmillan Canada for Canada; by Computer and Technical Books for the Caribbean Basin; by Contemporanea de Ediciones for Venezuela; by Distribuidora Cuspide for Argentina; by CITEC for Brazil; by Ediciones ZETA S.C.R. Ltda. for Peru; by Editorial Limusa SA for Mexico; by Transworld Publishers Limited in the United Kingdom and Europe; by Al-Maiman Publishers & Distributors for Saudi Arabia; by Simron Pty. Ltd. for South Africa; by IDG Communications (HK) Ltd. for Hong Kong; by Toppan Company Ltd. for Japan; by Addison Wesley Publishing Company for Korea; by Longman Singapore Publishers Ltd. for Singapore, Malaysia, Thailand, and Indonesia; by Unalis Corporation for Taiwan; by WS Computer Publishing Company, Inc. for the Philippines; by WoodsLane Pty. Ltd. for Australia; by WoodsLane Enterprises Ltd. for New Zealand.

For general information on IDG Books Worldwide's books in the U.S., please call our Consumer Customer Service department at 800-762-2974. For reseller information, including discounts and premium sales, please call our Reseller Customer Service department at 800-434-3422.

For information on where to purchase IDG Books Worldwide's books outside the U.S., contact IDG Books Worldwide at 415-655-3021 or fax 415-655-3295.

For information on translations, contact Marc Jeffrey Mikulich, Director, Foreign & Subsidiary Rights, at IDG Books Worldwide, 415-655-3018 or fax 415-655-3295.

For sales inquiries and special prices for bulk quantities, write to the address above or call IDG Books Worldwide at 415-655-3200.

For information on using IDG Books Worldwide's books in the classroom, or ordering examination copies, contact the Education Department at 800-434-2086 or fax 817-251-8174.

For authorization to photocopy items for corporate, personal, or educational use, please contact Copyright Clearance Center, 222 Rosewood Drive, Danvers, MA 01923, or fax 508-750-4470.

 is a trademark under exclusive license to IDG Books Worldwide, Inc., from International Data Group, Inc.

About the Authors

Kevin Savetz

Kevin Savetz (savetz@northcoast.com) is a computer technology writer specializing in the Internet, online services, and all things Macintosh. He is author of *Your Internet Consultant: the FAQs of Life Online*, and co-editor of *Internet Unleashed*. He is a regular contributor to *Internet World*, *Computer Shopper*, *Web Review* and other magazines. Kevin lives in Humboldt County, California with his wife, four kitties, three Macs, one dog, one PC, and an Atari 800, which he refuses to give up.

Neil Randall

Neil Randall (nrandall@watserv1.uwaterloo.ca) is the author or co-author of *Teach Yourself the Internet*, *The World Wide Web Unleashed*, *Using HTML*, and the forthcoming *Netscape Gold*. He is a contributing editor on Internet issues for *PC/Computing* magazine, and has also published in *PC Magazine*, *Windows*, *The Net*, *I*Way*, *Websight*, and *CD-ROM Today*. He is a professor of English at the University of Waterloo, where he conducts research into multimedia design and computer-mediated communications.

Yves Lepage

Yves Lepage (yves@cc.mcgill.ca) has worked at McGill University for over 3 years as a senior programmer. He currently runs the Canadian MBONE feed from a FreeBSD machine. A frequent MBONE user, Yves has begun porting the MBONE applications to NeXT computers. He has taught UNIX seminars at McGill University and has written articles in McGill's internal newsletter. As a senior programmer, his main tasks are to run, maintain, and enhance McGill's network services, such as e-mail, Web, gopher, ftp, IRC, manage the internal mailing lists, and provide internal UNIX support and consulting. Before working at McGill, Yves worked as a programmer, then as an analyst in the corporate world. He has a degree in Computer Science.

ABOUT IDG BOOKS WORLDWIDE

Welcome to the world of IDG Books Worldwide.

IDG Books Worldwide, Inc., is a subsidiary of International Data Group, the world's largest publisher of computer-related information and the leading global provider of information services on information technology. IDG was founded more than 25 years ago and now employs more than 7,700 people worldwide. IDG publishes more than 250 computer publications in 67 countries (see listing below). More than 70 million people read one or more IDG publications each month.

Launched in 1990, IDG Books Worldwide is today the #1 publisher of best-selling computer books in the United States. We are proud to have received 8 awards from the Computer Press Association in recognition of editorial excellence and three from Computer Currents' First Annual Readers' Choice Awards, and our best-selling ...For Dummies® series has more than 19 million copies in print with translations in 28 languages. IDG Books Worldwide, through a joint venture with IDG's Hi-Tech Beijing, became the first U.S. publisher to publish a computer book in the People's Republic of China. In record time, IDG Books Worldwide has become the first choice for millions of readers around the world who want to learn how to better manage their businesses.

Our mission is simple: Every one of our books is designed to bring extra value and skill-building instructions to the reader. Our books are written by experts who understand and care about our readers. The knowledge base of our editorial staff comes from years of experience in publishing, education, and journalism — experience which we use to produce books for the '90s. In short, we care about books, so we attract the best people. We devote special attention to details such as audience, interior design, use of icons, and illustrations. And because we use an efficient process of authoring, editing, and desktop publishing our books electronically, we can spend more time ensuring superior content and spend less time on the technicalities of making books.

You can count on our commitment to deliver high-quality books at competitive prices on topics you want to read about. At IDG Books Worldwide, we continue in the IDG tradition of delivering quality for more than 25 years. You'll find no better book on a subject than one from IDG Books Worldwide.

John J. Kilcullen

John Kilcullen
President and CEO
IDG Books Worldwide, Inc.

IDG Books Worldwide, Inc., is a subsidiary of International Data Group, the world's largest publisher of computer-related information and the leading global provider of information services on information technology. International Data Group publishes over 250 computer publications in 67 countries. Seventy million people read one or more International Data Group publications each month. International Data Group's publications include: **ARGENTINA:** Computerworld Argentina, GamePro, Infoworld, PC World Argentina; **AUSTRALIA:** Australian Macworld, Client/Server Journal, Computer Living, Computerworld, Digital News, Network World, PC World, Publishing Essentials, Reseller; **AUSTRIA:** Computerwelt, PC TEST; **BELARUS:** PC World Belarus; **BELGIUM:** Data News; **BRAZIL:** Annuário de Informática, Computerworld Brazil, Connections, Super Game Power, Macworld, PC World Brazil, Publish Brazil, SUPERGAME; **BULGARIA:** Computerworld Bulgaria, Networkworld/Bulgaria, PC & MacWorld Bulgaria; **CANADA:** CIO Canada, ComputerWorld Canada, InfoCanada, Network World Canada, Reseller World; **CHILE:** Computerworld Chile, GamePro, PC World Chile; **COLUMBIA:** Computerworld Colombia, GamePro, PC World Colombia; **COSTA RICA:** PC World Costa Rica/Nicaragua; **THE CZECH AND SLOVAK REPUBLICS:** Computerworld Czechoslovakia, Elektronika Czechoslovakia, PC World Czechoslovakia; **DENMARK:** Communications World, Computerworld Danmark, Macworld Danmark, PC World Danmark Supplements, TECH World; **DOMINICAN REPUBLIC:** PC World Republica Dominicana; **ECUADOR:** PC World Ecuador, GamePro; **EGYPT:** Computerworld Middle East, PC World Middle East; **EL SALVADOR:** PC World Centro America; **FINLAND:** MikroPC, Tietoverkko, Tietoviikko; **FRANCE:** Distributique, Golden, Info PC, Le Guide du Monde Informatique, Le Monde Informatique, Reseaux & Telecoms; **GERMANY:** Computer Business, Computerwoche, Computerwoche Extra, Computerwoche Focus, Electronic Entertainment, GamePro, I/M Information Management, Macwelt, PC Welt; **GREECE:** GamePro, Macworld & Publish; **GUATEMALA:** PC World Centro America; **HONDURAS:** PC World Centro America; **HONG KONG:** Computerworld Hong Kong, PCWorld Hong Kong, Publish in Asia; **HUNGARY:** ABCD CD-ROM, Computerworld Szamitastechnika, PC & Mac World Hungary, PC-X Magazine; **INDIA:** Computerworld India, PC World India, Publish in Asia; **INDONESIA:** InfoKomputer PC World, Komputek Computerworld, Publish in Asia; **IRELAND:** ComputerScope, PC Live!; **ISRAEL:** PC World 32 BIT, People & Computers; **ITALY:** Computerworld Italia, Computerworld Italia Special Editions, Lotus Italia, Macworld Italia, Networking Italia, PC Shopping, PC World Italia, PC World/Walt Disney; **JAPAN:** Macworld Japan, Nikkei Personal Computing, SunWorld Japan, Windows World Japan; **KENYA:** East African Computer News; **KOREA:** Hi-Tech Information/Computerworld, Macworld Korea, PC World Korea; **MACEDONIA:** PC World Macedonia; **MALAYSIA:** Computerworld Malaysia, PC World Malaysia, Publish in Asia; **MEXICO:** Computerworld Mexico, GamePro, Macworld, PC World Mexico; **MYANMAR:** PC World Myanmar; **NETHERLANDS:** Computable, Computer! Totaal, LAN Magazine, Macworld, Net Magazine; **NEW ZEALAND:** Computer Buyer, Computerworld New Zealand, MTB, Network World, PC World New Zealand; **NICARAGUA:** PC World Costa Rica/Nicaragua; **NIGERIA:** PC World Africa; **NORWAY:** Computerworld Norge, Computerworld Privat, CW Rapport Klient/Tjener, CW Rapport Nettverk & Telecom, CW Rapport Offentlig Sektor, IDG's KURSGUIDE, Macworld Norge, Multimedia World, PC World Ekspress, PC World Nettverk, PC World Norge, PC World's Produktguide, Windows Spesial; **PAKISTAN:** Computerworld Pakistan, PC World Pakistan; **PANAMA:** GamePro, PC World Panama, Electronics Today, Game Camp, PC World China, Popular Computer Week, Software World, Telecom Product World; **PERU:** Computerworld Peru, GamePro, PC World Profesional Peru, PC World Peru; **POLAND:** Computerworld Poland, Computerworld Special Report, Macworld, Networld, PC World Komputer; **PHILIPPINES:** Computerworld Philippines, PC Digest, Publish in Asia; **PORTUGAL:** Cerebro/PC World, Correio Informático/Computerworld, Mac•In/PC•In Portugal; **PUERTO RICO:** PC World Puerto Rico; **ROMANIA:** Computerworld Romania, PC World Romania, Telecom Romania; **RUSSIA:** Computerworld Rossiya, Network World Russia, PC World Russia; **SINGAPORE:** Computerworld Singapore, PC World Singapore, Publish in Asia; **SLOVENIA:** MONITOR; **SOUTH AFRICA:** Computing S.A., Network World S.A., Software World; **SPAIN:** Computerworld España, COMUNICACIONES WORLD, Dealer World, Macworld España, PC World España; **SWEDEN:** CAP&Design, Computer Sweden, Corporate Computing, MacWorld, Maxi Data, MikroDatorn, Nätverk & Kommunikation, PC/Aktiv, PC World, Windows World; **SWITZERLAND:** Computerworld Schweiz, Macworld Schweiz, PCtip; **TAIWAN:** Computerworld Taiwan, Macworld Taiwan, PC World Taiwan, Publish Taiwan, Windows World; **THAILAND:** Thai Computerworld, Publish in Asia; **TURKEY:** Computerworld Monitör, MACWORLD Turkiye, PC WORLD Turkiye; **UKRAINE:** Computerworld Kiev, Computers & Software Magazine, PC World Ukraine; **UNITED KINGDOM:** Acorn User, Amiga Action, Amiga Computing, Amiga, Appletalk, CD Powerplay, CD-ROM Now, Computing, Connexion, GamePro, Lotus Magazine, Macaction, Macworld, Open Computing, Parents and Computers, PC Home, PC Works, The WEB; **UNITED STATES:** Cable in the Classroom, CD Review, CIO Magazine, Computerworld, Computerworld Client/Server Journal, Digital Video Magazine, DOS World, Electronic InfoWorld, I-Way, Macworld, Maximize, MULTIMEDIA WORLD, Network World, PC World, PUBLISH, SWATPro Magazine, Video Event, WebMaster; **URUGUAY:** PC World Uruguay; **VENEZUELA:** Computerworld Venezuela, GamePro, PC World Venezuela; and **VIETNAM:** PC World Vietnam
10/17/95

Dedication

Dedicated to Wayne Miller (1946-1994)

"Never apologize, never explain."

— KMS

Credits

**Senior Vice President
and Group Publisher**
Brenda McLaughlin

Vice President and Publisher
Christopher J. Williams

Acquisitions Manager
Gregory Croy

Acquisitions Editor
Ellen Camm

Brand Manager
Melisa M. Duffy

Managing Editor
Andy Cummings

Editorial Assistant
Timothy Borek

Production Director
Beth Jenkins

Production Assistant
Jacalyn L. Pennywell

Supervisor of Project Coordination
Cindy L. Phipps

Supervisor of Page Layout
Kathie S. Schnorr

Supervisor of Graphics and Design
Shelley Lea

Production Systems Specialist
Steve Peake

Reprint Coordination
Tony Augsburger
Patricia R. Reynolds
Theresa Sánchez-Baker

Media/Archive Coordination
Leslie Popplewell
Melissa Stauffer
Michael Wilkey

Senior Development Editor
Erik Dafforn

Editors
Patricia Seiler
Nate Holdread
Kerrie Klein

Technical Reviewer
Larry Barr

Project Coordinator
Sherry Gomoll

Graphics Coordination
Gina Scott
Angela F. Hunckler

Production Staff
Cameron Booker
Mark Owens

Proofreaders
Henry Lazarek
Carl Saff
Robert Springer

Indexer
Sharon Hilgenberg

Cover Design
Kavish and Kavish

Acknowledgments

The authors would like to thank the following folks for their contributions to this project: Peace Gardiner (for the idea for this book), Yves Lepage (for sharing his MBONE experience), Mike Macedonia and Don Brutzman (for use of their article), Erik Dafforn and the folks at IDG (for putting up with us), Steve Casner, Henning Schulzrinne, and David M. Kristol (for their MBONE FAQ), Aaron Weiss (for letting Kevin liberate his ideas), Anders Klemets, Dave Hayes, and Piete Brooks (for their assistance and experience), Dwight Spencer (for his help in screen capturing), Jonathon Heiliger (for providing us with an mtrace output), the people at the JASON project (for their images), the people at NASA (for their images), the Saint John String Quartet (for their image), and to all the people who have worked to make the MBONE the great conferencing system that we use today.

Also, thanks to Scott Adams (for Dilbert), Tyco (for the Magic 8-Ball), and all the creative and talented people who have — and continue to — stitched together that magic thing we call the Internet.

(The publisher would like to give special thanks to Patrick J. McGovern, without whom this book would not have been possible.)

Contents at a Glance

Table of Contents

Tomorrow's Technology Today

The Internet and Multimedia

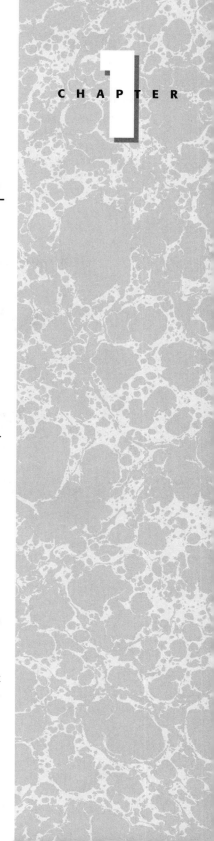

Once upon a time, not so long ago, the words *Internet* and *multimedia* were rarely mentioned in the same sentence. Although you could download GIF images or sound files from an FTP site and then view or listen to them on your PC, the Internet experience itself was far from a multimedia extravaganza. Indeed, until the advent of Mosaic and the phenomenal popularity of the World Wide Web, accessing the Internet was like reading the front page of the Wall Street Journal: lots of good information, but gray, without pictures, and dull on the eyes.

In 1993, a computer program called Mosaic changed all that. Mosaic is a browser — a program that allows users to use the Internet's World Wide Web. For the first time, true multimedia — the mixing of various media such as text, images, sounds, and movies — came to the Internet. Today, not only can you download those sorts of files, but you can also experience them while you are online. And, if you have anything to say, you can even present your information, complete with mixed media, on your own Web page.

The World Wide Web continues to grow in popularity, but most of us have limited bandwidth resources. We use poky 9600 bps and 14.4 Kbps modems to send and receive data, but in the world of full multimedia we're going to need much faster access. After all, 14.4 Kbps means 14,400 bits of information every second, and even with good data compression technology, we're lucky to hit 38,800 bits per second regularly. At these speeds, video or audio files that are more than a few minutes long can take an hour or more to transfer to a PC, so if you're waiting to see *Gone with the Wind* or hear Wagner's entire Ring cycle, forget it. Even users who are lucky enough to access the Internet with a 28.8 Kbps modem get tired of waiting for things to download.

As a result of this bottleneck, most people get only text and graphics files from the Web. Text and still image files are generally small, so you don't need to wait too long to view them, but anyone who has waited for a graphically heavy Web site, such as Time Warner's *Pathfinder* (Figure 1-1), soon realizes how frustrating even this experience can be. Although audio and animation are both possible on the Web, you need a much faster connection (or the patience of a saint) to send and receive the huge audio and video files that would enable you to take full advantage of Internet multimedia.

Figure 1-1: Time Warner's *Pathfinder* Web site — a great resource, but the images can make it slow going.

On the Internet, and typically in real life, new technologies are first available to a core group of inventors and experimenters. If the new technology is good enough, or interesting enough, or worthwhile enough, word gets out. Other folks begin to hear about the wonders of the new technology, and they want to try it. They find out what they need, and then they spend whatever time and money are necessary. Slowly, the technology gains wider and broader acceptance, with more and more people taking part, until at last it becomes so common that it's practically a household word. Consider, for example, electronic mail. Or the World Wide Web. Or the waffle iron.

What's interesting about the Internet these days is that new technologies don't get much of a experimental period. The Net had more than a decade to shake itself out, from the time of its inception in 1969 to the beginnings of its widespread use in the early 1980s. After that, especially beginning in the late 1980s, new technologies started moving from someone's brain to common use in a matter of a couple of years or even less. Mosaic, the famous World Wide Web browser, is an excellent example. First introduced in February 1993, and solely for UNIX's X Window platform, Mosaic became an important program for thousands of UNIX, Windows, and Macintosh users by the end of 1993, and it became probably the most written-about computer program in the world by the middle of 1994. If you want to invent an Internet technology today, you'd better plan to introduce it less than a year after you start working on it, or the technology will likely be out of date by the time it hits the Net.

Nevertheless, important technologies take time to develop. Sometimes, a technology is so complex that years of research are needed to get it to work at all. Other times, the technology demands so much of related technologies that only a few people in the world have the equipment necessary to even get an inkling of what the technology is about. Over the past few years, something called the *MBONE* has been making its way onto the Internet slowly and experimentally. But its use is about to increase exponentially, because even those of us who today rely on mere modems will soon have access to the technologies that are necessary to bring the MBONE into our homes and offices.

Today, "regular Internet users" are at the cusp of a new multimedia revolution. Users who are pushing the limits of a 14.4 Kbps connection can already use some cool new multimedia tools (some of which are discussed in Chapter 3). In the coming months, true multimedia will become more commonplace for "regular users" as bandwidth limitations decrease and as hackers continue to improve compression methods for stuffing more information down that thin 14.4 Kbps link. Then, too, 28.8 Kbps modems will soon be cheap enough to replace the 14.4s completely, helping to ease the data bottleneck even further.

What is bandwidth?

Throughout this book, we bandy about the word *bandwidth*. Simply, bandwidth is a measurement of how much information can be transmitted between two points in a given period of time.

If you own a modem, you are probably already familiar with bandwidth to some extent. Your modem operates at a certain maximum speed — the speed of a modem is its bandwidth. A 2400 bps modem can transmit 2,400 bits per second (bps) of information. (A *bit*, by the way, is the smallest particle of information that a computer can handle — a single digit: 1 for "on" and 0 for "off.") A 2400 bps modem can transmit and receive approximately 240 characters each second. (A *character* is a single letter, number, or punctuation mark.)

(continued)

(continued)

If you use a 2400 bps modem, you may feel that it's a bit on the sluggish side. Indeed, faster modems — modems with much greater *bandwidth* capability — are available. The authors use modems that work at 28,800 bits per second. At about 2,880 characters each second, those bad boys work 12 times faster than a 2400 bps modem.

Vanilla modems are not likely to go much faster than 28.8 Kbps (kilobits, or thousands of bits per second) because the phone system that they're designed to work with can't handle much faster data reliably. However, there are a variety of ways to move information at faster speeds. For example, a special data line called a *T-1* can move 1,544,000 bits per second. A *T-3* runs at 28 times the speed of a T-1.

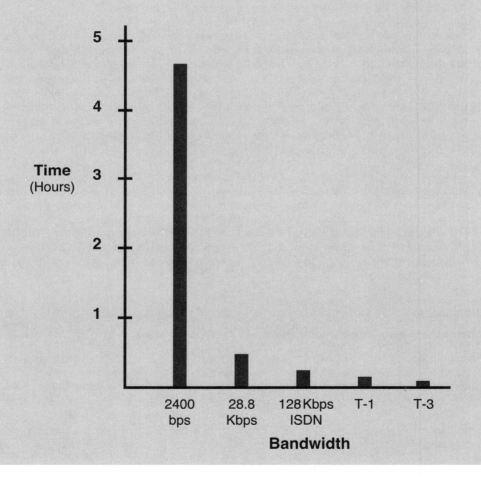

Time (Hours) vs Bandwidth

Most of us will never need the kind of band-width that a T-3 line provides, but a variety of systems can provide a happy medium of Internet bandwidth. One system, called *ISDN,* enables you to pump information around at a crisp 128 Kbps. ISDN equipment and service are more expensive than a plain old phone line and modem, but prices are dropping.

It can be hard to digest all those bits and bytes and get a clear picture of how much band-width we're really talking about. The authors sometimes use a less established measure-ment of bandwidth: *bibles per second.* Bibles per second gives us something we can readily understand: How long does it take to transmit the King James version of the Bible? Well, the text of the Bible is just under 5MB in size. A 2400 bps modem requires more than 4 ¹/₂ hours to transmit that size file. A 28.8 Kbps modem can duplicate the tome in about 23 minutes. A 128 Kbps ISDN link that's running at full tilt can do the job in 5 minutes. A T-1 line can do it in 25 seconds, a T-3 in less than a second. (The figure will give you a better idea.)

You can see why greater bandwidth is a necessary (and somewhat addictive) thing: Although most of us don't download a copy of the Bible on a daily basis, Internet users think nothing of receiving a 5MB program from an FTP site or sucking down 5MB of graphics from the World Wide Web.

Using a *bigger pipe* (more bandwidth) is one way to speed things up. Another solution is to use *compression* to reduce the size of the file that is being transmitted. Many modems include a built-in compression feature. Two similarly-equipped modems automatically compress data before sending it and then decompress it again after receiving it. As a result, more information can be transmitted more quickly. Text compresses rather well: A 5MB Bible, when compressed, requires only about 1.5MB of bandwidth. Unfortu-nately, some other types of data — such as certain graphic file formats and files that are already compressed (for example, .GIF images and .ZIP file archives) — can't be compressed much further, so your modem's compression doesn't save additional bandwidth.

Multimedia?!

But back up a second. What do we mean by *multimedia?* Loosely, *multimedia* is the blending together of more than one medium — such as text, graphics, sound, movies, smell-o-vision, whatever — on your computer. Multimedia has been around for years, of course, through movies and television, but the word *multimedia* refers almost exclusively to computer technology. For example, thousands of CD-ROMs, computer games, and educational programs offer on-screen text combined with video, music, and narration.

As an extended example of multimedia, consider the Jurassic Park and Back to the Future rides at Disney World. Here, computer technology takes multimedia two steps further. First, it hides the computer from view, and second, it incorporates the sense of touch. You feel these rides as much as you hear or see them. To a lesser degree, three-dimensional games such as Doom accomplish the same goal, although the "touch" in this case tends to be nausea.

The Internet has been home to multimedia — graphics, animation, and sound files — for years and years. But because graphics, animation, and sound files are so large, often several *megabytes* in size, they take a great deal of time (not to mention disk space) to download. For this reason, their availability has been sharply limited for regular users. Let's face it, hearing Bill Clinton's voice welcome you to the White House Web site (Figure 1-2) is mighty cute, but it's hardly worth the four-minute download time with a 14.4 Kbps modem. One possible vision of hell is being forced to listen to the Watergate hearings in their entirety through the World Wide Web and a 14.4 Kbps modem. Or the Lincoln-Douglas debates. Or, God help us, the O. J. trial.

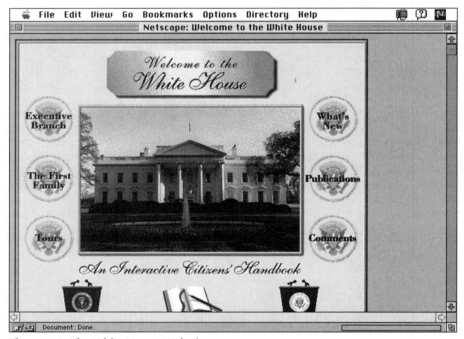

Figure 1-2: The White House Web site.

To us, *true multimedia* means, in part, being able to do all those things that you can already do, but without the interminable waiting. Multimedia is supposed to be an interactive endeavor, but for now Internet multimedia isn't interactive; it's click-and-wait. True multimedia will deliver information fast enough that you won't have time to — or want to — go for coffee while that speech is transmitted to your computer.

The intertwining of multimedia and the Internet (slowly and irrevocably) makes sense. People like multimedia on their computers. It's engaging, entertaining, and often makes otherwise complex computers a little easier to use. Certainly it works: Some multimedia educational CD-ROMs (such as Figure 1-3) are meant to be enjoyed by children who are barely old enough to walk. The Internet, once an ugly, text-only system, certainly needed some pictures, sound, and point-and-click simplicity to make it understandable to the masses.

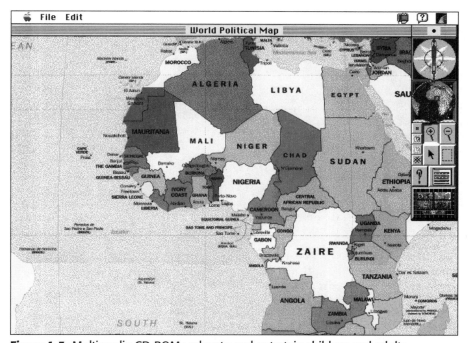

Figure 1-3: Multimedia CD-ROMs educate and entertain children and adults.

For example, a few years ago, using the Internet to find the weather forecast meant knowing how to log into a mainframe or minicomputer, remembering how to telnet to a remote computer (undoubtedly one that had an obscure, hard-to-type name), and navigating a series of text-based menus or prompts, as in Figure 1-4. You could get the forecast pretty quickly once you got good at the process, but the exercise wasn't for the faint of heart or computer shy.

Figure 1-4: Getting the weather, the old way.

Today, all you need to do to get the weather forecast is launch a World Wide Web browser and click on a "hotlist" item. Voila! You are greeted not with a lengthy description of weather trends but with a pictorial map of the weather situation, as shown in Figure 1-5. This example is only the beginning of how multimedia is changing the Internet. Consumer products and services, such as Mosaic in a Box and America Online, are making the Net still easier for all to enjoy.

Most people would agree that the advent of multimedia on the Internet is a change for the better, although longtime users (in Internet parlance, that's anyone who has been online for more than three months) may contend that the Internet's newfound ease of use is making Cyberspace a wee bit crowded for their tastes. Still, multimedia on the Internet is here to stay.

Figure 1-5: Getting the weather, the multimedia way.

Interactivity

The notion of interactivity is important, and it brings up another aspect of multimedia that doesn't get mentioned all that often — *live* multimedia. Even the fastest, prettiest, and most technologically advanced computer games and simulations take place in fabricated time, and their multimedia is packaged and programmed to take place at specific times and intervals. But the real world happens in real time, with interactions occurring constantly and things changing and adapting by the second. What about those transactions? How can they happen over a series of linked computers? How can they happen globally, over the Internet, which was designed from the beginning as an information-sharing resource, not a live communication technology? Here, too, the MBONE comes into play.

The wonders of Mosaic were first available only to users who had powerful workstations, but the Web was quickly embraced by the legions of "regular users" (dialing in from home, school, and the office) using their "regular computers" (relatively affordable PCs and Macs). Likewise, folks today who have powerful computer workstations and bandwidth to burn (say, 384 Kbps or more at their disposal) are using the hottest multimedia tools — programs that allow such marvels as real-time videoconferencing, collaboration using shared virtual "whiteboards," and media-on-demand servers.

What Is the Internet, Anyhow?

This book assumes that you are somewhat familiar with the Internet and some of the terminology that goes along with it. You don't need to be an Internet guru, or even have an Internet account. Our goal is to show seasoned Internauts and "clueless newbies" (as new users are so affectionately called) what's around the corner on the information superhighway. If you need some basic information about how the Internet works and what you can do with it, your bookstore probably has a billion different books on the subject. Two such books are *Your Internet Consultant — the FAQs of Life Online* by Kevin Savetz, and *Teach Yourself the Internet in a Week* by Neil Randall, both of which you should definitely buy in mass quantities. But just in case your bookstore isn't open at the moment, here are a few major points.

The Internet is the world's largest computer network. It's an international collection of smaller networks, computers, and the people who use them. By some estimates, as many as 25 million people have access to the Net. The commercial online services (CompuServe, America Online, Delphi, and so on) are all part of the Net. Your business's or school's computer system may be on the Net. The person sitting beside you at the doughnut store could well have an Internet account, as could that wazoo who cut you off on the freeway this morning.

Users on the Internet can exchange electronic mail with each other, copy files from computer to computer (even if those computers are thousands of miles apart), play games, access databases of information, chat it up in electronic re-creations of pubs, and lots more. In fact, folks on the Internet can use their computers to communicate in countless amazing ways — from the useful (getting live satellite images of the weather, for example) to the useless (such as finding out how many colas are left in a soft drink machine in a college dorm somewhere in Massachusetts). Some people spend many hours every day browsing the World Wide Web or reading and posting messages in newsgroups, and it's quickly becoming possible to buy everything from printers to pizzas by simply logging into your account.

Multicasting on the Internet

In its short history, the Internet has seen more than its share of revolutions. First came the revolution in global communications with e-mail and Usenet. After that, FTP and Gopher revolutionized information sharing. In the past few years, the World Wide Web has revolutionized the presentation of information. Governments, magazines, television networks, businesses, and any number of other organizations are turning to the Web as a new means of reaching their audience.

But the most significant revolution of all may well be the one that's just around the corner. The MBONE will make the Internet a hotbed of real-time multimedia communications. In essence, it will become a brand of interactive boardroom, classroom, television, cinema, video game, and edutainment of the kind only dreamed of in the hype about the information superhighway (Figure 1-6). The MBONE will make it possible, eventually, for all of us to start our own Internet-based TV shows, if we want to, without so much as an FCC license or a transmitter. Or teach in an online classroom with students from ten different states. Or hold an important meeting with researchers from around the globe.

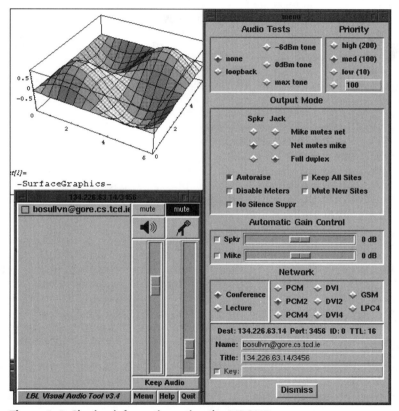

Figure 1-6: Sharing information using the MBONE.

The Internet has traditionally been built to send information to one person (or computer) at a time. The information being transmitted has a specific destination in mind, such as an e-mail message that tries to reach a specific (single) colleague. A request for a Web page is transmitted to a single host, and the host sends back the requested information to the single recipient. Although computers can handle hundreds (or thousands, or millions) of these requests every second, the information being moved around is still one-to-one: One computer is sending the information, and only one is receiving it.

This arrangement seems perfectly fine until you consider what happens when you want to send information simultaneously to more than one person. As an example, consider an e-mail message to which you've attached a graphics file. If you send that message to your friend in England, you'll chew up a certain amount of bandwidth. Now, as any seasoned Internaut knows, you can address an e-mail message to 2, 3, or 20 people at the same time. If you send this file to 20 people, you create 20 times as much Internet traffic. So if a band such as R.E.M. wanted to transmit a live concert across the Internet to 150,000 of their closest friends, well, you can easily imagine how quickly the Net would clog up.

The next generation of groundbreaking tools on the Internet will be *IP multicast* programs. MBONE (multicast backbone) programs are today's implementation of IP (Internet Protocol) multicast. IP multicast programs change the rules of the road by enabling users to "broadcast" packets of information to anyone who is "listening," rather than to a single specific individual or computer. The packets aren't sent individually to each recipient; instead, only one packet is sent, but it ends up at all the specified destinations at (more or less) the same time.

Why is that interesting? Because IP multicasting lends itself to a whole new way to publish information on the Internet. Instead of the electronic equivalent of a one-on-one chat, you use a megaphone to broadcast to everyone who cares to listen. And the people who do the listening can send something right back, not just to you, but to everyone else as well.

As the MBONE gathers steam, it promises a thorough and irrevocable shift in how the world communicates. It promises, in others words, a revolution of its very own.

You can use the MBONE to do the following:

✦ Collaborate with colleagues in real time by using a shared virtual "whiteboard"

✦ Hear and see live lectures from famous professors or scientists, and even ask them questions

✦ Listen to radio stations that "broadcast" on the Internet

✦ Start your own radio show

✦ See live pictures of spacebound NASA astronauts on the space shuttle

✦ Attend a virtual poetry reading where you hear the words in the author's own voice

✦ See and hear rehearsals of Silicon Valley garage bands

✦ Attend an Internet Engineering Task Force meeting without leaving your office

In the future, the MBONE may make it possible for you to do the following:

✦ Watch a customized version of CNN from your computer's desktop

✦ Engage 5,000 other people in a huge intercontinental computer game

✦ See reruns of "Gilligan's Island" and share your snide comments in real time with faraway friends

✦ Put your own garage band's rehearsals online for all to see (and hear)

✦ Automatically download and install authorized upgrades and bug-fixes to your computer software, without your intervention

✦ "Chat" in real time with 20 other users (as you can with Internet Relay Chat, except that you'll use your voice instead of your overworked fingers)

✦ Do plenty of other things that haven't been thought of yet

The next chapter explains IP multicasting and the MBONE more thoroughly.

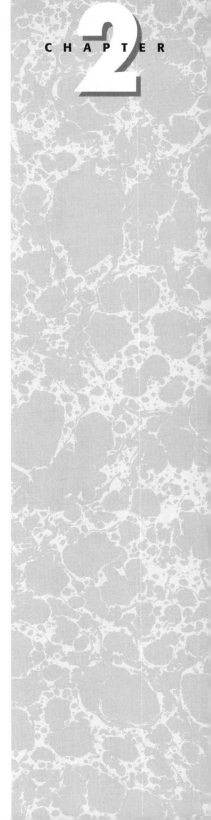

## CHAPTER 2

Today's Technology

Although some great new multimedia tools and toys will certainly be heading down the pike in the coming months and years, an impressive batch of programs that work multimedia wonders on the Internet is available today — now — this minute! The current lineup of audio and video tools works for ordinary users who dial into the Internet from home, using plain old phone lines and 14.4 Kbps modems.

This chapter examines some of today's multimedia programs. It isn't meant to be a complete roundup of what's available today, just a sampling of what's out there and what's in store. Multimedia tools for the Internet are becoming more common. Last year, you could count on one hand the multimedia Internet programs for Macs and PCs, but things are speeding up. In the first half of 1995, the number of these tools easily doubled, and the number will likely double again before the middle of 1996. It's a great time to be an Internaut, even one with a slow modem.

The Internet has been accessible in one form or another via dial-up links for many years, so why are multimedia tools for PCs just beginning to blossom? It may be that software developers are just beginning to see the light of multimedia. A bigger reason, however, is that the SLIP and PPP connections that are necessary to use these tools have become commonplace enough and (thanks to products such as Internet in a Box and Internet Chameleon) easy enough to use that the user base is large enough to warrant creating these tools.

Conferencing Tools

The Internet has always been a superb tool for conferencing, but not, unfortunately, for *real-time* conferencing. Electronic mail enables you to conference with other users, and conferencing is the very basis of Usenet newsgroups; but you can't have a real-time discussion by using e-mail or a Usenet newsgroup because the point-counter-point exchanges are separated by minutes, hours, and, sometimes, even days.

Of course, real-time communication over the Net has been available as well. Early *chat* programs, such as UNIX's *Talk* (see Figure 2-1), enable you to engage in real-time typing with another Internaut, while Internet Relay Chat, or IRC (see Figure 2-2), expands on this idea to include multiple typists all doing their thing at the same time. As anyone who has participated in *Talk* or IRC sessions can tell you, however, both experiences can be extremely disorienting. IRC sessions typically consist of reading lines of text and then trying to type something in fast enough to see it before it scrolls away. And Talk sessions, which seem like a good idea, quickly degenerate into a competition over who can type faster or better. The point is, typing was never intended as a real-time communication activity, and no amount of fancy programming can make it one.

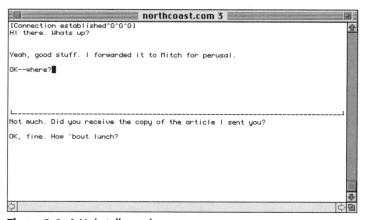

Figure 2-1: A Unix talk session.

That's why today's conferencing tools show such promise. Instead of typing, you spend your on-line time watching and listening, two activities users are far more familiar with in face-to-face or voice-to-voice communications. Significant hurdles remain, particularly in the area of access speed and bandwidth, but even now the potential for conferencing is clear.

```
▤▤▤▤▤▤▤▤▤▤▤▤▤▤  northcoast.com 3  ▤▤▤▤▤▤▤▤▤▤▤
*** (irc@gauss.elee.calpoly.edu).
*** Or try /msg Rogue_F help me please!
*** savetz (~savetz@redwood.northcoast.com) has joined channel #hottub
*** Topic for #hottub: everybody wish Xap a happy birthday!!!!!!
<sQyrm> aKasha: all cuz of a stolen nick?
* Blurry lights the Pittsburgh Steelers on fire and watches them die painfully
+and excruciatingly.
*** Te-deum has left channel #hottub
*** Signoff: bobm (Leaving)
*** Signoff: sQyrm (EOF From client)
<Akkasha> no...BAD weekend.....
<Akkasha>  VERY VERY bad...
* FastFredi huggerz hiz mom
* Blurry leaps over to Cassy and huggers her again and again until she hurts
+no more...
<Exapno>
<Vespyr> Ciao, Tigress, happy hunting!
<FastFredi> exap: yer speechless?
*** MCSAM (~Sam@Dial24.Solutions.Net) has joined channel #hottub
*** MCSAM has left channel #hottub
*** Vespyr has left channel #hottub
*** Signoff: Akkasha (it's like USELESS and stuff....bye)
[1] 14:34 savetz on *private* (+nst) * type /help for help
```

Figure 2-2: An IRC session.

Audioconferencing tools

I am not a fan of long-distance telephone companies. Their simpering television ads and pathetic bickering just grate my soul. You've probably never heard of my long-distance company. It doesn't advertise on television, its salespeople don't call you up during dinner to ask you to switch to its service, and its prices are better than prices of the big three companies. Who needs 'em? There's an even better way to annoy the phone companies — I don't use the phone at all.

If the newest crop of Internet tools is any indication, fewer and fewer Internet users may be making traditional phone calls. The early months of 1995 saw the advent of a new type of application: live voice conferencing over the Internet. Armed with the right hardware, a common modem, and special software, you can chat over the Internet in your own voice. Although the technology is relatively new, audioconferencing software has the potential to change the way people use the Internet, just as the World Wide Web did. Dare I say it? One of these programs could be the Internet's next "killer app."

Imagine doing your regular on-line thing — maybe reading your e-mail or checking out some Web pages — when the computer signals an incoming call. You switch to your audioconferencing software, click Answer, and you're chatting in real time with your boss, your mom, or anyone else who has an Internet connection, anywhere in the world. This scenario is not a fantasy. A variety of programs exist today that can put that magic in your machine. All you need are a Mac or a PC that is running Windows or OS/2; a microphone and sound card; a SLIP or PPP Net connection; and a modem or a LAN. Amazingly, for most of these programs, a 14.4 Kbps modem can transmit intelligible voices, and 9600 bps is sometimes enough bandwidth.

I'm not suggesting that your PC and modem will replace Ma Bell anytime soon. The obvious drawback of on-line audio is that you can talk only to associates who have similarly-equipped hardware. Although millions of folks have Internet accounts, it will probably be many years before all of your friends and relatives are on the Net.

How does audioconferencing work?

Audioconferencing programs work by digitizing your speech as you talk and sending the digital data over the Internet. But there's a problem. A typical modem connection has limited bandwidth: 14.4 Kbps modems can send and receive a maximum of 1,800 bytes of noncompressible data each second. Telephone-quality speech needs 8,000 bytes per second of bandwidth. The two solutions to the problem are to get a faster modem or to compress the sound information before transmitting it. Most programs compress the audio. For example, one audio application, NetPhone, finesses the problem by compressing each second of audio into fewer than 1,300 bytes before transmitting it. At the receiving end, NetPhone uncompresses the audio and plays it out of the computer's speaker.

A variety of methods for encoding and compressing sound data are available, and as you might expect, the standards aren't necessarily very standard, yet. The quality of the audio that you can send and receive depends on the application that you're using, the speed of your computer, and the compression method that's used. In my tests, audio is understandable, albeit less clear than a phone call. Still, talking across the country or around the world for the cost of an Internet connection is kind of amazing, and easy on the wallet.

Audio quality and compression

Depending on the software that you use, talking over the Internet may be more like using CB radio than like using a telephone. In a phone conversation, you can interrupt or inject "uh-huhs," but many of today's programs allow only one person to speak at a time. This type of communication is called *half-duplex* conversation, and it means that you have to wait for the speaker to release the line before you can respond.

Even if your software provides full-duplex, real-time conversation, a short but sometimes noticeable gap occurs between when you speak and when the person to whom you're speaking hears your words. The modems themselves introduce about $1/4$ second of "latency" in the sound transmission because of the buffering, error correcting, and data compression that they do. The result is a bit like talking over an intercontinental satellite telephone link. If the time lag bothers you, you may be able to reduce this effect by turning off your modem's compression bells and whistles.

The audio quality can vary, but generally, no matter what program you use, voice quality is acceptable. Surprising to most people, if you have a good Internet connection, then the sound quality is comparable to a regular phone call. However the sound quality varies dramatically between applications. In nearly all cases, the limiting factor will not be the speed and capacity of the Internet but will depend on the local work at each end. If both parties have fast network connections, some applications provide sound quality significantly better than a regular telephone call because they use 16-bit signals rather than 8-bit signals in regular phone lines.

Audio compression introduces distortions into the sound that are made worse by the lousy speakers that are built into most computers. If the speaker in your computer doesn't sound good enough, try using headphones. They eliminate the worst of the distortion by bringing the source of the sound closer to your ear. Compression causes audio to lose intensity in important frequencies, but the loss is less noticeable when the source of the sound is closer to your ear.

CVSD (continuous variable slope deltamodulation) is a compression method that isn't very CPU intensive, but it provides a respectable 8:1 compression ratio. CVSD-encoded voices are understandable but not terribly crisp. Another encoding type, *GSM* (which stands for *Global System for Mobile telecommunications*) requires faster computers on the sending and receiving ends, but the quality is quite a bit better than with CVSD. In fact, GSM at a sampling rate of 6 kHz (6,000 sound samples per second) is clearer than CVSD at 12 kHz (12,000 samples per second).

Other encoding methods include *raw* or *linear* encoding, which uses one byte per sample without compression, and *Intel DVI,* which is a common standard that does some compression (about 2:1).

The protocol that everyone is waiting for is *RTP (real time protocol).* RTP is a standard that is being created by the people who created vat, which is the UNIX audioconferencing tool that started it all. So far, the developers of audioconferencing programs have been working in isolation. RTP is emerging as an elegant protocol that can provide better interoperability to bridge the gap between the many audio tools that don't currently talk to one another.

Maven

Maven (see Figure 2-3) was the first Internet audioconferencing tool for Macintosh. Maven is free software, but it is a bandwidth hog. Maven requires a minimum of 13 Kbps. Maven can talk to other Macs that are running Maven, as well as to the UNIX vat program.

Maven was the first real-time Internet audio program to work on an affordable home computer. According to Charley Kline, the programmer who started the Maven project, "Maven started out as a challenge to me when I heard at the Audio-Video Transport (AVT) working group at the Internet Engineering Task Force (IETF) meeting a couple years ago that the 'only serious platform' for multimedia network conferencing was a high-end UNIX workstation. I knew that the Macintosh had better audio processing ability than a Sun (true!) and set about to write a little 'toy' that would interoperate with the existing UNIX conferencing tools. Within a few weeks, I had something demonstrable."

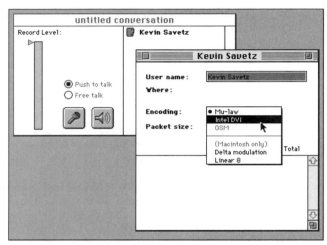

Figure 2-3: Maven.

According to Kline, Maven "sort of escaped to the Internet" when a friend passed the program around on the *Global Schoolhouse,* a network of K–12 schools that uses Internet videoconferencing tools. "Before I knew it, I had a phone call from the National Science Foundation asking if I would be interested in continuing work on Maven under a grant." The rest, as they say, is history.

Maven is a free program that you can get via FTP in `k12.cnidr.org :/pub/Mac/`.

For more information, join the Maven e-mail discussion list. To subscribe, send e-mail to `listserv@cnidr.org` with a message body of `subscribe maven Your Name`.

NetPhone
NetPhone, like Maven, gives an Internet-connected Macintosh the ability to do audioconferencing (see Figure 2-4). But NetPhone has the upper hand over Maven because it works over slower connections. It works reliably using only a 14.4 Kbps modem. At a sampling rate of 10,000 samples per second, the sound quality isn't wonderful, but the voices of my NetPhone compatriots are certainly understandable. NetPhone shines because it can handle various sound encoding methods, and sampling rates from 4,000 to 16,000 samples a second. All you need is a Mac, a microphone, and a SLIP or PPP connection. You can use NetPhone to talk to users of NetPhone and Maven, as well as to users of any program that uses the UNIX vat protocol. Sadly, Netphone is not available for Windows, so you're limited to talking to Mac and UNIX people. (A version for Windows may be available by the time you read these words.)

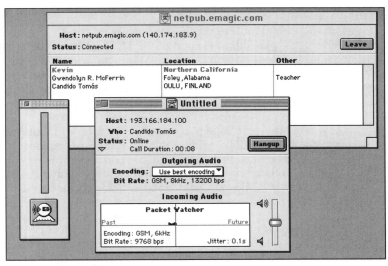

Figure 2-4: NetPhone.

NetPhone requires a Mac LC or faster computer. It is a commercial program that costs $75 per copy or $125 for two copies. NetPhone certainly won't be the only program on the Mac to follow in Maven's footsteps, but it's a great program nonetheless, especially if you're not lucky enough to be connected to a high-speed network.

You can try a free demo version of NetPhone that limits calls to 90 seconds. For information, send e-mail to `netphone-orders@emagic.com` or visit NetPhone's Web page at `http://www.emagic.com/`.

Speek Freely

Speak Freely, available for Windows and UNIX systems, is free and one of the best applications available. It offers many advanced features such as voice mail, multicasting, encryption, and usually offers excellent sound quality. Its GSM compression routine requires a high-end 486 or Pentium processor. It will work for 14.4 Kbps modems with GSM, but sound quality is degraded. The current version is not compatible with other software except for Speak Freely for UNIX. Complete source code is available.

For information, visit the Web page `http://www.fourmilab.ch/netfone/windows/speak_freely.html`.

Internet Phone

Internet Phone is a $69 voice communications program for Windows 3.1 or higher. It requires a 33 MHz 486 or faster machine, Winsock 1.1, and a 14.4 Kbps modem over SLIP or PPP. The Internet Phone software uses a proprietary compression algorithm, so it won't talk to other programs. Internet Phone runs on top of Internet Relay Chat, providing you with a list of on-line users and topics of conversation; so should you be inclined, you can easily find perfect strangers to talk with.

In mid-1995, a new version of Internet Phone was released that added full-duplex capabilities. What full-duplexing means, from the standpoint of audioconferencing, is that both users can speak at the same time. Because telephone conversations obviously work this way, full-duplexing software is important if audioconferencing is to catch on; and Internet Phone (which has become extremely popular among Windows users) will almost certainly help it to do so. In order to use the full-duplex version, you need either an audio board that will support this technology or two separate audio boards, one for receiving sound and one for transmitting it. Given the pure hell of configuring peripherals for PCs, most of us will experience the joys of full-duplexed conversations only when audio boards that support full-duplexing become commonplace.

For more information, see the Vocaltec Web page at `http://www.vocaltec.com/` or send e-mail to `info@vocaltec.com`. The software is available via FTP from `ftp.vocaltec.com` in the `/pub` directory.

Internet Global Phone

Unlike the other audioconferencing programs mentioned in this chapter, Internet Global Phone is not a clean, ready-to-use application. In fact, it is very much a work in progress. Internet Global Phone (IGP) is a technology demonstration project that provides a code platform for two-way, real-time voice exchange over the Internet. The details of the project are documented in an article in *Dr. Dobb's Journal* in December 1994. If you like hacking in Microsoft Visual C++, you too can hack on Internet Global Phone.

"The state of the software is currently an engine without a user interface. The voice digitalization, compression/decompression, and transmission mechanisms are built-in and functional, but the user interface is simplistic," according to Sing Li of microWonders, codeveloper of the program. "Users and programmers are encouraged to add their own user interface and functions to this base code; essentially constructing their own phone," he said.

Internet Global Phone is based on the GSM compression standard. To run IGP (after you compile it), you need an Internet connection, a Windows-supported PC soundboard, and a microphone. A 20 MHz 386 or faster machine is recommended for best performance, as is a 14.4 Kbps modem link.

You can get the source code via FTP from `ftp.cs.tu-berlin.de:/pub/local/kbs/tubmik/gsm/ddj`. You can find a newer, ready-to-run version on CICA or any mirror under the `win3/demos` directory. Get the file IGP8_102.ZIP for 8-bit sound cards, IG16_102.ZIP for 16-bit sound cards, and IGS_102.ZIP for the source code. The version numbers will certainly change by the time you get there. That's the price of progress.

More to come? Certainly

In the coming months, more companies will help Internauts to reach out and touch someone. The future will certainly bring more audio tools and features, limited only by imagination. Some audioconferencing tools already provide a sort of digital answering machine to answer your digital telephone when you're not online. Others provide encryption. What about the ability to have a conference call of three or more people? How long will it take for anonymous Internet phone sex services to be available? Will people really use Internet telephones for long-distance calling on a regular basis? Will the long-distance companies wither away, or will they revel in the increased bandwidth that they'll be able to sell to the Internet Service Providers?

For updated information on Internet audioconferencing software, get the FAQ "How can I use the Internet as a telephone?" from the World Wide Web at `http://www.northcoast.com/~savetz/voice-faq.html`. Or you can receive it via electronic mail by sending a message to `voice-faq-request@northcoast.com` with a subject of `archive` and a body of `send voice-faq`.

A videoconferencing tool

If you really want to push the limit of your modem, you might try playing with CU-SeeMe, a videoconferencing program. CU-SeeMe sends and receives video in real time, enabling you to see the people you're chatting with onscreen. It doesn't work well for two-way communication using anything less than 56 Kbps, but those of us without a fast link can still be voyeurs by watching well-connected netizens wave to each other in blocky, slowly-moving windows. OK, so it's not perfect, but it is an interesting start.

Currently, video images over CU-SeeMe are black and white, using a very low frame rate (1 – 2 frames per second is typical). As faster links to the Internet become more commonplace, performance and video quality will improve.

CU-SeeMe consists of a client program (available for the Mac and Microsoft Windows) and a server-like component called a *reflector*. CU-SeeMe's person-to-person connections for video phone calls provide real-time interactive video and voice communication over the Internet. When several users connect to a reflector rather than directly to another CU-SeeMe user, group videoconferencing is possible. Figure 2-5 shows the basics of reflector technology.

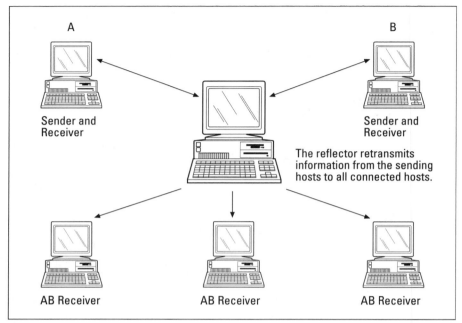

Figure 2-5: How a reflector works.

Reflectors simulate multicasting by sending audio and video signals to multiple Internet sites at the same time. A reflector acts as a mirror. CU-SeeMe users can connect to the reflector and bounce their AV signal off the reflector; other users can connect to the reflector and receive the signal or signals being reflected. This system works well as long as only a few users are sending video signals and only a few are receiving them. Unlike with multicasting, reflectors must send out a stream of IP packets for each user who wants to receive the signal; so running a reflector requires a tremendous amount of bandwidth. Similarly, although you may be able to receive one low-quality video signal with a 14.4 modem, a five-person videoconference requires five times the bandwidth, too much for most of us. Sending your own picture into the ether requires yet more bandwidth.

CU-SeeMe is available as free software and will work with just about any video capturing hardware. According to Tim Dorcey, a CU-SeeMe senior developer, "one of the central objectives in developing CU-SeeMe was to make it available to the widest possible range of users, under the belief that the value of a communication technology is in large part determined by the number of people with access to it."

When the time comes that regular users have enough bandwidth to send *and* receive video, you'll still need a video camera to beam your mug into Cyberspace. Luckily, cheap hardware is already available. A company named Connectix has a gadget called the QuickCam, a $99 black-and-white snowball-size job that works with CU-SeeMe. Word has it that a color version will be available by the time you read this. QuickCams are available for Windows and Macintosh.

Another product, LogiTech's VideoMan, is even cooler (although a bit more pricey at $399). It's a sound and full-color video capture card for Windows. Besides working with CU-SeeMe, the VideoMan can do CD-quality audio and 30 frames-per-second video, and it includes its own digital camera.

CU-SeeMe was developed at Cornell University, where it has grown from a simple experiment into the de facto standard for Internet videoconferencing. The Cu-SeeMe development team began work on desktop videoconferencing in 1993. In May 1995, Cornell selected White Pine Software to enhance CU-SeeMe and create a commercial version of the program.

The CU-SeeMe development team is preparing a new version with a slide projector and a plug-in interface to support externally developed function modules, such as on-screen chat windows.

CU-SeeMe has been used for more than simple talking-heads style videoconferencing. Other "broadcast" events with Cu-SeeMe have included speeches, lectures, and even a kitschy low-budget comedy flick. On June 3, 1995, a film called *Party Girl* made Internet history as the first full-length movie broadcast on the Internet with CU-SeeMe. The one-time Net showing of the black-and-white flick coincided with its premiere at the Seattle International Film Festival.

Information about the film and its Internet debut is available at `http://www.polis.com/firstlook/party/default.html`. Information about the Seattle International Film Festival is available at `http://www.film.com`.

Unlike with audioconferencing software, CU-SeeMe is the only choice available for Internet videoconferencing. When the masses have faster modems and higher-bandwidth connections, other software options will certainly appear. For now, though, CU-SeeMe is in a class of its own and does a fine job.

For more information about CU-SeeMe, point your Web browser to `http://www.wpine.com/cuseeme.html` or subscribe to one of the CU-SeeMe mailing lists. CU-SeeMe-L is for discussion of the program. To subscribe, send e-mail to `listserv@cornell.edu` with a message body of `subscribe cu-seeme-L <first name> <last name>`. CU-SeeMe-Announce-L is a low-volume mailing list dedicated to announcements about the CU-SeeMe software. To subscribe, send e-mail to `listserv@cornell.edu` with a message body of `subscribe cu-seeme-announce-L <first name> <last name>`.

To obtain CU-SeeMe for Windows, use anonymous FTP to `cu-seeme.cornell.edu` in the directory `/pub/video/PC.CU-SeeMe W0.xxx`. Download the ReadMe file from that directory in text mode and the CUSEEME.ZIP file in binary mode.

To obtain CU-SeeMe for the Macintosh, use anonymous FTP to `cuseeme.cornell.edu` in the directory `pub/video/Mac.CU-SeeMe0.xxx`. Download the ReadMe file from that directory in text mode. Read it and obtain the other files you need.

Collaboration Tools

Today, the Internet can provide more than the equivalent of the telephone and videophone. Using so-called collaboration tools, two or more people separated by any distance (for example, a department, a task force, or just two authors working on a book) can share ideas, outlines, art, text, and other information in real time.

Collaboration tools often work with the metaphor of a *shared whiteboard,* an area on each user's computer screen that can be written to, erased, drawn upon, or scribbled upon. Imagine a meeting in a boardroom with a large chalkboard or one of those nifty white-boards that you write on with colored pens. Collaboration tools put the whiteboard on each participant's screen, enabling all of the participants to create outlines, diagram ideas — and even play Pictionary — without schlepping to the same physical location.

Some collaboration tools provide public and private chat windows and shared text editing fields, and some even enable participants to vote on issues. Some collaboration tools provide a *WYSIWIS* (what-you-see-is-what-I-see) feature, which allows a moderator to run other applications on his computer and have the moderator's screen be mirrored on each of the participants' computers.

NCSA (the National Center for Supercomputing Applications, the same folks who brought you Mosaic) has created a program called *Collage* for the analysis and sharing of scientific data. Collage's functions include image display and analysis, color table editing, and spreadsheet display of floating-point numbers.

For more information on Collage, see `http://www.ncsa.uiuc.edu/SDG/Software/Brochure/Overview/MacCollage.overview.html`.

Another collaboration tool, Co-Motion Lite, focuses on group idea generation, annotation, evaluation, and issue resolution. Co-Motion Lite is commercial software. For more information, contact Bittco at `bittco@ccinet.ab.ca` or by phone at 403-922-5514 or fax at 403-922-2859.

Because most collaboration tools transmit text and line art rather than bandwidth-intensive data, you can use these tools reliably with Internet connections of 9600 bps or even slower. Coupled with a traditional conference call for voice communication, collaboration tools can be a useful way to share information and ideas, even if you can't share the same office.

Radio

Because audio works better than video on modem connections, when Internauts try broadcasting on the Internet, the most-successful experiments involve audio broadcasting — Internet radio.

Note

As I write this section, my computer is blaring a song by Sunfish, a Canadian band that I've never heard of before. I downloaded the tune from Virtual Radio (`http://www.microserve.net/vradio`), an online warehouse of, well, bands that I've never heard of. The song, "Difference," is online in it's entirety. It's about 2MB, and it took several minutes to download, but it was definitely worth the wait. It has a beat; you can dance to it.

Yes indeed, there's music on the Net. Another Web site offers news and commentary from National Public Radio's "Morning Edition" show. Yet another site houses an impressive collection of music from California garage bands.

Sound on the Internet is in its infancy. Standards are still being hashed out, and no "killer apps" are available for audio (yet). But as the Internet takes its slow course toward being the source for 500 channels of multimedia superhighway mayhem, the ability to transmit sound is becoming essential. Today's experiments with audio on the Net are a great first step. They provide interesting content, and they work on almost any computer that can play audio. However, the technology still has hurdles to overcome. Most notably, the sound quality of most of these services is low, scratchy, and low fidelity. Despite the emerging press releases and corporate propaganda, don't believe that the current uses of sound on the Net are anything more than experiments.

Still, it's fun to be on the cutting edge, listening to songs from bands that I didn't know existed.

Today's audio on the Internet loosely falls into two categories:

✦ Traditional broadcasters (such as National Public Radio and the American Broadcasting Company), who are looking to the Internet for added exposure

✦ A new kind of Internet-only broadcaster (such as the Internet Underground Music Archive), who is looking to the Net for the only realistic chance at a widespread audience

Both categories are interesting for different reasons. The traditional broadcasters know very well that the Net threatens to grab the attention of their listeners (and is, therefore, a threat), and they're actively looking for ways to use the new medium to enhance the old. A wide range of radio stations now offer Web sites that advertise their programming, make programs available as downloadable files, and point to the home pages of local and regional musicians whose music they feature.

For the Internet-only broadcasters, the challenge lies in getting people to tune in beyond the first try. They depend completely on listeners' bookmarking their sites and returning to them, and thus they have a much harder task than the traditional broadcasters. On the other hand, Internet-only radio is ultracool, and Internet-savvy bands are beginning to make their music available on the Net. Similarly, Internet-savvy listeners are tuning in, and as access becomes faster, broadcasting on the Internet could very well change the way that people experience radio.

Internet Talk Radio

Internet Talk Radio (ITR) was one of the first well-known experiments in "broadcasting" on the Internet. Actually, ITR doesn't do broadcasting — or even multicasting. It publishes audio files that you can download and then listen to on your computer. A typical half-hour radio show consumes a whopping 15MB of disk space.

Carl Malamud is the founder of ITR. "The idea for ITR came from my frustration with the trade press. I knew they weren't providing the information I wanted, and [I] was looking for an alternative." He noted that the trade press focuses on marketing and reviews, leaving a gap for a general-interest, technically-oriented publication for Internet users. "I couldn't start a magazine, because it takes money to print and distribute a magazine," he said. Malamud turned to the Internet as a general-purpose distribution method.

Some Net users have criticized the talk radio concept as a grandiose waste of network bandwidth, given the fact that the same information in text format could fit into only a few kilobytes. "The reason that you get audio information from a $3,000 (or $30,000) computer," Malamud said, "is because ultimately this gives you a very new medium. We're not trying to replace radio, just as the trucks didn't replace the railroads and the telephone didn't replace the telegraph. There are things we can do that you can't do on a radio, like go interactive or add WAIS databases to support a program, or make an audio-on-demand server."

Internet Talk Radio began in 1993, and although it was innovative, it seems to have fallen by the wayside. It has been surpassed by newer technologies (some of which we examine later in this chapter), and Malamud has moved on to newer avenues of Internet multimedia.

Note

For more information on Internet Talk radio, visit `http://www.town.hall.org/radio/index.html`.

RealAudio

Fast forward to 1995, when a company called Progressive Networks created a program called the RealAudio player, software that deals with the biggest shortcoming of Internet Talk Radio — those huge time-sucking, hard-disk-eating audio files. Instead of making you download a complete audio file prior to listening, RealAudio uses audio *streaming:* It plays the sound as it downloads. Its audio-on-demand technology reduces the wait to hear a program to just a few seconds. Because RealAudio uses strong audio compression, you can listen to audio by using only a 14.4 Kbps modem. So you don't need to wait to download 15MB to hear a radio program. With RealAudio, you can (theoretically) listen to "live" broadcasts, such as sports events and news as it breaks.

The RealAudio software (see Figure 2-6) runs on Windows, Macintosh, and UNIX. The RealAudio Player is free, and it works from within your Web Browser. When you click on a RealAudio file, the Player launches and begins to play. Progressive Networks is lining up traditional broadcasters, including National Public Radio and ABC, to provide material for RealAudio. Net notables including former MTV veejay Adam Curry. Radio Canada and C-SPAN are using RealAudio to publishing information, and certainly more broadcasters will be announced.

Figure 2-6: RealAudio player.

The RealAudio player presents the listener with a set of stop, play, rewind, and fast-forward buttons. Unlike with "real" radio, you can stop the music if you need to step away from your desk, and then pick up where you left off when you return. Even better, you can index radio shows so that you can jump straight to the material that interests you. For example, if you want to hear Radio Canada's news story on why huge chunks of ice are breaking off Antarctica, you can go directly there, skipping over the program's introduction and never hearing the feature about how sex may control the cockroach population.

RealAudio's sound quality isn't wonderful — it's something akin to AM radio — but speech is certainly understandable. Unfortunately, whether you're connected to the Internet with a 14.4 Kbps modem or a T-1 line, RealAudio sounds the same. It's too bad that higher bandwidth doesn't bring better-quality sound. Then again, better sound is coming, according to Progressive Networks, although almost certainly not in the range of CD-quality audio files. RealAudio's true future appears to be in Internet-based talk radio; and because the Net spans the globe, this alone is reason to be excited.

Note

About five minutes before this book went to press, RealAudio 2.0 was released — the new version is said to support better-quality audio for users with faster connections.

Figure 2-7: The RealAudio Web site.

Note

For more information check out RealAudio's Web site: `http://www.realaudio.com`. (See Figure 2-7.)

National Public Radio

For years, National Pubic Radio's primary outlet for its news and features has been hundreds of public radio stations throughout the United States. Now, NPR is experimenting with using RealAudio to publish its material on the Internet. (See figure 2-8.)

Richard Dean, producer of New Media Services at National Public Radio, is excited about the benefits of publishing audio on the Internet. He notes that audio-on-demand has its benefits and drawbacks. "As a listener, it's a great thing. As a radio programmer, maybe it's not such a great thing — it disturbs the continuity of the program," he says. "Instead of pushing info at someone — that's what radio broadcasters do — you allow listeners to come get it from you."

"The biggest problem with radio is that your work is really ephemeral; it hits the ether, and it's gone. No one can hear it again, unless they go buy the tape or the transcript." Because a transcript can't capture the nuances of a news story, and audio-tapes take several days or weeks to arrive, the Internet gives NPR listeners the ability to hear — or hear again — a story at any time, when it's convenient. "This is where radio broadcasting — information providing — is going," Dean said.

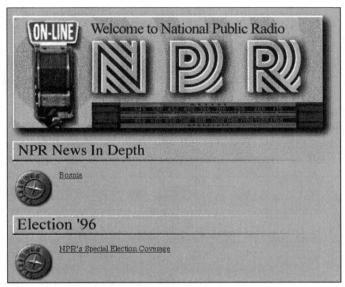

Figure 2-8: National Public Radio on the Web.

"Here's my problem with the MBONE: Nobody's on it. I think MBONE is a really neat technology, but it doesn't reach who I want to reach; it reaches a bunch of guys with UNIX boxes. With NPR, our goal is to get our content to the end user. That end user is using a dial-up Internet account," he said. RealAudio technology may not be the ultimate in Internet multimedia, but for NPR, it's the best of the technologies available today. "I look at things two ways — one is what's now, what can I do today, and then, where is the technology going?"

As faster connections become available to the masses, "the MBONE will become something more important than it is right now. But I need to reach listeners now, not in years." He equates today's audio technology to the hand-crank phone: "It may not be the right solution in the long run, but in the short run it is." People don't want to wait. When the technology reaches the next level, you jump to the next level.

Note

For more information about NPR and its Internet broadcasts, point your Web browser to http://www.npr.org/NPR.

Dean says that one of the drawbacks of RealAudio is that the sound quality is the same no matter the speed of your Internet connection. RealAudio sounds like an AM radio whether you're using a 14.4 Kbps or a T-1 connection to your desk, unlike with an emerging protocol, MPEG-2 streaming. In contrast, if you have the hardware and software necessary to handle MPEG-2 streaming and you have plenty of bandwidth to spare, you can hear audio with excellent quality. If you don't have the speed, you can increase the compression — dialing up less quality for less bandwidth.

Another issue for National Public Radio has to do not with technology but with copyright law. Currently, NPR needs to edit the musical "bumpers" from the Internet broadcasts. Although NPR can legally play songs (or portions of songs) on the air by virtue of paying ASCAP and BMI fees, the music organizations don't yet dole out on-line broadcast rights. It's still unclear how these organizations, who traditionally get paid based on the broadcast range of radio stations, will charge on-line broadcasters. Should a radio station pay royalties based on a potential on-line audience of 30 million? Or can tracking software be developed so that stations can tell exactly who is tuning in to e-broadcasts and when they are tuning into them?

Small college radio stations are experimenting by broadcasting their signals live on the Internet (Figure 2-9). What they're doing may be illegal (at least according to the music clearinghouses ASCAP and BMI), but these stations are pushing the envelope of what can be done and pushing us to contemplate these issues sooner rather than later.

Dean says this reflects a fundamental change in how radio broadcasters must think about their function. His advice to radio stations entering the Internet realm is to "Think of yourself as an information provider, not a radio station." To avoid obsolescence, today's broadcasters need to care about the information they're providing rather than about the medium itself. If the railroads realized that they were in the transportation business, they would be airlines today.

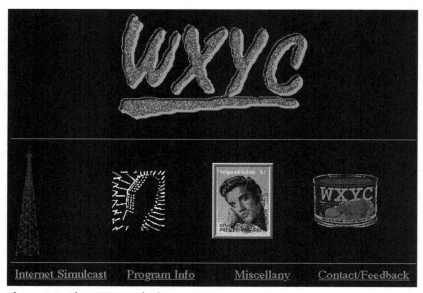

Figure 2-9: The WXYC Web site.

Like everyone else who is hawking wares on the infobahn, NPR needs to make money. NPR uses underwriting sponsorships and sells products (T-shirts, mugs, and the like) online.

Traditionally, NPR gets money from member stations, who in turn solicit funds from their listeners. If NPR and other broadcasters-turned-Internet-multimedia-info-pushers want to stay in the black, the rules of where the money comes from must shift. Today, NPR's on-line audio is free to the listener. "In several years, it might not be free to the end user," Dean said. "But there is no model yet. The price will have to be something incredibly low. The on-demand audience is skyrocketing. The money may not be there, but the audience is, and the money will follow."

The same technology that enables NPR to publish information on the Net enables anyone else — J. Random Hacker — to create an on-line cyberstation. Could these basement stations create competition for traditional broadcasters who are trying to find a home on the Internet? Certainly. "Competition is a good thing. It only makes what we are going to be doing better," Dean said.

Voice of America

For more than 50 years, the Voice of America has earned the reputation of providing up-to-the-minute, accurate, and balanced news and features, as well as music and other entertainment, to its international audience. Competing with nearly 125 broadcast services worldwide, VOA is one of the top three international broadcasters in today's vast global media market, along with BBC World Service and Radio Moscow. An estimated 92 million listeners around the world tune in to VOA programs in English and 46 other languages via direct medium wave (AM) and shortwave broadcasts. Millions more listen to VOA programs on local AM and FM stations around the world, giving VOA a vast and almost unequaled global reach.

And, as you might expect, VOA broadcasts on the Internet as well. Its Gopher site, `gopher.voa.gov`, offers news broadcasts in English, Spanish, Cantonese, Hungarian, Slovak, Urdu, and other languages. (See Figure 2-10.)

Voice of America doesn't use audio streaming, so as with Internet Talk Radio, you need to download a large audio file before listening in. According to the service, "These audio files are necessarily large. We have done what we could to keep them manageable, even sacrificing sound quality to some extent in an attempt to minimize their size and, consequently, the time and network bandwidth required to collect them." Downloading the audio for a ten-minute newscast through a modem can take an hour or more.

VOA's on-line audio files are encoded with Sun Microsystems' 8-bit u-law encoding at a rate of 8,000 samples per second. This format, the de facto standard for cross-platform audio files, is relatively compact and offers good sound quality. VOA's on-line news offerings are one of the most reliable and useful venues for Internet multimedia to date.

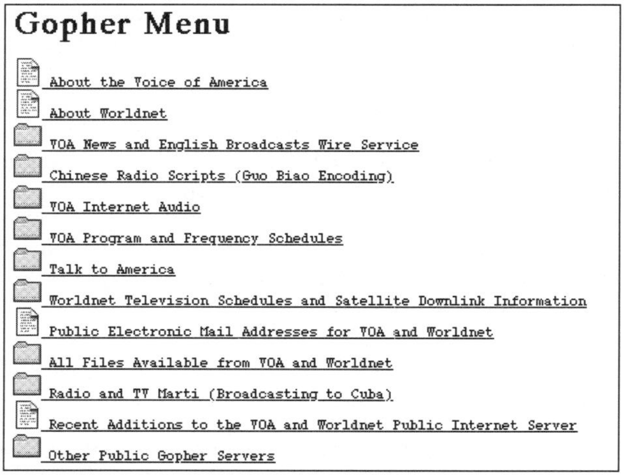

```
Gopher Menu

▢  About the Voice of America
▢  About Worldnet
▭  VOA News and English Broadcasts Wire Service
▭  Chinese Radio Scripts (Guo Biao Encoding)
▭  VOA Internet Audio
▭  VOA Program and Frequency Schedules
▭  Talk to America
▭  Worldnet Television Schedules and Satellite Downlink Information
▢  Public Electronic Mail Addresses for VOA and Worldnet
▭  All Files Available from VOA and Worldnet
▭  Radio and TV Marti (Broadcasting to Cuba)
▢  Recent Additions to the VOA and Worldnet Public Internet Server
▭  Other Public Gopher Servers
```

Figure 2-10: Voice of America.

IUMA

You can't think of the cutting edge of music on the Internet without thinking of *IUMA* — the *Internet Underground Music Archive.* Combining a unique retro WWW interface and a flair for pushing the limits of the technology, IUMA is helping to bridge the gap between tomorrow's technology and today's. (See Figures 2-11 and 2-12.)

IUMA has helped pioneer much of the multimedia that's common on the Internet today, from getting college radio stations on the Net, to live audio and video broadcasts. First and foremost, IUMA is an archive of music — it provides a forum for bands and record labels to exhibit their wares online. It also sponsors live performances on the MBONE and helps college radio stations put their signals online. Besides the increasingly common feat of putting traditional radio stations on the Internet, IUMA has done the opposite: It helped a radio station program a radio show entirely from IUMA's digital archives.

With IUMA's help, San Jose College radio station KSCU-FM broadcast a full three-hour show live and direct from the IUMA computer archive. On September 14, 1994, KSCU and IUMA played 28 songs during the show. Raji Rai, the DJ for the show, commented that the new system would revolutionize the way DJs format their shows. "Having a resource of over 300 bands, easily searchable in a graphic user interface that is constantly updated from the IUMA site headquarters and complete with full biographical information about the artists is a DJ's dream come true," she said. "It means that we can format an entire show in a fraction of the time it used to take and readily provide listeners with all the band information they could ever want." According to IUMA, "despite some last-minute technical chaos and a quick run to Circuit City, the show came off very well."

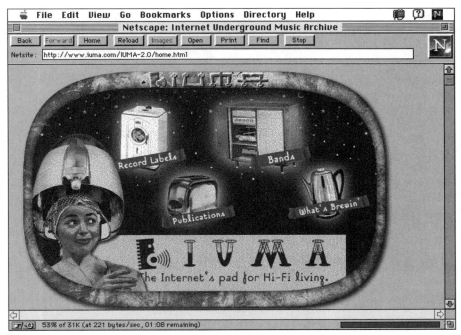

Figure 2-11: Internet Underground Music Archive.

IUMA has plans to make its archives, along with the technology of the Internet, available to college radio stations around the country. Implementation will be through a combination of CD-ROMs that contain the IUMA site and special hardware and software.

Note

See IUMA for yourself: `http://www.iuma.com`.

Virtual Radio

Virtual Radio went online in August 1994. Its goals are to provide a forum for exposure for bands and to sell music. On its face, it appears to be a lot like IUMA, providing information on bands as well as downloadable songs and song excerpts. (See Figure 2-13.)

But when it comes to making music available on the Internet, the folks at Virtual Radio take a different approach than IUMA's. "IUMA is way ahead trying to pioneer the new technology — they are really big on going for high-quality CD sound," said Brent Marcus of Virtual Radio. Of course, high-quality sound means big files to download. "We cut back on that for two reasons," Marcus said. "First is file size, and second is copyability. We don't want to give away free CD-quality music. We want people to sample the music and then buy CDs."

Figure 2-12: Crusing through IUMA.

Figure 2-13: Virtual Radio.

Virtual Radio sees its role "as an on-line promoter of bands — versus IUMA, which is a music archive," Marcus said. "To outside people, it appears much the same. Our goal is to put the radio station concept online."

Because Virtual Radio can use its World Wide Web server to track exactly how many times each song has been downloaded, it can gauge the bands and music genres that are most popular.

The administrators of Virtual Radio want it to be heard by as many people as possible, so they post music in a variety of audio formats. Since each platform — Mac, Windows, and Sun, to name a few — uses a different audio format, Virtual Radio's music is posted in a format that's native to each platform. That way, users can download and hear music quickly, without going through a time-consuming (and possibly confusing) audio conversion process. "We want to reach the most people with the least work for them," Marcus said, even at the cost of disk space and staff time to prepare the sound files.

Marcus's vision of the middle future? "In five years, it would make sense to put a whole CD-quality album on the Internet and just sell that. That would be the ultimate music format."

To see Virtual Radio for yourself, point your Web browser to `http://www.microserve.net/vradio`.

More radio on the Internet

Check the following sources for more information about radio on the Net:

✦ A list of radio stations that use the World Wide Web for broadcasting or informational purposes is accessible at `http://american.recordings.com/wwwofmusic/radio.html`.

✦ Yahoo's Index of Radio Stations on the Net is at `http://akebono.stanford.edu/yahoo/Entertainment/Radio/Stations/`.

✦ The MIT List of Radio Stations on the Internet is at `http://web.mit.edu/afs/athena.mit.edu/user/w/m/wmbr/www/otherstations.html`.

✦ WXYC. `http://sunsite.unc.edu/wxyc/`.

Electronic Mail

Even tools as pedestrian as electronic mail benefit from the addition of multimedia. Although most e-mail that is sent and received today is composed of boring ASCII text, without the interesting fonts, color characters, or formatting tools that are available in the simplest word processors, electronic mail is beginning to see a multimedia shift of its own.

MIME

Today, *MIME* (the *Multi-purpose Internet Mail Extensions* specification) enables Internet users to send e-mail that contains graphics and text and has simple layout features.

MIME is a specification that offers a way to interchange text in languages that have different character sets and exchange multimedia e-mail among various computer systems. In addition to plain old ASCII text, MIME messages can include other character sets, images and sounds, PostScript files, pointers to FTPable files, and more.

Note

For more information about MIME, read the `comp.mail.mime` FAQ, which is available on the Internet at `ftp://rtfm.mit.edu/pub/usenet-by-group/news.answers/mail/mime-faq/` and at `http://www.cis.ohio-state.edu/text/faq/usenet/mail/mime-faq/top.html`.

Not all e-mail clients can handle MIME, although an increasing number of them do. We use Eudora (for the Mac and Windows) and TCP/Connect II (for the Macintosh) for our MIME e-mail needs.

VideoMail

VideoMail is another example of how multimedia is enhancing electronic mail. This shareware program for the Macintosh makes it easy to e-mail a QuickTime movie of yourself hamming it up.

Using VideoMail, you can digitize yourself (using audio and video, or just audio, depending on the hardware attached to your Mac), enter an e-mail address, and watch VideoMail encode the multimedia message and fire it off to an associate in just a few seconds. The recipient receives e-mail with an encoded attachment — a QuickTime movie — of your face and voice. (See Figure 2-14.)

VideoMail works great for short messages, but you're likely to annoy your friends if you send them a 10-minute video of yourself with a cat on your head. As with all other multimedia, sending audio and video messages with VideoMail takes a good chunk of bandwidth — about 7 Kbps for audio only and 30 Kbps for audio and video. The program's author recommends keeping AV messages to 15 seconds or less, and audio-only messages to under 45 seconds. A 15-second VideoMail message with audio and video can take about 4 minutes to download at 14.4 Kbps. Many users would agree that although that time could be much faster, it approaches an acceptable download time for a message of that length.

VideoMail is not an end-all e-mail program. It was designed to be a simple, send-only multimedia mailer and is a fine complement to a full-featured e-mail program such as Eudora. Perhaps soon, full-featured mail programs will include the ability to capture and send audio and video without the help of a separate program such as VideoMail.

Figure 2-14: VideoMail screenshot.

For more information about VideoMail, check out `http://www.spyglass.com/~dtrinka/videomail.html`.

Multimedia mail for the masses?

Multimedia electronic mail will likely become a staple of Internet communications in the coming months — certainly sooner than real-time applications such as CU-SeeMe. Live multimedia applications such as CU-SeeMe and Internet Phone need to be able to send and receive information in real time. Should your network connection slow down below a certain limit, packets of information will arrive late or get lost. If you're participating in a videoconference, a constant stream of packets (arriving in more or less the same order in which they were created) is important. Receiving a snippet of video that should have arrived ten seconds ago makes for a conversation that is, at best, hard to follow.

But electronic mail doesn't occur in real time; it doesn't matter terribly whether the message you send is received in ten seconds or two minutes. So, with multimedia e-mail, the information can travel at a more leisurely pace than it can with real-time applications. If packets arrive out of order, they can be reassembled in sequence with no loss of continuity. When your e-mail program barks that mail has arrived, you'll receive a clear message, complete with video and audio.

Some people say that in the Internet's middle future, your service provider's charges may be based on how much information you send and how quickly you want that data to arrive, rather than on how long you're online. Under this scheme, real-time audio and video, which use a large amount of bandwidth and require fast distribution to the recipient, would be expensive. On the other hand, a multimedia e-mail message would cost less to send because although it might use the same amount of bandwidth, data could be sent at a lower priority because precise timing is not critical.

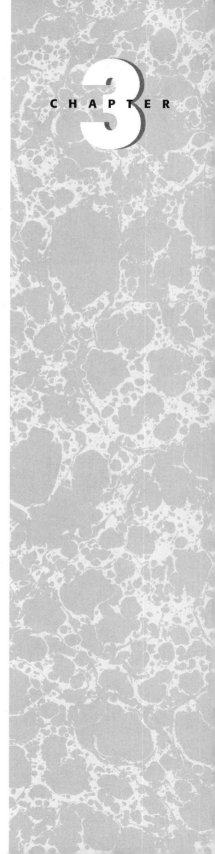

The MBONE and Multicasting

In this chapter, we take a closer look at the MBONE and multicasting: what they are, how they work, and what people are doing with them. Since we want this book to be interesting to people other than network engineers (although we have nothing against network engineers), we don't want to frighten you off. So although we endeavor to explain the concepts and background involved, we don't delve into the nitty-gritty details of multicast encapsulation, the pros and cons of reliable and unreliable datagram multicasting, or the specifics of how tunneling works. If you want to know about these scary details, you can find information about them on the Internet.

Today, the MBONE is a critical piece of the technology that's needed to make multiple-person data, voice, and video conferencing on the Internet — in fact, sharing any digital information — cheap and convenient.

Internet researcher John December says, "MBONE is truly the start of mass-communication that may supplant television. Used well, it could become an important component of mass communication."

How so? December thinks that a number of scenarios are possible: The culture of the MBONE may develop like the e-zine (electronic magazine) culture, eventually giving rise to hundreds of "channels" of programming. Some channels would be professionally produced; others would be quirky homebrew channels.

Another possibility is that organizations will adopt MBONE as a low-cost way to conduct meetings without all the expenses of telecom-equipped conference rooms. Smaller, informal organizations could use MBONE as well as large companies, because MBONE would be controlled personally, not commercially. Certainly, both of these MBONE scenarios, and others, could coexist.

What Is Multicasting?

Multicasting is a technical term that means that you can send a piece of data (a *packet*) to multiple sites at the same time. (How big a packet is depends on the protocols involved—it may range from a few bytes to a few thousand.) The usual way of moving information around the Internet is by using *unicast* protocols — tools that send packets to one site at a time.

You can think of multicasting as the Internet's version of broadcasting. A site that multicasts information is similar in many ways to a television station that broadcasts its signal. The signal originates from one source, but it can reach everyone in the station's signal area. The signal takes up some of the finite available bandwidth, and anyone who has the right equipment can tune in. The information passes on by those who don't want to catch the signal or don't have the right equipment.

On a multicast network, you can send a single packet of information from one computer for distribution to several other computers, instead of having to send that packet once for every destination. Because 5, 10, or 100 machines can receive the same packet, bandwidth is conserved. Also, when you use multicasting to send a packet, you don't need to know the address of everyone who wants to receive the multicast; instead, you simply "broadcast" it for anyone who is interested. (In addition, you can find out who is receiving the multicast — something television executives undoubtedly wish they had the capability to do.)

How Is the MBONE Different from Multicasting?

Unfortunately, the majority of the routers on the Internet today don't know how to handle multicasting. Most routers are set up to move traditional Internet Protocol (IP) *unicast* packets — information that has a single, specific destination. Although the number of routers that know how to deal with multicast are growing, those products are still in the minority.

Router manufacturers have been reluctant to create equipment that can do multicasting until there is a proven need for such equipment. But, as you might expect, it's difficult for users to try out a technology until they have a way to use it. Without the right routers, there's no multicasting. Without multicasting, there won't be the right routers. Catch-22.

In 1992, some bright fellows on the Internet Engineering Task Force (IETF) decided that what no one would do in hardware, they could do in software. So they created a "virtual network" — a network that runs on top of the Internet — and wrote software that allows multicast packets to traverse the Net. Armed with the custom software, these folks could send data to not just one Internet node, but to 2, 10, or 100 nodes. Thus, the MBONE was born.

What is a router?

A *router* is a device that connects a local area network — such as an interoffice LAN — to a wide area network — such as the Internet. The router's job is to move information between the two networks.

Most routers today are *unicast* routers: They are designed to move information from a specific place to another specific place. However, routers that include multicasting capabilities are becoming more common.

The MBONE is called a *virtual network* because it shares the same physical media — wires, routers, and other equipment — as the Internet.

The MBONE allows multicast packets to travel through routers that are set up to handle only unicast traffic. Software that utilizes the MBONE hides the multicast packets in traditional unicast packets so that unicast routers can handle the information.

The scheme of moving multicast packets by putting them in regular unicast packets is called *tunneling*. In the future, most commercial routers will support multicasting, eliminating the headaches of tunneling information through unicast routers.

When the multicast packets that are hidden in unicast packets reach a router that understands multicast packets, or a workstation that's running the right software, the packets are recognized and processed as the multicast packets they really are. Machines (workstations or routers) that are equipped to support multicast IP are called *mrouters* (multicast routers). Mrouters are either commercial routers that can handle multicasting or (more commonly) dedicated workstations running special software that works in conjunction with standard routers.

So, what's the difference between multicasting and the MBONE? *Multicasting* is a network routing facility — a method of sending packets to more than one site at a time. The *MBONE* is a loose confederation of sites that currently implement IP multicasting.

The MBONE — or *multicast backbone* — is a fancy kludge, a hack. It is at best a temporary utility that will eventually become obsolete when multicasting is a standard feature in Internet routers. By then there will be an established base of MBONE users (which should make the router manufacturers happy). The utilities and programs that work on today's MBONE will undoubtedly work on the multicast backbone of tomorrow.

Pavel Curtis, a researcher at Xerox PARC (Palo Alto Research Center) says, "I believe that IP multicast is very likely to remain an important part of the Internet for quite a long time, and that it will be the primary audio/video transmission medium on the Net."

"On the other hand," he continues, "I think that the MBONE as an identifiable subset of machines on the Net is already beginning to fade away, as more and more router and computer vendors supply IP multicast support in their products; when multicast support is ubiquitous, the MBONE ceases to be identifiable as something other than the Net as a whole."

What's on the MBONE?

Today, multicasting is used for videoconferencing, audioconferencing, shared collaborative workspaces, and more. Conference multicasts generally involve three types of media: audio, video, and a *whiteboard* — a virtual note board that participants can share.

Perhaps the most sought-after function that the MBONE provides is videoconferencing. The MBONE originated from the Internet Engineering Task Force's attempts to multicast its meetings as Internet videoconferences. MBONE video is nowhere close to television quality, but at a few frames a second, video quality is good enough for many purposes.

In the spirit of the IETF's early technically-oriented offerings, many of the MBONE events that take place are technical conferences, ranging from the SIGGraph '94 conference in Orlando, Florida, to the International Conference on High Energy Physics in Glasgow, Scotland, to the Second International Conference on Intelligent Systems for Molecular Biology from Stanford University. Users also were able to tune into the MBONE to see astronauts on the space shuttle Endeavor repairing the Hubble space telescope and panel discussions at the 1995 annual meeting of the Congress of Neurological Surgeons.

What is the IETF?

The Internet Engineering Task Force is the branch of the Internet Architecture Board that addresses the immediate technical problems and challenges of the Internet. The IETF is a voluntary committee of technical people such as network operators, engineers, and telecommunications equipment vendors.

The IETF's parent organization, the Internet Architecture Board, concerns itself with the technical challenges facing the Internet now and in the long term. Such challenges include how to effectively handle the continued burgeoning growth of the Internet, how to keep the Net operational even when each of us can pump 2 megabits per second through the fiber-optic cable that will one day be plugged into our computers, and how to help the network better handle the demands of real-time audio and video.

The MBONE's capability to carry remote audio and video makes it a wonderful tool for seminars, lectures, and other forms of "distance education." Imagine sitting in on a lecture that's being given live thousands of miles away and even asking questions or contributing to a panel discussion. According to Navy Lt. Tracey Emswiler, whose experiments with the MBONE are the basis for her master's thesis in information technology management, "Some people believe that teaching over the MBONE can't be done. We've proven that you can send regular live-broadcast lectures over the MBONE." An average of 10 to 12 universities and labs tune into each distance education lecture that is sent over the MBONE, including institutions in the United States, France, Great Britain, Japan, and Germany.

Indeed, much of what happens today on the MBONE is of a technical nature, information that most of us would find dull. However, the nerds don't get to keep the MBONE to themselves. Besides esoteric engineering events, the MBONE is home to more-exciting fare, such as multicasts of concerts, a do-it-yourself radio station, and even poetry readings.

The Seattle-based techno-ambient band Sky Cries Mary performed the first live rock concert on the MBONE, and the Rolling Stones multicasted 20 minutes of their November 18, 1994, Dallas Cotton Bowl concert as a promotion for a subsequent pay-per-view TV special.

Radio broadcasts, in part because of their lesser bandwidth requirements, have become common on the MBONE. Some examples include episodes of "The Cyberspace Report" (a public-affairs show from KUCI 88.9 FM in Irvine, California), Internet Talk Radio, and Radio Free vat.

Some MBONE users are experimenting with distributing Usenet news via the MBONE instead of with NNTP (Net News Transport Protocol). NNTP has been used to pass netnews traffic around since the early days of Usenet, but sending Usenet traffic via multicasting could significantly reduce the total amount of bandwidth used to transmit netnews. Rather than having thousands of copies of a message travel from site to site, each message could be broadcast on the MBONE only once and grabbed by each site as it passes through.

Note

For more discussion about what's on the MBONE, see Chapter 6.

How Large Is the MBONE?

Today, about 1,700 networks (in about 20 countries) are on the MBONE (see Figure 3-1), making the MBONE approximately the size that the entire Internet was in 1990. Unfortunately, there is no way to know how many people within each of the 1,700 networks can access the MBONE.

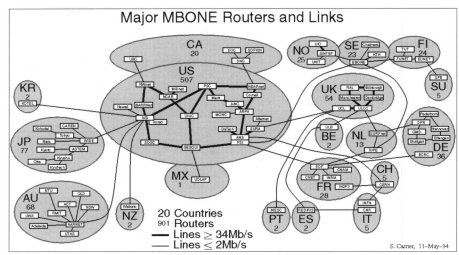

Figure 3-1: Topology of the MBONE.

The size of the MBONE, compared to the Internet as a whole, is relatively small. As of February 1995 the Internet was home to 48,500 subnetworks, so the MBONE was available on roughly 3.5 percent of the Internet.

Pavel Curtis estimates that by 1996 or 1997, multicasting will be broadly supported in routers. When that happens and upgraded routers are installed in place of unicast routers, the MBONE and the Internet will effectively be one entity. (See Figure 3-2.)

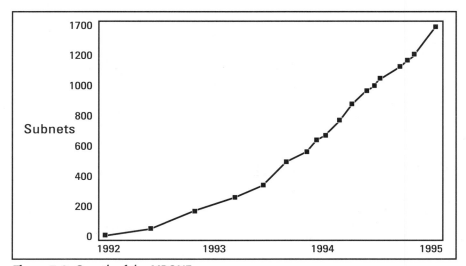

Figure 3-2: Growth of the MBONE.

Can Your Computer Handle the MBONE?

Although anyone who has the right equipment can use the MBONE, the hardware and connectivity requirements for using the MBONE are much greater than what's available on the equipment that most Internet users have in their homes. A PC or Macintosh system coupled with a standard modem doesn't have enough computing power or bandwidth to send or receive MBONE transmissions.

You need a good deal of power to handle multicast IP. Today, *multicasting software* — the behind-the-scenes tools for moving, encoding, decompressing, and manipulating multicast packets — is available only for high-end UNIX workstations, such as those from Sun, DEC, HP, IBM, and Silicon Graphics.

UNIX is a powerful, multitasking, multiuser operating system. UNIX was developed in 1969 by AT&T's Bell Laboratories, and today UNIX-based computers comprise a large portion of Internet-connected computers.

This situation is changing, however. Multicasting tools are becoming available for Linux — a free UNIX-like operating system that runs on relatively cheap IBM PC-compatible computers. Since MBONE tools can work on a Linux-based PC, it's not too much to imagine that MBONE tools will soon be available for home computers — PCs that are running Microsoft Windows and Macintosh computers. It will probably take the mostpowerful home computers (with Pentium and PowerPC chips), but it seems to be a likely eventuality. The software tools are being built: PC/TCP Version 2.3 from FTP Software Inc. supports multicasting for PCs, as does Windows 95, and it is rumored that the next version of MacTCP will support multicasting.

The ability to process multicast IP packets is one thing, but multicasting software is not much use without some multicast packets. Because the MBONE and Internet are not (yet) one and the same, before you can receive multicast packets, your network provider needs to get you hooked to the nearest MBONE node and to configure a "tunnel." This project should keep even expert network administrators busy for at least a week or two.

How Much Bandwidth Is Necessary?

Even if users had the hardware to do multicasting today, another huge hurdle would prevent the MBONE from taking over the Internet: Most users don't have enough bandwidth. A multicast video stream of 1 to 4 frames per second eats about 128 Kbps of bandwidth and gives you slow, grainy, bandwidth-hogging video. (By comparison, television-quality video scans at about 24 frames per second.)

Remember though, that a video stream uses the same bandwidth whether it is received by 1 workstation or 100.

Incidentally, 128 Kbps is about nine times the speed of a 14.4 Kbps modem. A dual-channel ISDN line can move data at 128 Kbps, so if you are one of the lucky few who have ISDN, you have barely enough bandwidth to receive multicast video. (Sending video requires another 128 Kbps, which makes using ISDN for two-way videoconferencing barely tolerable, if not impossible.) Most experts agree that in order to do multicasting effectively and get other work done, you need a T-1 or faster link to the Internet (although some users have managed to make the tools work with as little as 56 Kbps). That 128 Kbps video stream uses nearly 10 percent of a T-1 line; several simultaneous high-bandwidth sessions can easily saturate network links.

High-speed connections to the Internet can cost thousands of dollars a month. Lower-speed connections cost much less. The faster you go, the more you pay.

In their paper, "MBONE Provides Audio and Video across the Internet," authors Michael Macedonia and Donald Brutzman write, "Only a few years ago, transmitting video across the Internet was considered impossible. Development of effective multicast protocols disproved that widespread opinion. In this respect, MBONE is like the proverbial talking dog: It's not so much what the dog has to say that is amazing, it's more that the dog can talk at all!" Macedonia and Brutzman's paper is reprinted in Chapter 8.

What is ISDN?

ISDN — Integrated Services Digital Network — is a type of telephone service that enables you to get high-speed data connections through your phone line. ISDN is basically the telephone network turned completely digital, using existing wiring.

ISDN is much cheaper than many other methods of moving data at high speeds, but it is still expensive relative to a normal phone line. (Normal phone lines — the kind that work reliably with your 14.4 Kbps modem, fax, answering machine, and the *Sports Illustrated* football phone—are known in some circles a *POTS*— plain old telephone service.)

ISDN is new, but it is catching on. A major drawback to ISDN is that because it moves digital data instead of analog data, it doesn't work with your regular modem, answering machine, or football phone. You need special, expensive equipment to perform those functions at ISDN speeds.

On the bright side, ISDN is faster than a standard modem. ISDN is available in various parts of the world, including Australia, Western Europe, Japan, Singapore, France, and portions of the United States.

The World Wide Web site `http://alumni.caltech.edu:80/~dank/isdn/` is one of the best Internet resources for finding out about ISDN. For more information, check out that site.

Audio multicasts, partly because of their lesser bandwidth requirements, are more common on the MBONE than are video multicasts. Multicast audio typically uses 56 Kbps to 64 Kbps of bandwidth. (Thanks to heavy hacking and experimental compression tools, MBONE audio and interactive whiteboard traffic have been demonstrated by using as little as 9600 bps lines. These demonstrations are one indication that eventually those of us who access the Internet from home at 14.4 Kbps will be able to have some access to the MBONE.)

"For the multicast broadcasting model that the MBONE establishes to succeed as a mainstream medium, current technologies simply have to advance," writes Internet guru Aaron Weiss. MBONE services simply eat more bandwidth than most of us can afford. Before multicasting becomes commonplace, either bandwidth needs to be available more cheaply or our ability to compress bandwidth-hogging information into a limited bandwidth space needs to improve. "Network bandwidth has to fatten or audio-video compression schemes have to flatten," Weiss writes. "Presumably, both will occur, which also will require increased CPU power at the home computer level. Although it's probable that all three of these developments will take place, the time frame is not clear," he says.

Even if you could push 128 kilobits (or more) each second around the Internet affordably, it's a good bet that when enough of us could push that much data around that fast, the sheer load of all that data pulsing though the Internet would bring it to a standstill. One of the IETF's jobs is to plan for this eventuality.

"Until recently, experts believed that the MBONE could not be used for transmission of simultaneous video, audio, and data because of limited bandwidth," notes Professor Don Brutzman. "This effort to push the envelope of computing technology has provided valuable data to computer scientists and has shown that methods can be employed to work around the bandwidth problem."

There's a ceiling to the amount of information that can move around on the MBONE as a whole: 500 Mbps (million bits per second). At full tilt, the MBONE itself can handle no more than four simultaneous videoconferencing sessions or eight audio sessions.

"Although there is much to experience on the MBONE, there isn't much space for everyone. There is only about 500 Kbps of bandwidth available to the entire MBONE community at any one time. With video streams typically running at about 128 Kbps and audio streams at 64 Kbps, there is a small and finite limit on the number of simultaneous transmissions the MBONE can handle," writes Weiss.

This limited resource environment presents MBONE users with what Weiss calls "the classic sandbox scenario": sharing and playing nice. Sharing means planning multicast events in advance and scheduling them with the rest of the MBONE community to eliminate conflicts. Internet e-mail lists have been set up for announcing scheduled events.

Special multicast programs are announced on the rem-conf mailing list. To subscribe, send e-mail to `rem-conf-request@es.net` with a message body of `subscribe`.

Sometimes two planned events conflict (for example, a High Energy Physics conference conflicted with a planned IETF meeting, so the physics conference was broadcast at a later time). At times, oversight or naiveté can wreak havoc. "In mid-1994, a host in Japan was found to have been sending 650 Kbps video streams over the entire MBONE, effectively trashing it," according to Weiss. The problem, as it turned out, was caused not by malice, but by a program bug that enabled the multicast packets to escape a local network. Such unintentional flooding happens periodically and is a testament to the experimental nature of the MBONE.

Who operates the MBONE?

You may be surprised to learn that no one is actually in charge of the MBONE's topography of event scheduling. Much like the Internet itself, the MBONE's growth has been based on mutual cooperation between network service providers and users.

The MBONE community is active and open. Work on tools, protocols, standards, applications, and events is a cooperative international effort. Cooperation is essential due to limited bandwidth on many networks (for example, on intercontinental links).

How do TTLs limit the life of MBONE packets?

An infinitely loud megaphone, one that could be heard anywhere in the world, would be a bad thing: Once a few dozen of us had them, we wouldn't be able to get useful information from the din. The MBONE is no exception. Broadcast packets need to have a finite life lest they bounce around the network forever. The MBONE includes procedures for limiting how far multicast packets may travel, to prevent them from saturating the entire Internet. Each packet has a *time to live (TTL)* value, a counter that is decremented every time the packet passes through an mrouter. Because of TTLs, each multicast packet is a ticking time bomb.

If an MBONE broadcast were a TV station (as in the analogy at the beginning of this chapter), TTLs would be the station's signal area — the limitation of how far the information can travel before petering out.

Those multicasting something that's of little interest to the outside world (for example, a company board meeting) might produce a packet that had a small time to live (perhaps 10). As the packet moved around the company's internal network, its TTL would be notched down every time it passed through an mrouter. When the packet's TTL reached 0, the packet would die and not be passed further. With careful planning, those multicasting can keep their multicast packets on their internal networks or within their state or country.

Events of interest to the world at large are generally multicast with long TTLs — perhaps 200 — to guarantee that the information will reach around the world.

What Alternatives to the MBONE Are Available?

The MBONE shows promise for the future, but other tools are now available for using multimedia on the Internet. For example, CU-SeeMe is a videoconferencing tool for the Mac and PCs that works without the MBONE. CU-SeeMe uses *reflectors* — computers that provide the multipoint distribution functionality that multicasting would normally handle. Reflectors allow multiperson videoconferences without multicasting. Chapter 2 has more information on CU-SeeMe.

Multimedia on the Internet can also be handled by *streaming technology software,* which sends and receives an ongoing flow of information that can be interpreted and displayed (or heard) in real time. In this way, streaming technology software works like the MBONE; but this software does not use multicasting, and it does not require as much bandwidth as multicasting does. One example of streaming technology software is RealAudio, which is covered in Chapter 2.

John December believes that in order for MBONE and multicasting on the Internet to flourish, they must be allowed to continue their growth as they have been doing, "finding a niche from the ground up, according to the needs people have, rather than commercially introduced and presented and hyped by telecom companies." December points to the repeated failure of picture phones after more than three decades of hype by telecommunications companies. The MBONE has potential because it is controlled by the people, not by telecommunications companies.

Today, the MBONE offers users a certain degree of functionality as well as the opportunity to participate in and perhaps influence the gestation of a medium that will one day become predominant — interactive multimedia multicast communications.

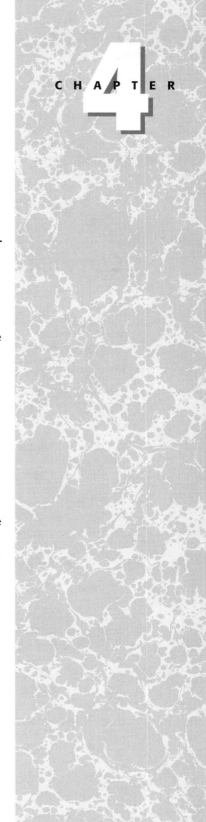

## CHAPTER 4

Where the MBONE Came From

I t's never necessary to know a technology's origins. Technologies exist to be used, and as long as you can do so, it really doesn't matter where they came from. At least, that's the practical view of things. For anyone hoping to *understand* a technology rather than just *use* it, however, origins matter a great deal. And for any technology that promises (or even threatens) to change the nature of entertainment, interaction, and communication, using it without understanding it just doesn't seem sufficient.

Does the MBONE really promise to change the nature of entertainment, interaction, and communication? Actually, it doesn't promise anything at all; nor would its inventors and developers be comfortable suggesting any such significance. But one thing we've all come to realize over the course of this century is that the most lasting technological designs often begin with very little sense of significance, whereas those designed with significance in mind often come up short — or not at all. Who knew, for instance, that the microwave oven or the videocassette recorder would find their way into practically all households in, at least, the U.S. and Canada? Who knew that the home computer would become practically ubiquitous? Who knew, for that matter, that the Internet would take off as it has? In all cases, certainly not the designers. On the other side, of course, we have the technologies that were supposed to change our lives but didn't. Quadraphonic sound. Ted Nelson's Xanadu. The Wankel rotary engine. And who knows how many more?

To say that the MBONE promises to enact change means, of course, that it holds the promise to do so. Nothing more, and nothing less. We'll look at some of that promise in Chapter 8, but for now let's examine the reasons for the MBONE's existence. By this, we're not referring to the *technological* history of the MBONE itself, at least not expressly. In this chapter, we'll look at the underpinnings of the MBONE from the standpoint of the major developments over the past decades in communications, broadcasting, and multimedia. It will be all too brief, naturally, but since its goal is to provide a *context* for the MBONE, rather than a detailed history, that brevity will serve us well.

Communications

The history of twentieth century communications begins, quite probably, in the latter part of the nineteenth century. After a series of experiments conducted by a number of people, Alexander Graham Bell put together a device that would become the telephone. Of all the technological inventions of the past 150 years, surely none has affected the course of human communications as much as this one, at least not in the nations where telephone service has become a *sine qua non* of day-to-day existence. Through this one device, businesses thrive, relationships evolve, people's lives are both made and destroyed. It is as difficult for most North Americans to imagine a world without telephones as it is for them to imagine a world without electricity. The two, it seems, go hand in hand.

Since the middle of this century, the telephone has taken on a new role. Whereas previously phone lines were relied on to transmit voice messages, they have since become the primary means for transporting digital data as well. When you log on to your Internet account and download a file from an FTP site, you are using the same telephone system you use when you call your loved ones from the other side of the continent. The difference is that the latter scenario transmits *analog* signals, and the former transmits *digital* signals. Because the phone system is an analog transport system (fiber-optics technologies are changing all this), the digital signals from your computer have to be changed into analog signals for transmission to occur. The device that does this is the *modem* (*mo*dulator-*dem*odulator), a device that has become almost as ubiquitous as personal computers themselves.

There's a problem with the combination of modems and phone lines. They aren't very fast. That is, they allow data to be transferred at a limited rate, and the 28.8 Kbps (kilobits per second) modem is approaching the analog phone system's technological limit. (Probably. But that's what they said about 2400 bps modems, too.) By compressing the data it is sending and receiving, your modem can reach an effective transmission speed of 115,000 Kbps, but in practice, this rate is rarely achieved. Even if it were, it would be too slow to handle the huge quantities of data necessary for the transmission of audio and (especially) video files, so from the standpoint of the MBONE, the modem isn't an issue. Far greater speeds are needed, along with increasingly effective data compression technologies.

But the telephone-modem combination has provided the basis for theorizing about the MBONE or any other kind of digital communications technology. With the telephone, long-distance real-time human communication became possible (*telephone* means *to speak far*), and with the modem, direct transfer of data from one machine to another, by means of the widespread global telephone system, also became possible. The main point here is that people from all over the world could communicate with each other or exchange information with each other, and they began to expect to do so more or less instantaneously. People could pick up the phone and say hello from one side of the world to the other, or they could log into their accounts and transfer files to machines every bit as far away.

Or, by using these same computers and these same phone lines, they could replace telephonic communication with computer-based communication. To do this, they used the messaging capabilities of their networked computers — electronic mail, newsgroups, or various forms of network "chat." Electronic mail and newsgroups (the latter primarily through a subnetwork called Usenet) weren't real-time communications; you composed and sent your message, then waited for the recipients to read it, compose a reply, and send it back to you.

As for network chat, which allowed real-time communications between two Internet users, or the more popular Internet Relay Chat (IRC), in which several people linked themselves together simultaneously and communicated that way, the major problem was the fact that communicating was done through typing. To see how significant this problem is, arrange with a friend to use a chat program such as UNIX's *talk* while you're logged on together, and try to carry on a "conversation" through typing. You'll quickly discover that the typing itself becomes a topic of conversation, and that for most people typing impedes the actual communication. Then, for a really fascinating time, hook up to an IRC channel and carry on a conversation with not just one, but potentially a dozen or so other users, all trying to make themselves heard, with several different conversations going on at once. It's a great deal like a loud, active family dinner conversation, except that our eyes are much less effective than our ears at filtering through the din.

Over the years, electronic mail and newsgroups haven't changed much. Nor, for that matter, has postal mail. With their capabilities essentially at their limit, and with the telephone limited by the fact that conversations are timed for the sake of charging money (we've all experienced the nearly debilitating effect of that imaginary clock ticking while we're talking on the phone), new communications mechanisms became desirable. Then, too, there was the advent of videoconferencing, in which people from distant locations set up equipment and conducted live conversations with a full video complement. That meant that you could see each other while you talked, and therefore you could draw diagrams, demonstrate things, and otherwise make use of the sense of sight, something that the telephone and its associated audioconferencing (conference calls) didn't allow. The problem with videoconferencing was that it was (and is) extremely expensive, prohibitively so for anyone outside a well-funded organization.

During the past few years, two communications methods have appeared on the Internet, neither of them new but both promising to be revolutionary. The first is real-time audio communication; the second is real-time video communication. Real-time audio communication effectively means the ability of two Internet users to converse with each other by voice and in real-time — in other words, the ability to use the Internet like a telephone. The demands of real-time video over the Internet are much higher, and until a few years ago, this technology was considered impossible. The MBONE is the primary means of effecting real-time video, and its research was begun in earnest, in fact, nearly four years ago.

The first basis for the coming of the MBONE, then, is the constantly growing need for more and better forms of human communication.

Broadcasting

Today, it's extremely difficult to imagine life without broadcasting. Broadcasting is the means by which we receive, by far, the greatest portion of the information we take in each day, and to be cut off from it is considered both unusual and, if done for any length of time, dangerous. At the same time, the sheer volume of advertising has probably led to a growing inability to separate important from unimportant information, and indeed, to think about what we receive at all. That's why many of us vacation in places that actually deny our access to information. We seem to realize, somewhere underneath it all, that information overload is unhuman.

Given a choice, though (not to mention absolute political and societal power), few of us would eliminate the means by which broadcasting is accomplished. Radio is a continuous noisemaker, but it's a noise most of us have come both to accept and to expect. Television is criticized by many as notoriously ineffective as a worthwhile entertainment medium, but the TV set has become an almost inevitable fixture in today's home (in the "have" countries, at least). Another, older form of broadcasting is the newspaper, which does not broadcast "signals" per se but which unquestionably operates as a daily disseminator of information in much the same way as radio and TV. In fact, as has been well noted, a newspaper like *USA Today* is little more than a print version of televised information, complete with graphical design and brevity of detail. Still, newspapers and similar publications are not typically considered broadcasting, at least not electronic broadcasting, and we'll stick to that norm here, restricting our discussion to radio, television, and computer networks.

Radio

Radio came first. It broadcast sound, and when it did so, it completely revolutionized information dissemination. How? Consider the days before radio. To hear a political speech or debate, you and hundreds of others went to a meeting hall. To hear a new musical composition, you and hundreds of others went to a concert hall. To hear the news, you and hundreds (well, maybe not hundreds) of others went to the town square. If you wanted a slightly dated version of the news, you bought a newspaper, took it home, and read it.

All these events still go on, of course. But radio changed them. With radio, it was suddenly possible for you and thousands of others to hear a political speech or debate while sitting, isolated from one another, in the comfort of your living room. You could sit in the same room, again all by yourself, and hear musical concerts and even full operas. And the news could be offered to you every hour of the day, constantly updated and less time-consuming to digest. You and everyone in your town, your entire state for that matter, could hear the same material without ever appearing in the same physical location.

What this did was to change forever our expectations about receiving information. For information to be considered useful, it had to be timely, and it also had to be conveniently available. Newspapers quickly became a means of fleshing out pieces of information and of providing information of more personal interest but less regional or national interest. Real news was available immediately after it happened, and it was suddenly your responsibility to keep up with it all. It's possible, in fact, that the advent of broadcast radio was the beginning of today's obsession with absolutely up-to-date current events on a global scale. Before radio, you could be up-to-date about local events through the "grapevine," but a knowledge of the outside world had to wait for the newspapers. And even here things were changing, as the grapevine quickly became a function of another growing technology, the telephone. The radio and the telephone, exclusively aural media both, cast a huge shadow over the future history of the dissemination of information.

Radio changed one other thing — the experience of theater. On the one hand, you were able to receive broadcasts of theatrical events, such as operas. On the other, a new type of theater emerged, short dramas and comedies designed and written specifically for the new medium. Knowing that you were willing to sit in your living room with the radio on, producers decided to supply entertainment (both frivolous and serious) of a kind never before available. The weekly broadcast of ongoing series began with radio, taking advantage of the the medium's immediacy, convenience, and ephemerality. These were programs for the moment, and they became fully accepted as such.

Television

Television expanded on radio's capabilities by adding video. That's so obvious it seems pointless to write down, but it's no less significant for being obvious. Radio offered a limited view of information and performance, after all; you could hear, but you could not see, and as such it was precisely the opposite of the newspaper and the magazine. Cinema fed both senses — seeing and hearing — but it was much less immediate than radio. A medium that would combine radio's immediacy and comfort with the visual capabilities of cinema, newspapers, and live theater was yet to be developed. That medium proved to be television.

It is impossible to overstate the significance of television as a medium of information in this century. Liking or disliking this medium has nothing to do with it; the fact remains that it has utterly dominated all other methods of acquiring information. Think of the great moments in television history — assassinations, space journeys, natural disasters, political events, van chases, Sally Field's Oscar acceptance speech — and they all point to television. Think of the enormous effect of the coverage of the Vietnam War on the U.S. populace, another television experience, and then, years later, of the brilliant (if scary) manipulation of television by the U.S. military during the Gulf War. For information to be considered completely useful today, it must not only be immediate and convenient, it must also engage our visual and auditory senses together. Especially the visual.

In many ways, television is a perfect medium for disseminating information. And, to be sure, it has single-handedly conveyed more information to more people than any other medium. As it turns out, however, it has become severely limited in this capability, largely because of a commercial model that preaches audience size above all other concerns. In other words, and ironically, television has become limited by the very fact that it is a *broad*cast medium, that the broadness is expected (by its inevitable financiers, the advertisers) to grow larger at all times. The result has been a limitation in programming types and topics, a point that remains true even with the variety of specialty channels coming to the fore.

Perhaps the most important effect of television on the MBONE has been our acceptance of television's audio and visual ability to convey information. As soon as we realized that we could experience live video on television, it was only a matter of time until we wanted to use the medium for an enormously important genre in business communication, the meeting. Meetings are nothing more than a limited number of people getting together to discuss issues of common interest, and their main limitation is the fact that all the participants have to be in the same room at the same time. Why not have a meeting with people at a remote location, with their faces displayed on a television screen and their voices coming in over the airwaves? And, in return, they'll see and hear you via TV screens as well.

The idea caught on, and it became known as videoconferencing. This idea is at the heart of the MBONE, but it's important to realize its close relationship with television, particularly television's capability to convey information on a real-time basis using both video and audio capabilities. Videoconferencing via the MBONE is one of the most exciting immediate applications for business, and videoconferencing is a seemingly natural extension of the communications capabilities of television itself.

In discussions of broadcasting, radio and television are two obvious phenomena. Less obvious, perhaps, but equally important for our purposes, is the advent of computer networking, in particular wide-area networking and internetworking. Had it not been for the capability of computers to exchange data with each other across large distances, the MBONE could not have come into existence. What must be said, however, is that the MBONE uses the Internet's broadcasting capabilities, and these aren't frequently talked about.

The Internet is well known as a person-to-person communications system. Electronic mail, in fact, remains its primary application. But electronic mail and newsgroups are broadcast technologies as well. When you send a message to a newsgroup or a mailing list, you are broadcasting on a one-to-many basis. You, an individual, broadcast information to whoever happens to be tuned into the channel — such as the newsgroup or mailing list — to which you transmit. This is, however, broadcasting of a different kind, because unlike with TV or radio, the message is not received in real time. To watch a newscast, all viewers turn on their TVs at an agreed-upon time (11 p.m., for instance); newsgroup subscribers, by contrast, can read your message whenever they feel like it, secure in the knowledge that it will be there. When it comes to time-dependent broadcasting, the Internet is only beginning to demonstrate its usefulness.

But the MBONE is not bound to time-dependant broadcasting — "on demand" technology allows MBONE users to download speeches, lectures, and concerts at any time (stopping and restarting at the user's whim) without waiting for a predetermined "broadcast" time.

Multimedia

The third technology necessary for the MBONE's development was computer multimedia. Much hyped and coming to us with endless promises, multimedia is nothing more than the incorporation of video and audio technologies into computer programs. Nothing more, but also nothing less. Most of us can remember when computers couldn't do these things at all.

A long, long time ago (which in computer terms means about 30 years), computers didn't have graphics. In fact, they didn't even have monitors on which graphics might be displayed. It wasn't until a full ten years after the beginnings of the Internet/ARPAnet in 1969 that a home computer with even rudimentary graphics capabilities became available, and from the time it debuted, the Apple II became a mecca for multimedia designers. People bought the Apple II, it seemed, for two main reasons: They wanted to use a revolutionary program called VisiCalc, the very first spreadsheet package; and they wanted to play games.

The Apple II had sound in the form of beeps. Soon, a peripheral became available that allowed better sound. With that sound, and combined with graphics that looked notably like line drawings, artists and game designers had a multimedia environment. Back then, they didn't call it a "multimedia environment," but they had it nonetheless.

While this was going on, of course, serious multimedia research was taking place in computer labs around the world. Most of us saw the results in media such as cinema, where computers were beginning to be used for the creation of special effects. But for home computer buyers, two hugely popular products brought multimedia's potential home. First came the Atari 2600, a game machine that was in its day what the Nintendo became about several years later. This was a machine that connected directly to the television, the most popular multimedia device of all time, and delivered interactive entertainment with both graphics and sound into the living room.

And then, in the early 1980s, the Commodore 64 exploded onto the scene, changing the public's perception of computers for good. Right out of the box, the 64 offered sophisticated graphics and sounds capabilities, and in a move atypical for the company, Commodore actually promoted it. It became the favorite design platform for designers of games, educational software, easy-to-use art programs, and early music packages. It's easy to dismiss the 64's influence because of its rapid decline, but doing so would be wrong. The machine mattered.

Shortly after the introduction of the 64, IBM introduced its first PC, and multimedia development took a huge step backward. The IBM-PC was expensive, monochromatic, and text-only. Its idea of sound was a beep whenever something went wrong, and it offered no graphics capabilities whatsoever. It was bland, it was ugly, and corporate America thronged to it. Graphics and sound might be nice for home use, as the Commodore 64 proved, but real computer users didn't need these things at all.

In 1984, Apple brought the Macintosh onto the scene. In many ways, it was a less capable multimedia machine than the Commodore 64, and well behind the soon-to-be-introduced Atari ST and Commodore Amiga. But Apple did two things very right. They introduced the graphical user interface and the mouse to the public, and they marketed their machine extremely well. Artists and others in the nonbusiness and non-science communities picked up on the Mac immediately, and it wasn't long until it became the favored machine for graphics designers and desktop publishers. It remains so to this day.

When the Amiga hit the market in 1985, it had built-in multimedia capabilities beyond all but the most multimedia-driven computers today. It had separate chips for sound and graphics (taking the load off the main processor), and it spawned games with graphics and animation quality that PC designers are only now beginning to match. The Amiga never became the machine it could have been for a variety of reasons, but its influence was widespread.

From the standpoint of multimedia, the decade since the the arrival of the Macintosh and the Amiga has been little more than an attempt by PC designers to catch up to these two machines and their enhancements. Sound cards and video boards are now available by the score for PC owners, while the Mac continues its multimedia excellence. CD-ROM at least partly took care of the huge expansion of file sizes and now allows computers to play lengthy video sequences with top-quality sound. Computer makers want their machines to look and sound like enhanced televisions (miniature cinemas if you will), and this goal is beginning to be realized.

For the MBONE, computer multimedia was a prerequisite. The MBONE relies on the fact that video and audio can work together, and that computer users can display and hear it. Without multimedia-capable computers, an MBONE broadcast would be pointless, even worse than listening to a TV station through your radio. The MBONE's future relies on the convergence of multimedia with several other related technologies.

Summary

The key to the MBONE's existence is convergence. Communications concepts and technologies are added to broadcast concepts and technologies, and then are mixed with multimedia concepts and technologies, with the final result being nothing less than an interdependent joining of all three. Unfortunately, like most media convergences, the result often receives less credit than it should because it seems like such a natural idea in the first place. The MBONE, a technology that is remarkable for existing at all, will almost certainly become a technology that Internet users — especially those who join during the next few years — will take entirely for granted.

But then, that's what happens to all successful technologies. Ask most 20-year olds if they're in awe of television's capability to bring live video and audio signals into their house from somewhere halfway around the globe, and you're likely to be greeted with stares of incomprehension. For that matter, try to explain to them how truly wonderful it is that your PC plays the video introduction to Wing Commander III without burping even once; the incomprehension continues. Then turn around and wax eloquently about how amazing it feels to be talking on the phone with someone three time zones away, or that you're listening to a baseball game in another city, or that you turn the key in your ignition and the car seems to start by itself.

If the MBONE works well, it will quickly be taken for granted. Indeed, its name may even disappear. You'll walk into a room and ask, "How's the MBONE performing today?" and someone at the table will say, "MBONE? No idea. Let's just get on with the videoconference." It's only a matter of time.

An Armchair MBONE Session

If you've never used the MBONE, you may be wondering just what it's like. In this chapter, we will cover how to watch MBONE sessions and create your own MBONE events.

Watching a Session

In order to watch a session, we first launch SD — the session directory tool. After a few minutes, session names begin to appear in the SD window, shown in Figure 5-1. SD shows "advertisments" — information about MBONE sessions that are currently active.

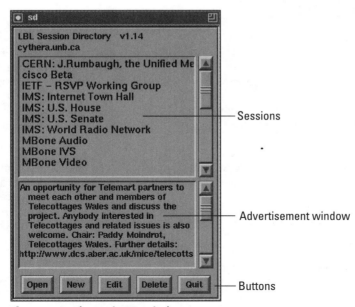

Figure 5-1: The main SD window.

An advertisement is composed of the following information, which is accessible via SD:

✦ a session title

✦ a session description

✦ a multicast group

✦ audio and/or video and/or whiteboard ports

✦ the identity of the session creator

✦ creation date and time

Watching a session is as simple as selecting the desired session in the SD window and clicking the Open button. When you choose a session, your workstation automatically runs the appropriate client for participating in the event—each application has a specific function. NV gives you the video data, vat enables access to the audio, and wb displays a whiteboard. Other tools also can be used. MMCC, similar to SD, can be used for session management. IVS, which is also used for video data, implements a different video compression algorithm than NV. SDR, the newest sessions management tool, implements much more functionality than SD and is destined to replace SD in the future. IMM is a different type of tool. It slowly downloads images from the MBONE and displays them. IMM is used mostly for picture galleries. (For more information on MBONE clients, see Chapter 9.)

Creating Your Own Session

Ready to create your own session? With SD running, select the New button. The New button brings up a window in which the information for the advertisement is entered. In this second window, the name parameter is the title others will see in their own SD windows. We'll create a session with the unimaginative title "My New MBONE Event."

The next field describes the session. It should ideally contain useful information, such as the targeted audience, whether the session is private or public, the main speaker, and so on.

Next, select what kind of data the session will be made of. You can select any combination of video, audio, and whiteboard. There are various protocols available for different types of data — examples of available video formats are NV, VIC, and Cu-SeeMe.

Next, select the scope, perhaps the most delicate aspect of the creation of an MBONE event. The "scope" is also known as the TTL, or time to live, as explained in Chapter 4.

A scope too high sends your session to parts of the world that may not be interested in participating. Too low, and you unknowingly limit your audience. The scope should reflect your intended audience. If, for example, a session is created to allow the deans of California universities to share some ideas, selecting *World* as a scope would not be appropriate.

In the SD window, a World scope means that the TTL is set to 255, a Region scope is 128, and a Site scope is 64. These numbers will not always produce the desired effect for your situation. The scope depends heavily on the configuration of the various mrouters between you and the remote parties. You should inquire about the correct values from your network provider.

Finally, set the creation time and date and the duration of the event. Note that time zones affect the session. If you specify a time of 16:00, the creation time of the session is effectively 16:00 locally in all the time zones. If a remote party is in a time zone that is delayed by two hours relative to you, and you really want the session to start at 16:00, you should make the start time 14:00 so that the remote party in the other time zone can see it, too. See Figure 5-2.

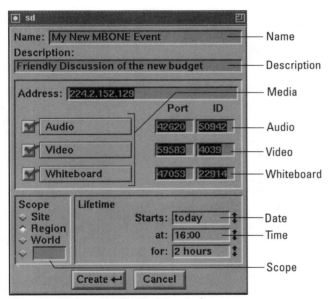

Figure 5-2: SD session creation window.

When everything is set up, click the Create button. The session immediately appears in the main SD window, as shown in Figure 5-3. The session can be opened by clicking on the Open button. The MBONE applications corresponding to the data types you have selected at the creation step are now launched.

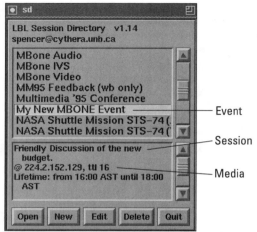

Figure 5-3: SD main window with a newly created event.

It takes a few minutes for the session advertisement to propagate to the rest of the MBONE. When users see the advertisement appear in their own SD window, they will be able to join the session by opening the advertisement. In your vat window, you will begin to see the advertisements appear as joined to the event.

Video in Your New Event

The network video package, nv, is a videoconferencing tool that uses a default bandwidth of 128 Kbps and offers video rates of three to five frames per second. Versions are available for Sun, Silicon Graphics, DEC, and Hewlett-Packard systems. In Figure 5-4, you can see the main NV window. NV was one of the MBONE tools that was started as part of our new session.

The NV window is divided into five parts:

✦ The participants who are sending video. You can see them and their identity in the form of fingernail video clips.

✦ The conference information. This part includes the multicast address of the conference (which really is a group), a port number, your name, the TTL of the session, and a channel number.

✦ I do not have a video camera and a frame grabber for my workstation, but I can still send video by choosing the X11 grabber from the Grabbers menu. In this section, you have the controls for the X11 grabber. By selecting Pointer, I can send that part of my desktop that surrounds my mouse pointer as a video signal. I also can choose to grab from a fixed area of my screen or a single window.

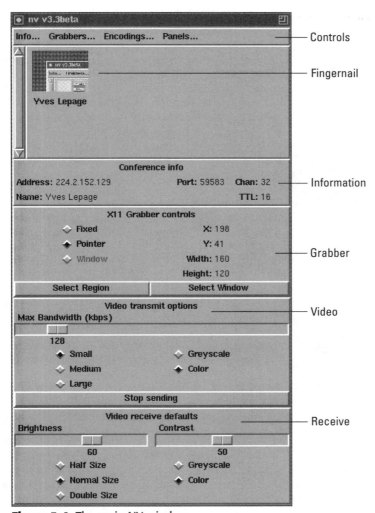

Figure 5-4: The main NV window.

✦ The video transmit options are used to limit the amount of video data I'll be sending onto the network. The default is 128 Kbps. I am sending a small color image so that I use the least possible amount of bandwidth.

✦ The video receive options are used to control how I see the video I am receiving. Selecting double size for the size of the picture window, as shown in Figure 5-5, makes the window bigger, but the pixels of the image get bigger, also. It can be useful if you have an audience watching at your screen. Selecting double size also asks more of your machine in terms of processing. If you have a machine that would benefit from a smaller image so that the load of the machine does not suffer too much, selecting half size will do that for you. You can also adjust the contrast and brightness of the image to your liking.

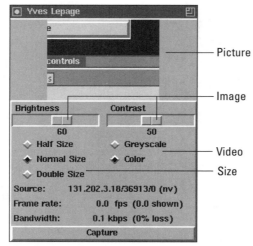

Figure 5-5: The NV picture window.

When you click on a fingernail picture, the image of the fingernail appears in a normal-size picture window, as shown in Figure 5-5. You can have as many windows as there are people sending video to your event. In this window, you see the status of the actual broadcast in terms of frame rate, bandwidth, and packet loss. The brightness and contrast controls are still there, so you have per-picture control of these parameters. A Capture button allows you to capture a frame and save it to a file.

Audio in Your New Event

The visual audio tool, or vat, is a program for sending and receiving audio via the MBONE. The main vat window, shown in Figure 5-6, is a fairly simple window with few controls. On the left you can see a list of people who are participating in your event. At the moment, I am the only one. On the right you have two volume sliders, one for received audio and one for the microphone. Next to each volume slider is a meter. The meter for received audio indicates the volume of the audio you receive from the event. The meter for the microphone level indicates the volume of the sound when you talk into the microphone. Two buttons at the top right allow you to mute the sound from the session and also mute the microphone. Selecting the Menu button gives you a second window in which you can set various parameters. See Figure 5-7.

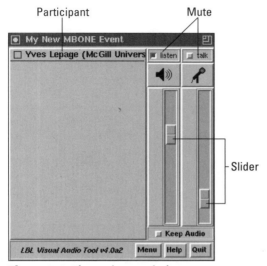

Figure 5-6: The main vat window.

In this second window, various settings can be adjusted, including the priority of the sound. High-priority sound uses more bandwidth but sounds better; low-priority sound allows more packets to be dropped if necessary, due to network congestion, so your audio may not sound as clear to other listeners.

Watching an Event with SDR

SDR is a new session directory tool destined to replace SD. It includes many more features and functionality than SD. The SDR main window appears when SDR is launched, as shown in Figure 5-8. The main window contains five buttons and a scrollable list. The list contains session names. The five buttons are for showing the calendar of events, creating a new session, making the settings window appear, invoking help, and quitting the application.

The calendar of events, shown in Figure 5-9, provides you with an overall view of all the scheduled events for the current month and for the next two months. The calendar helps you plan your sessions and, at the same time, avoid conflicts with other sessions. Since only two or three MBONE sessions can exist at the same time, careful planning is easy using this calendar feature.

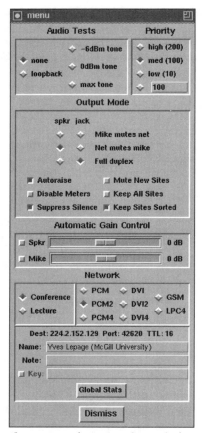

Figure 5-7: The vat settings window.

Shortly after SDR launches, session names begin to appear in the scrollable list. The left and right mouse buttons each perform a different function when you either left-click or right-click on a session name.

You can set various parameters in the settings window, as well as turn on the balloon help. With balloon help enabled, when you position the mouse pointer over part of the SDR window, a help balloon tells you what each button does. You'll want to turn on balloon help during the first few times you use this software. You also can set how the WWW links specified at event creation time will be handled. If you choose *Send to browser*, the links are passed on to SDR's internal Web browser. This Web browser allows you to see the supplementary conference information that can be found on the Web page.

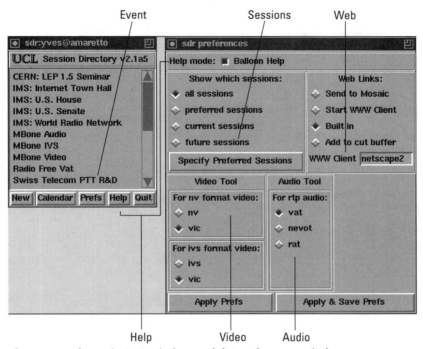

Figure 5-8: The main SDR window and the preferences window.

SDR's internal browser does not download images; it just presents you with the text. Only presenting text is faster and saves colors from the 256 colors availavble on an 8-bit display. Downloading images and assigning colors to them would steal colors from your MBONE applications. You can also select *Start external browser* so that a browser like Mosaic or Netscape can be started, enabling you to see the images from the Web page. In the Start external browser window, you also can choose your favorite MBONE tool, depending on the format of the data, and you can select which sessions you want to see from the scrollable list of the main window. These choices are all pretty obvious, except for *Preferred sessions*. If you select this one, all the sessions are shown in the list, except those that you have specifically chosen to hide using the third mouse button in the scrollable list of the main window.

If you select a session name from the main window with button one (the leftmost mouse button), the session information window appears, as shown in Figure 5-10. This information window shows you the conference information and also allows you to join the session. Selecting a session name with the second (middle) mouse button allows you to join the session without putting the conference information window on the screen.

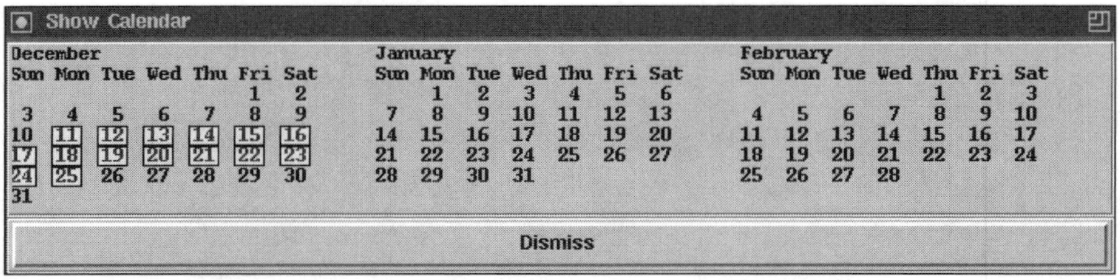

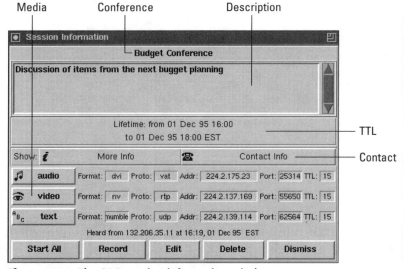

Figure 5-9: The calendar of events window.

Figure 5-10: The SDR session information window.

The session information window shows you the session name, the description, time and date information, and the various media involved with the event. Selecting the Contact Info button shows you who created the event and an e-mail address and a phone number in case you want to reach the person.

To join the event, you can select either one or more of the media buttons (audio, video, text) or the Start All button, which starts the tools for all the media for that session.

You may also choose to record an event in case you won't be present to watch it or you want to replay or rebroadcast it later. If you choose to record an event, make sure that you have plenty of disk space: for audio — 64 Kbps of audio × one hour (3600 seconds) = 1.84MB of data (for a monaural event). You also have to plan disk space for video data, text, and whiteboard data. Video is not as easy to calculate, because the various video encoding algorithms will most often send you variations (deltas) from one frame to another.

If you are the person who created the event, two supplementary buttons are present in the session information window: Edit and Delete. The Edit button allows you to change almost everything in your event, from the contact information to the format of the audio and video. In fact, the Edit window is nearly identical to the event creation window, except for the Create button, which is called Modify in the Edit window.

Now that you know how to watch an event with SDR, it's time to create one.

To create an event using SDR, follow these steps:

Creating an Event with SDR

Assuming that you have something to share with the MBONE-watching world, you can create an event using SDR. This is similar to the process of creating an event with SD, except that SDR provides stronger functionality and more features to the session creator. To create an event using SDR, follow these steps:

1. Start SDR. From the main window, select the New button to get the event creation window, as shown in Figure 5-11.

2. Enter the session name in the field at the top of the window. This name appears in the scrollable list of the SDR main window.

3. In the next field, enter the session description. You may be as verbose as you want here.

4. Now enter a URL. URL stands for Uniform Resource Locator. It represents a document address in a form that the Web browser understands.

   If you have a WWW server at your site, you may want to create a Web page for your event so that when users see the session in the SDR list, they can go to that Web page and learn more about the session you created. Next to the URL field is a button for testing the URL to make sure that it works.

5. Next, decide if your conference will be open to anyone or restricted to a select group of people. If you select Public, anyone can join the session. If you select Private, only those who possess the correct encryption key are able to join the session.

6. Now choose the distribution scheme, either one group per conference or one group per media.

   One group per conference gives you all the media, audio, video, and text. Choose this option if all your participants are on fast network links. Because all participants won't have the luxury of choosing which media they want, they will receive everything.

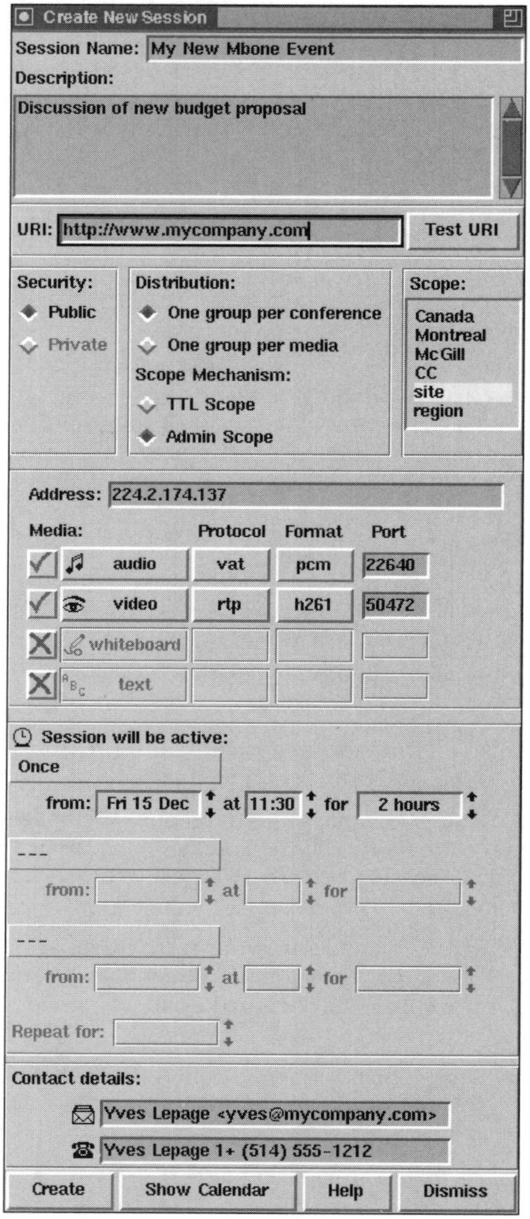

Figure 5-11: The SDR session creation window.

One group per media allows your participants to choose to receive only the media they desire, be it audio, video, or text. Choose this option if your event will be worldwide, because not everyone on the Internet has access to fast, non-congested links.

7. The next option to set is the scope mechanism, either TLL or Administrative Scopes. See Chapter 10 for a discussion on administrative scopes. Depending on which mechanism you choose, the box to the right changes so that you can choose the correct value for the chosen mechanism. Since Mycompany is not necessarily in Canada, choosing McGill, Montreal, or even Canada is not appropriate here.

8. Now select the media you want to use, along with their protocol, format, address, and port. The address and the port are assigned by SDR, but you can change them if you need to do so. For the protocol, there is only one choice except for audio, for which you can choose either rtp (Real Time Protocol) or vat. For the format, the choice really depends on the medium. For example, for sound you can choose PCM, DVI, PCM, and so on, which are all sound formats with different qualities.

9. Finally, set the date, the time the event will be active, and the contact information as people will see it. If the session will not be a continuous event but will be on and off, you can specify up to three active periods. Specifying active periods is useful when your participants don't want to remain joined in the event, but they want to know in advance when to join.

Notice that SDR supports a new MBONE medium: text. The application that handles this new medium is called mumble. Mumble implements textual conversations using the MBONE. It works on a principle similar to IRC in that when you create an event with text as a medium, the event has a group assigned to it (on IRC they are called channels). Users join your event, their own SDR starts mumble, and they are able to enter text that you receive and vice-versa. The fun part is that icreating your event with other media adds a great deal of power to the conversation. Users also can join your event using mumble's internal set of commands. The best advantage of using MBONE text over electronic mail is that it is real-time communication and takes up a very small amount of bandwidth.

Last but not least, SDR supports extensive hypertext help. When you select help from the main SDR window, shown in Figure 5-12, the help window appears with a menu inside. You can select items in that list that are dark blue to get to a new help section (or submenu). The help in SDR uses the same built-in Web browser that is used for getting to a session URL for more information about the session.

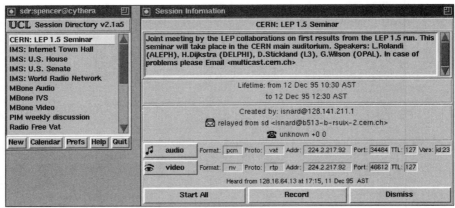

Figure 5-12: The SDR help window.

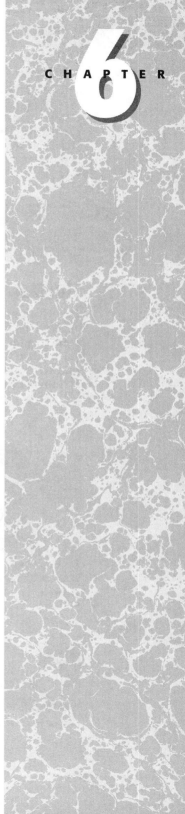

## CHAPTER 6

MBONE Events

A number of events are always happening on the MBONE. Some of them are "regulars," — they are always there for you to join. Other events occur from time to time. The number of people who are now using the MBONE to facilitate the exchange of information is growing rapidly, and this growth assures you that the MBONE schedule is getting busier and busier.

Basic Events

I call those basic events because they are the base of the MBONE. They are what the MBONE has been created for. I am referring to the broadcasts of the IETF (Internet Engineering Task Force) meetings.

During these meetings, people from various workgroups meet, exchange, adopt resolutions, and so on. Results from workgroups are broadcasted on the MBONE. These events are a great source of information on upcoming technology or protocols. Sometimes, the slides of the presentation are made available via the whiteboard, and most often you see them in the video session. These sessions are among the most popular. The IETF holds these meetings several times per year, and some of them are used as testbeds for new protocols or new tools. (The December 1994 IETF meeting was the one in which VIC was tried for the first time. We discovered that VIC could produce a frame rate about 30 times higher than that of NV's, for the same amount of bandwidth!)

For testing purposes, some sessions are always present. These sessions have titles such as "MBONE video" or "MBONE audio." All users can join them and test their setup by sending small amounts of video or audio.

The Research Events

On the Internet, researchers often use the MBONE for exchanging ideas and working with remote colleagues.

Seminars from the MICE project are an example of research events. MICE is a research project at UCL, in England. It stands for Multimedia Integrated Conferencing for Europe, and its goal is to develop a multimedia conferencing platform — in fact this project has been a major contributor to the development of the MBONE. The MICE staff regularly presents seminars about various topics related to networking and computing.

Educational Events

Educational research has always been very popular on all parts of the Internet, and the MBONE is no exception.

The JASON Project

JASON is a project founded by Dr. Robert Ballard (Figure 6-1).The project makes expeditions to various places. Its goal is to educate children and students and allow them to interact with scientists. For the two weeks that the JASON expedition VI was in Hawaii in March 1995, the topic was volcanos (Figure 6-2) and how they played a role in the Earth's formation and how it compares to other planets in our solar system in terms of volcanic issues.

Figure 6-1: Dr. Robert Ballard introducing the event to a student. (Photo courtesy of JASON Project.)

Figure 6-2: Dr. Ballard and a lava field. (Photo courtesy of the JASON Project.)

The broadcasts were sent to satellite links, and hundreds of thousands of students participated and interacted directly with the scientists on the site. The broadcasts focused on the research activities of the scientists, students, and teachers who participated in the program. The expedition went one more step by allowing students to try to control ROVs (remotely operated vehicles), like the one in Figure 6-3, from their remote location. Using the Web, people were able to register their location in a map of viewers' locations, and this map was later used in the event itself.

Figure 6-3: A remotely operated vehicle. (Photo courtesy of JASON Project.)

The missions of the Space Shuttle

Had enough of Earth-bound affairs? NASA broadcasts space shuttle missions onto the MBONE.

During these broadcasts, we can follow the astronauts during their space walks, their experiments, and their everyday life in space.

We are also provided with spectacular views of the Earth and space (Figure 6-4), and we can view live historic events like the rendezvous between the shuttle and the MIR space station (Figure 6-5).

Figure 6-4: A view of the Space Shuttle's launch. (Photo courtesy of NASA.)

Figure 6-5: A rendezvous between the shuttle and the MIR space station. (Photo courtesy of NASA.)

These space shuttle events are a great source of information, and the MBONE is the medium for viewing them live when most human beings only hear about these events through the news on TV. The shuttle missions are very popular, and seeing more than a hundred sites joined to view them is not uncommon.

The SUNergy broadcasts

Sometimes, a group of people sharing an interest presents a series of seminars on a topic and invite other people to come and share.

The events are held by Sun Corporation, and they consist of a discussion about issues involved in a larger topic. For example, on January 11th, 1994, the broadcast was about Global Information Infrastructures, and it featured people from Sun Corporation and the Internet Society.

Musical Events

Severe Tire Damage was the first live band on the Internet. On June 24, 1993, Severe Tire Damage was broadcast live from the patios of Xerox PARC onto the MBONE, both audio and video. The band was seen and heard live as far away as Australia. Severe Tire Damage multicasts their jam sessions on the MBONE weekly. For more information, see `http://www.ubiq.com/std/band.html`.

Rolling Stones

One of the most publicized MBONE sessions ever was the Rolling Stones Cotton Bowl concert in Dallas. It was advertised in advance, and they had setup a Web site for people to come and get early information about this upcoming MBONE session. The session was a 20 minute clip of their live concert in Dallas. Even though the event was mostly a clever way of advertising their pay-per-view ™ offer, it was a technical achievement. The announcement of this session was received with a bit of coolness by the MBONE community because they felt that such a frivolous event was not appropriate on the MBONE, mainly because the MBONE is supposed to be a research platform. However, this event began a new era for the MBONE as it would not only be used for computer and networking research and education, but also more artistic domains could now profit from it. The Rolling Stones concert event is one of the most popular MBONE events ever.

It was nice to hear Mick Jagger say, "I wanna say a special welcome to everyone that's, uh, climbed into the Internet tonight and, uh, has got into the MBONE. And I hope it doesn't all collapse."

The Ryuichi Sakamoto concert

Recently, Ryuichi Sakamoto, a famous New Age musician, broadcasted a show on the MBONE.

The concert was presented live from the Nippon Budohkan in Tokyo. Mr. Sakamoto performed with Daizaburo Harada. For this concert, a temporary satellite station was installed at the Nippon Budohkan. This satellite station broadcasted IP datagrams to several satellite stations of WIDE Network Operation Centers at 2 Mbps.

The Saint John String Quartet concert

The Saint John String Quartet held a concert from the Christ Church Cathedral in Fredericton, New-Brunswick, Canada, on November 23, 1995. They were performing with Andrew Miller, a double-bassist. This classical concert was the first ever to be broadcasted on the MBONE. The producers of the event were using computel (a proprietary video conferencing system) machines that were connected to a VCR that was doing live conversion to standard video. This concert was broadcasted on both the MBONE and to the CU-SeeMe world using a specially configured reflector.

Vat Radio

For some of us, just listening to the radio isn't good enough — we want to be the D.J., spinning discs for all the Internet to hear. In fact, folks are already doing this with a resource called Radio Free vat. RFv allows anyone who's connected to the MBONE to check out a chunk of time on a virtual radio station, and play virtual D.J. for a couple of hours to an audience of, well, dozens.

Dave Hayes, a network and systems administrator for the Network Engineering group of JPL, created Radio Free vat. The idea was born quite by accident. "One day, I cross-connected the CD output (of my workstation) with the vat input and wound up broadcasting a couple minutes of a Chick Corea tune over the MBONE audio channel. I quickly noticed my error, cut off the CD, and made apologies on the audio channel." Someone answered back, "If you play music like that, you can play music anytime you want to." "Then it hit me," Hayes said. "I used to D.J. in college... Why not do this over the Internet? So, I started Radio Free vat. I began to play CDs that I liked. Soon, the idea caught on. I wrote a Perl server which handles session conflicts, and we went from there."

The number of MBONE users is rather small, so RFv doesn't have a huge audience — "The most people I've seen at one time is about 75," Hayes said.

As more users get access to high-bandwidth Internet connections, thanks to affordable services like ISDN, the audience for Radio Free vat will grow. If you thought self-publishing on the web was popular, wait until everyone with a Net connection and microphone can have their own radio show, without so much as a nod from the FCC.

Recreational Events

The Internet Town Hall broadcasts a news bulletin at specific times every day. The news bulletin originates from the Canadian Broadcasting Corporation (CBC).

The radio free vat often broadcasts music just for people who would like some music playing while they work. Anyone can broadcast music to this event simply by reserving a slot. The information for this is contained in the session advertisement.

You can often see test sessions between various people on the planet. These sessions are created so that one of the parties can test a setup or a tool. Once the testing is done, the parties involved almost invariably start a conversation, begin exchanging whiteboard data, and so on.

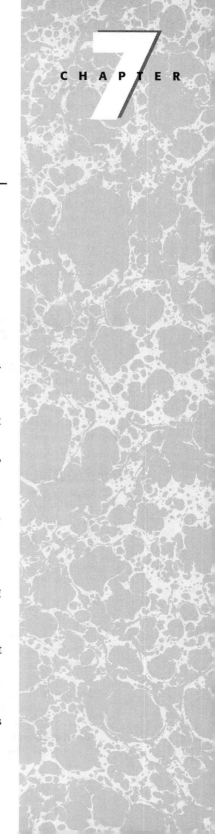

## CHAPTER 7

Why the MBONE Matters

If one certainty exists in the last gasp of the twentieth century, it is that technological change is rampant. You can barely open a newspaper or a newsmagazine without reading about some new advance in technology, whether or not it is couched in technological terms. Some people grow numb at the mention of computers, but they happily discuss the features on their fancy new coffeemaker, their VCR, or their programmable phone. For many people, the less technologically phrased an invention is, the more acceptable they find the technology itself. New technologies are scarcely daunting if you can easily incorporate them into your everyday life.

Many of the most important technologies, or at least those most readily accepted, are difficult to grasp in how they operate but not in what they do. Television is a perfect example of this concept — how many people can actually tell you how it works? Word processing, photography, and the internal combustion engine are other good examples. The MBONE fits this paradigm as well. Try to explain the sophisticated convergence of transmission and multimedia technologies at work, and you'll usually be rewarded with some glazed-over eyeballs. Sit someone down at a computer to participate in a continent-wide videoconference, however, and suddenly the point becomes clear. The only problem is that the user isn't likely to care whether he or she is using the MBONE, the Turner Broadcasting System, or video walkie-talkies. The only thing that the user cares about is that it works.

Even if it works, works well, and works easily, a technology must still be justified. In particular, people want to know why it matters at all, especially if, as in the MBONE's case, the technology is in a relatively early stage of development. Technologies come and go so quickly that getting anyone to invest their time or resources in a new one is a difficult task (that concept applies to book buyers as well).

With a technology as broad-ranging as the MBONE, the justification is doubly difficult. People not only have trouble immediately grasping its significance but also, for the most part, they can't even see the technology in operation. And even if they can, they're likely to be underwhelmed. At this point in the MBONE's life-cycle, the MBONE has hit the terrible twos: too old to be cute and too young to be useful.

So why does the MBONE matter? Very simply, it offers a means of taking the Internet to the next level. The Net is already a medium for live communication and for the distribution of visual information, but it is limited in that its live stuff isn't visual and its visual stuff isn't live. When television first started, people referred to it as radio with pictures, but live television also became the equivalent of real-time books and real-time movies. The convergence of visual information and live communication is what made the 1969 moon landing such a spectacularly gripping event, and that convergence of live and visual information is exactly what the Internet currently lacks.

A Technology in the Making

Of course, the question remains of why the Internet actually needs this convergence. Isn't the Net, as it stands in the middle of the '90s, sufficient for the purposes it was originally designed to fulfill? The answer is a definite "yes." But that question assumes that you care about what the Net's original purposes were, or that those purposes even remotely matter to today's Internet users. The fact is that the Net was designed to be a fairly limited interconnection of computers that would help researchers and military personnel transfer files to one another quickly and efficiently; even e-mail was a kind of accident born out of using the Internet.

Nobody really foresaw the exponential growth of the Net, or if they did, they probably expected that growth to slow well before it reached its current level. The evidence for this fact lies in the history of the Internet's addressing technology. In the Internet's beginning, the addressing system was constructed to enable a total of 64 addresses. Since that time, the addressing system has been expanded, but the Internet is running out of IP (Internet Protocol) addresses so quickly that developers are working furiously to create a new system that will enable everyone on the planet to have one or more Internet addresses.

This unexpected growth points to the fact that the Internet's original purposes are largely irrelevant to what you can do with it today. Who would have guessed that millions of users would fight out issues in Internet newsgroups, or that the newsgroups themselves would become the focus of outrage and outrageous arguments in the U.S. Congress? Who could have predicted that you'd be able to fire up a World Wide Web browser and order CDs, pizzas, computer equipment, and even condoms? Who would have foreseen the Internet as a value-added tool for entertainment companies, or as a technology for offering frog-dissection simulations? Indeed, who in their right mind would have even begun to suggest that you could hear e-mail addresses and Web URLs while cruising the highway listening to your radio?

The MBONE has nothing to do with the Net's original intentions. Back then, nobody could have predicted the possibility of real-time multimedia over a global network of networks, because neither the network nor multimedia were in place. From that perspective, the need did not yet exist for the convergence of networking and multimedia technologies that comprise the MBONE, but the need, or at least the desire, for it eventually set in. If you ask some Internet users today, they may tell you that the network *still* doesn't need this convergence. Some users feel that the Internet's tools are already sufficiently advanced for their purposes or that the Net is already too busy and that multicasting will simply destroy it.

Whether or not a technology is strictly *necessary* isn't always the issue. It could be argued, after all, that television wasn't necessary, and many critics insist that it still isn't. The way that television has changed North American society, everything from its culture to its economy, cannot be argued, however, so at least it has been *significant*. The difference between necessary and significant has a great deal to do with whether or not you're talking about foresight or hindsight. Necessity is something you predict; significance is something you see only with after-the-fact analysis.

At this stage in the MBONE's history, we remain firmly in the area of foresight. We simply have no idea how significant these new technologies will prove to be. As far as necessity is concerned, we wouldn't be writing this book if we didn't believe that the MBONE was much more than a toy. In fact, we predict that multicasting, and the multimedia capabilities that go with multicasting, will become at least as important to the Net's future as the World Wide Web is today.

Why "at least?" Because the Web, for all its current glory, is a relatively slow means of disseminating essentially printed information. The Web is evolving with the introduction of technologies (such as Sun's HotJava, which enables built-in programs) and the incorporation of a variety of document types into the browsers; but not much exists on the Web that couldn't be done, often better, on paper. Although paper documents cannot provide easy-to-use hypertext links, too many Web documents contain hypertext whose primary purpose is to disguise the fact that the site itself doesn't offer much. The authors of these documents seem to think that if they provide enough links, users will feel that the authors have given them something.

The MBONE promises to do for Internet information what the telephone did for letter-writing, what the motion picture did for reading, and what television did for nearly all paper publications — change it completely, whether for the better or for the worse. Video (through television) and audio (through radio) are such dominant forms of information dissemination today that any technologies that make use of them automatically vault to the center of media and popular attention. Make those technologies interactive, and the MBONE will be at its best. Although interactive technologies are currently not as popular as passive media such as TV and radio, the growing interest in multimedia CD-ROMs and computer games suggests that this fact may be changing.

So far, this book has insisted that the MBONE has enormous potential. For the remainder of this chapter, we examine that potential in greater detail. Specifically, we look at how the MBONE will affect business, entertainment, and education. As you're reading, keep in mind that very little of this potential has been realized yet, but also remember that the MBONE has reached a stage of development which makes it possible to say that these projections are not just pie in the sky.

Still, keeping the current limitations of the MBONE in mind is extremely important. If you're waiting breathlessly for the capability to see numerous live concerts happening simultaneously via videoconferences and live radio broadcasts, you're going to be disappointed, at least for now. The MBONE simply isn't designed to do all that. On the other hand, advances in multimedia and data compression promise that the Internet itself will focus more attention on multimedia, and you can definitely expect more downloadable information in a variety of media formats in the near future. The result — being able to experience multimedia and even real-time communication online — will at least be similar.

The MBONE and Business

After the initial period of funded testing, MBONE activity will almost certainly be dominated by business applications. The reason is simple: MBONE connectivity is expensive. ISDN (Integrated Services Digital Network) has brought reasonably high-speed home connections just around the corner, but until mid-1996 or later, these connections will be only sporadically available, and even these connections are barely fast enough for today's MBONE needs. For the MBONE to work well, especially in a fully interactive mode, you need a T-1 connection. Unless you're a very lucky individual (like, say, a successful baseball player), however, you probably can't afford it.

New technologies may soon provide individuals with T-1 speeds without the expense of an actual T-1 line. One promising technology, *ADSL* (*asymmetrical digital subscriber line*), may be capable of providing home Internet access over existing copper lines at a whopping 1.544 megabits per second, and possibly at rates as fast at 6 megabits per second. ADSL technology is decidedly one-sided, however: it enables you to quickly receive information from the Internet, but sending information from your computer *to* the Internet is still a relatively slow process — about 16 kilobits per second. For some multimedia applications (provided that you don't want to send live video from your computer), this rate is acceptable. ADSL may be available in certain (lucky!) cities as early as the fourth quarter of 1995. It remains to be seen when — or if — the technology will be available to the rest of us at any time soon.

Business activity on the MBONE can generally be divided into three major categories — collaboration, sales, and service.

Collaboration

When we say collaboration, we're not talking about different companies working together on the MBONE. That concept is technically possible, but because this ideal has not been a huge focus of business in the past, the MBONE is not likely to change that fact. Instead, collaboration means intra-company communication for the purpose of performing specific tasks. These tasks will certainly include meetings, but activities such as demonstrations and training will also be possible.

Consider what happens during a business meeting (if you've never attended one, stop reading, fall to your knees, and give thanks to whomever you like to thank for life's blessings). Typically, the participants sit around a table, the meeting leader (typically a manager or executive) runs through the agenda point-by-point, and everyone adds their comments as the occasion insists and as protocol allows. Items are resolved, assignments are given, and new meetings are set. The meeting consists of give-and-take, all for the sake of reaching specific goals.

The problem that large businesses have with meetings is these meetings frequently cover essentially the same topic; they just occur at various locations around the country (or even around the world). More frequently, meetings demand the participation of knowledgeable employees who work in geographically separated areas. To bring all these people together requires either a videoconferencing setup, which can be extremely expensive, or more commonly, extensive travel.

Here's where the MBONE enters. For videoconferencing, the expense is still there, because T-1 lines don't come cheap (they cost more than $1000 per month, not including setup), and a well-stocked Sun workstation (another expensive piece of equipment) is the recommended computer for receiving MBONE multicasts. Then you have to factor in the cost of image projection, because expecting a room full of employees to watch a small window on a small monitor seems a bit counter-productive.

Multicasting's benefit over videoconferencing is two-fold. First, once you have the lines and equipment in place, you can hold MBONE videoconferences whenever you want without making special arrangements. Second, you can use the T-1 line to hook up the company's local area network to the Internet for a fast, 24-hour connection (although a busy network will impair MBONE reception). In other words, because many companies are already hooking up T-1 lines to obtain Internet capabilities, extending the connection to include MBONE capabilities really isn't that expensive, and the convenience you get from having MBONE capabilities is high.

With the connections and equipment in place, all kinds of opportunities open up. National or international sales meetings, once semi-yearly or even yearly events involving large travel and accommodation costs, now become possible monthly, weekly, or even daily if that serves a purpose. Demonstrations of new products or services to geographically separated sales and service personnel also become easier, with instant feedback possible and the resultant elimination of misunderstanding and misinformation. You can conduct employee training without worrying about location, and existing seminars can be multicast from the seminar site to employees around the world. You can also use MBONE to multicast talks by expert speakers, an equally important area of corporate education.

The caveat is that this kind of activity on the MBONE requires careful scheduling because the MBONE can handle only a limited number of sessions at a time. But time has a tendency to work around limitations in technology and eventually eliminate them, and the MBONE's capabilities are continually being improved.

Sales

Companies sell things. That's how they get money. As a result, companies utterly depend on their sales staffs. That staff may work in a show room, a retail outlet, a direct-order desk, or on the road. Regardless of their location, they have to deal with customers and potential customers, and they need all available tools at their disposal to open and close a sale. How can the MBONE help in this regard?

First, the MBONE will enable regional sales people to invite customers to product demonstrations and unveilings that they conduct from a remote site. Obviously, this application has institutional purchasing in mind rather than single-item consumer sales, but for many firms, that area of sales is the sole or primary mode of their business. Consider an automobile company launching a new utility van designed for use in transportation fleets: a good MBONE multicast, complete with a question and answer period involving sales, service, and technical staff, would make a far bigger impression on potential buyers than another batch of brochures delivered by a single salesperson.

Consider also the electronics firm attempting to introduce a new portable CD player (quite a crowded market) for sales in a large department chain. Why not unveil it early via an MBONE broadcast, offering a comprehensive look at its features and benefits, as an adjunct to standard sales measures? Finally, consider a pharmaceutical firm about to introduce a new migraine medication: all the product brochures in the world couldn't possibly deliver as strong an impression as an MBONE multicast with video demonstrations, relevant charts and graphs, participation from researchers, and a full question-and-answer session with the audience.

Several forward-thinking companies have already experimented with Internet-based press conferences and online product announcements. Some companies have held "live" events on the World Wide Web, whereas others have used proprietary collaboration software to introduce their products. But these events lack the luster — and the audience — that most product managers want when they display their wares.

The MBONE also has the capability of becoming an important consumer sales technology. Assuming that we'll all have ISDN or ADSL connections one day for high-speed online access, the possibility of an interactive home shopping network becomes very real. If you've spent any time watching your home shopping station, you've probably realized that the current product lines are minimal and the interaction possible with it weak. To find a product worth buying, you have to wade through seemingly endless descriptions of ugly jewelry and portraits of sports heroes you've barely heard of, and then you have to pick up the phone to order whatever you want, largely on trust.

Now compare shopping via TV to the sales experience you get at the retail mall, which is more personal and varied, but also more tiring; and the mail-order catalog, which frequently provides you with extensive choices but is easy to ignore or dispose of. The MBONE could combine the best traits of these experiences to create the ultimate shopping forum, complete with personal interaction, ease of ordering, and extensive product selection.

The Internet has already taken huge strides in that direction in recent years. Hundreds of Internet "malls" have popped up — everyone with a Web server and an Internet connection is trying to make an extra buck hawking their (or someone else's) products on the Internet. Of course, opinions vary vastly on whether those online shopping experiences are worthwhile, or even profitable.

It's unlikely that you'll see a 24-hour MBONE link to a remote retail store any time soon, but what *is* possible is that a retail outlet, especially one with a niche clientele, could offer MBONE-based sales once a week by setting up a multicast and announcing it — via the Internet and other marketing channels — to whomever is interested. Such events would enable the store to show their goods in detail to interested customers, who could then ask questions, watch or hear demonstrations, and engage in discussions with one another about the products. You won't have much difficulty thinking of several potential sales and marketing applications of this kind, and as long as you give full play to both the multimedia and interactive aspects of the technology, the cost will easily justify itself.

This type of sales experience should have a strong effect in real estate sales and rentals. If you've ever had to move from one city to another, you know the enormous commitment of time and energy it takes to search for a new home. Even a move within your own city can be time-consuming and frustrating. But consider the home-shopping opportunities available via the MBONE. You can fire up your Internet connection and Web browser and head for the real estate pages that list houses for sale or rent in your new city. You could choose one you like, then fill in a form and send off a request for an MBONE "visit." The real estate firm would then contact you (maybe even by real voice phone), and agree to a time and date for the session. At the appointed time, you log in again, load your MBONE client software, and a sales agent greets you from the destination city, standing in front of the house. You're given a video and audio walkthrough of the house and the grounds, and the agent answers all your questions. If you want, you may even be able to meet with a local financing officer at the same time. Then, when you've narrowed down four or five houses that you're really interested in, you hop a plane and do a non-virtual visit, just to make sure that the floors actually exist.

You should realize that this kind of interactive, online sales experience is not yet available. Figure 7-1 shows the home page of one of the Web's most talked-about sales sites, the Internet Shopping Network. The ISN is enjoyable to shop and offers some significant deals at times, but it hardly provides a rich interactive experience. No one is there to answer your questions about the purchases you're making (product reviews are sometimes available, but that's about it), no product demonstrations are available, and you do not even have the opportunity to touch the goods. Admittedly, an MBONE multicast may not be feasible for selling hard drives, but for other goods, interactive multimedia presentations could certainly help.

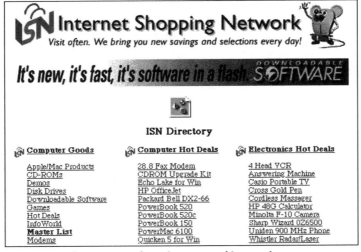

Figure 7-1: The Internet Shopping Network's opening page (http://www.internet.net).

Yet another example of Web-based sales can be seen in Figure 7-2. Noteworthy Music, whose home page resides at `http://www.netmarket.com/noteworthy/bin/main,` offers an extensive collection of music CDs for sale. This site is great if you're looking for older CDs or specific songs because you can search CDs according to various parameters. Noteworthy Music has a much wider selection than most music stores, offers good prices, and the site keeps track of the total amount of money you're spending. But while the site offers multimedia in the form of several album covers (Figure 7-2 is an example), it offers very little audio or video multimedia. Well-developed MBONE sales sessions could dramatically improve both interaction and sales capability, because customers could hear selections, talk to sales staff, and even hear live mini-concerts that Noteworthy could set up (every Thursday evening, for example). Until now, those capabilities haven't really existed, but with the MBONE, they suddenly do.

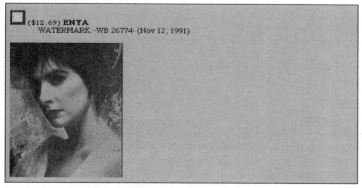

Figure 7-2: Noteworthy Music features the album covers of several popular releases (`http://www.netmarket.com/noteworthy/bin/main/:grm|:mode=text`).

Service

Supposedly, we live in economic times where service is extremely important to businesses. In reality, "service first" is little more than a catch-phrase because the only reason companies emphasize service is to increase sales. As a result, the service that many companies provide is not always that good. Sit on the phone waiting for technical service from a computer company, or try to get a repair person for your new refrigerator, and you'll understand just how bad it can be.

That said, however, service matters a great deal to other companies because it matters to their customers. Already we see companies using the World Wide Web as a service tool, and although this practice is currently limited primarily to computer firms, the potential of using the Web to provide service exists for other firms as well.

Figure 7-3 shows Digital's interactive catalog of Learning Services (`http://www.digital.com/.i/digest/htdocs/digest/home.html`), which includes prices, schedules, and descriptions of courses designed for Digital's customers. Elsewhere in DEC's site, you'll find software patches, technical documentation, and other useful service items, making this site one of the best service sites on the Internet.

Figure 7-3: The main page from Digital Equipment's Learning Services Interactive Catalog.

Another great service site is the Web site for Compaq Computer (`http://www.compaq.com`), whose downloadable files area of their Service and Support section is shown in Figure 7-4. Owners of Compaq computers go here rather than to phone technical support to get their upgrade files, and as a result, this site provides good service for Compaq's customers.

Bell Canada provides yet another type of service on the Web. The site at `http://www.bell.ca` offers a do-it-yourself guide to installing telephone wire inside your house. The reason? Early in 1996, Bell will no longer be responsible for this installation (for single-line residences only), so they offer this service as a means of helping with the transition.

These service sites each provide a definite degree of usefulness to consumers of their related products. But consider how much that usefulness would increase if customers were offered the same benefits via a high-speed MBONE session. A scheduled session would enable technicians to answer questions for a number of users simultaneously (an advanced version of the Frequently Asked Questions idea) and could demonstrate to users how to perform upgrades, installations, and so on. Other representatives could schedule times to explain, demonstrate, and answer questions about add-ons, upgrades, and other important, product-related issues, using audio and expanded video information as, well as text.

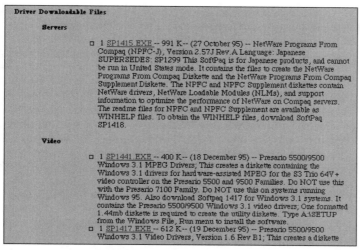

Figure 7-4: Downloadable files from Compaq Computer's Web site.

The secrets to successful customer service are speed, reliability, knowledgeability, and — if you will — humanity. Telephone hotlines can be fast, but they're often unreliable (busy), and technical help representatives often find that diagnosing a problem over the phone is impossible. Web sites and other online services (BBSs, CompuServe or AOL, and so on) are useful tools to turn to if you know what you're looking for, but the contact they provide is anything but "human." The MBONE will enable these qualities to come together (as long as companies structure these sessions wisely), and the result will be increased customer satisfaction at a reasonable cost.

The MBONE and Entertainment

Entertainment incorporates audio, visual information, interactivity, and the excitement of live performance. Few forms of entertainment use all of these components, but all entertainment forms use at least two of them. You could argue that reading involves only one (visual information), but many books and practically all magazines include illustrations, and for many readers, the imagination fills in the visual and auditory details. As for other entertainment forms, computer games offer the most obvious mix of multimedia and interactivity, whereas live theater features all components.

Television and movies are restricted to using audio and video signals, but the industry surrounding these two popular entertainment forms uses interaction and, in the awards programs and talk shows, live performances as well. Musical entertainment has long incorporated audio and video information, with live performances (and the resulting audience interactivity) considered to be one of the most important aspects of that entertainment mode.

Given the number of entertainment mediums already available, you may wonder why we need another one. We don't, probably. We can happily chew up untold hours by watching TV, sitting in front of the stereo, going to the movies, dressing up for the theater, playing computer games and board games, or — to slightly alter Neil Postman — amusing ourselves into oblivion. But one thing that humans seem to have proven over the course of this century is that we have a nearly insatiable appetite for entertainment, to the extent that even shows exist devoted solely to discussing entertainment media — the making of entertainment, the reporting of entertainment, and so on — that we watch on TV (itself an entertainment medium). We want to be entertained, and we're willing to spend a great deal of money to make it happen.

But will we pay for the MBONE? That's a question that we cannot yet answer, but the answer will at least partially determine if — and how — MBONE development continues. As a comparison, television was originally foreseen as an educational medium, but whether it would have survived, had the entertainment industry not co-opted it almost entirely, remains a subject for debate. Likewise, the Internet has undergone a shift in priorities, away from the scholarship and research purposes of its early years and towards business and entertainment. Entertainment dollars make a difference in the North American economy, and the survival of many technologies rides on the infusion of some of those dollars.

The next sections look at three promising entertainment modes for the MBONE — live performance, radio and television, and games.

Live performance

Indeed, the most visible cases of early MBONE activity have been entertainment-related. On November 18, 1994, the Rolling Stones decided to try out this new medium, offering about 20 minutes of a concert from their Voodoo Lounge tour via the MBONE. Figure 7-5 shows the Web page where information about the multicast is stored, as well as links to related items of interest.

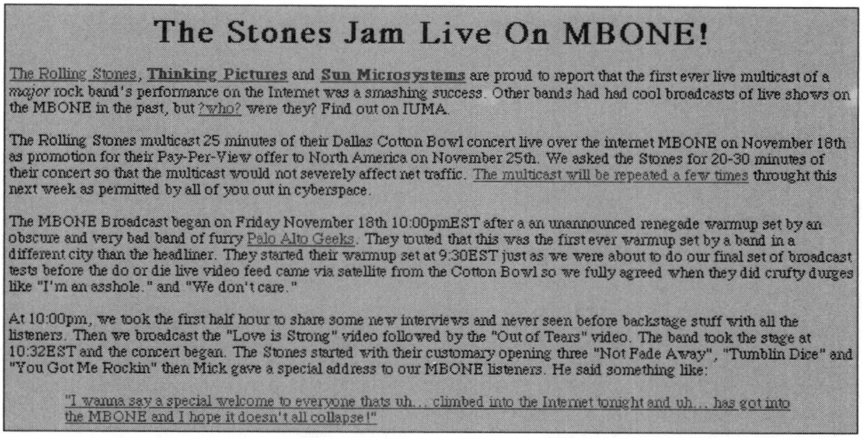

> ## The Stones Jam Live On MBONE!
>
> The Rolling Stones, Thinking Pictures and Sun Microsystems are proud to report that the first ever live multicast of a major rock band's performance on the Internet was a smashing success. Other bands had had cool broadcasts of live shows on the MBONE in the past, but ?who? were they? Find out on IUMA.
>
> The Rolling Stones multicast 25 minutes of their Dallas Cotton Bowl concert live over the internet MBONE on November 18th as promotion for their Pay-Per-View offer to North America on November 25th. We asked the Stones for 20-30 minutes of their concert so that the multicast would not severely affect net traffic. The multicast will be repeated a few times throught this next week as permitted by all of you out in cyberspace.
>
> The MBONE Broadcast began on Friday November 18th 10:00pmEST after a an unannounced renegade warmup set by an obscure and very bad band of furry Palo Alto Geeks. They touted that this was the first ever warmup set by a band in a different city than the headliner. They started their warmup set at 9:30EST just as we were about to do our final set of broadcast tests before the do or die live video feed came via satellite from the Cotton Bowl so we fully agreed when they did crufty durges like "I'm an asshole." and "We don't care."
>
> At 10:00pm, we took the first half hour to share some new interviews and never seen before backstage stuff with all the listeners. Then we broadcast the "Love is Strong" video followed by the "Out of Tears" video. The band took the stage at 10:32EST and the concert began. The Stones started with their customary opening three "Not Fade Away", "Tumblin Dice" and "You Got Me Rockin" then Mick gave a special address to our MBONE listeners. He said something like:
>
> > "I wanna say a special welcome to everyone thats uh... climbed into the Internet tonight and uh... has got into the MBONE and I hope it doesn't all collapse!"

Figure 7-5: The Web page with details about the Rolling Stones' MBONE multicast in 1994 (`http://www.stones.com/MBONE/`).

One of those links calls up another page, which shows the sites that tuned in to the MBONE concert. The interesting part about this page is the number of participants shown, as well as the range of locations from which the connections came. In November of '94, you needed more expensive hardware than you do today to connect to the MBONE, so a large MBONE audience was not guaranteed. Furthermore, some of these locations were "multicast viewing parties," something similar to an MBONE Super Bowl or World Cup party, where one person set up the connection and a bunch of friends gathered to experience the event. In this sense, the MBONE acted like a satellite television broadcast.

This fact is an important one: Although the MBONE may have the capability to be an interactive medium, nothing prevents it from working more or less like satellite broadcasting, with one source and many destinations. If people only use the MBONE in this way, it can't possibly develop to its full potential. One of the promises of the MBONE is that it will offer *narrow*casting rather than *broad*casting, catering to specialized interests and enabling full interaction between individual participants. Still, that the Stones' MBONE concert happened at all is significant in that marketers realized the commercial potential of the MBONE.

Much more interesting, from the standpoint of the MBONE's potential, was the concert that Sky Cries Mary gave, which was multicast on November 10, 1994, just eight days before the Stones' show. Figure 7-6 shows the main page for that event, stored at the Internet Underground Music Archive (`http://www.iuma.com/`), an organization that promises to provide regular MBONE entertainment. Here is an excerpt from the press release that you can access from that page:

On Thursday, November 10, at 7:00pm PST, World Domination Records, Windswept Pacific, the Internet Underground Music Archive (IUMA), Starwave Corporation, and Nick Turner of Firstars Management present the Seattle-based techno/ambient rock band Sky Cries Mary performing a live show in one of the first ever real-time rock concert broadcasts over the Internet.

This multicast broadcast will reach tens of millions of Internet computers world wide. This technology will allow anyone with access to a high end computer and a high-speed network connection to access the broadcast and view the concert live.

This experimental broadcast will utilize the fullest capabilities of the Internet today. While not yet up to MTV specs, it will be in color with telephone-quality audio. Note that this kind of broadcast is not at all possible using the commercial online providers like America Online and Prodigy. This represents a first step and is absolutely free of charge!

The concert will be broadcast at 7:00 PM PST over the MBONE.

The MBONE is an experimental multimedia broadcast service, using the Internet as a prototype of the broadband networks that will be provided in the future by telephone and cable TV companies.

To see the broadcast you must be at a site that has a powerful computer and a high speed network connection. Currently only powerful workstations like those from Sun Microsystems, Silicon Graphics, and Digital Equipment Corporation can receive MBONE broadcasts.

The network connection required is pretty heavy too, a T1 line connection is currently required (a T1 line is the equivalent of 24 regular telephone lines, or 12 ISDN lines). Don't despair too much, a T1 line is a fraction of the capability that is provided in many of the Interactive Television trials. Many of the trials of ITV are using a technology called ADSL which includes the equivalent of a T1 line and an ISDN line.

If you already have access to MBONE broadcasts, just select "skycries", and you'll be watching.

The press release stresses the uniqueness of the event, but what's interesting is the contrast between its claim that the broadcast will reach tens of millions of Internet computers worldwide and the statement that you need to be at a site equipped with a sophisticated workstation and a high-speed connection to take part in the event.

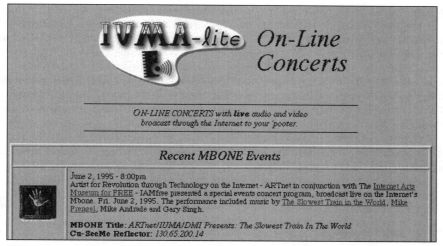

Figure 7-6: Web page with information about the Sky Cries Mary concert in 1994 (http://www.iuma.com/IUMA2.0/brew/concerts/Sky_Cries_Mary/index.html).

The most interesting item on the Sky Cries Mary site is the page of screen captures of the "whiteboard." Whiteboards are software items that are becoming prevalent in computer videoconferencing packages (whether on the MBONE or not). Whereas some conferencing software packages enable users to speak to one another, other (typically less expensive) packages offer a whiteboard instead for user-to-user communication. Even the speech-enabled packages contain the whiteboard, because it allows users to draw diagrams and demonstrate other communications that can be better handled visually than audibly. You'd expect a speaker in front of the room to use a whiteboard or blackboard for demonstration purposes, and there's no reason to expect conferencing software to offer less.

In this case, the whiteboard was available to anyone logged onto the MBONE to watch the concert. The comments weren't exactly replete with memorable content, but the impressive thing is that the comments were made in real time, from many different locations, during the concert. Extend this concept to a series of different whiteboards, each dedicated to a different "subject," and you have the basis for interaction during entertainment events. If you've ever wanted to talk about an entertainment event while you were watching it, you know how valuable that capability can be.

Sky Cries Mary was on the MBONE through the efforts of the Internet Underground Music Archive (IUMA). IUMA, which lists numerous independent artists (and some who have signed with labels) among their acts, is constantly offering Internet experiments in the entertainment field. After you log on to the IUMA site (`http://www.iuma.com/`), click on Enter IUMA and then the What's Brewing link to see whether IUMA plans to provide any new MBONE multicasts. You won't find anyone as well known as the Stones, but many people consider that fact to be a plus. One of the MBONE's capabilities, after all, is to provide lesser known artists with a way to reach the world.

Live performances on the MBONE are not restricted to musical concerts. Plays, poetry readings, ballets, and holiday choirs could use the MBONE as a forum for their productions as well. Setting up such a session takes planning, initiative, and frequently, corporate donations of equipment and connections, but it can be done.

Radio and television

Television and radio represent two existing mediums that stand to gain from the emergence of the MBONE. Network television probably won't make extensive use of the new technologies because it already has a wide broadcasting area, but for specialty stations and independent programmers, the MBONE offers a means of reaching extended audiences. The secret to using it successfully here deals with identifying and informing the audience.

Even for niche stations that now occupy positions on cable or satellite networks (such as the Home & Garden channel, the Cable Health Club, or the satellite TV network aimed solely at truckers on the road), the MBONE may prove a worthwhile investment, especially for early adopters. Cable and satellite subscribers now have an overwhelming number of channel choices, and their choices will only increase in the future. Because MBONE activity is still quite rare, television-type stations have a chance to define the MBONE's entertainment programming before the big players get hold of it. Once commercial interest in the MBONE increases, the paradigm will already be in place. This scenario is basically what happened with the Internet.

Television-like activity on the MBONE is practically non-existent as of this writing, however. The more interesting forays into the MBONE are the radio initiatives that include multicasting as a distribution strategy. The point is that you can now use the Net essentially for radio programming. With the advent of technologies such as RealAudio (`http://www.realaudio.com/`, also covered in Chapter 2), we will also begin to see "near-live" radio — taped programming that is immediately converted to RealAudio format and placed on the Net within minutes of the original taping.

One possible use for this format is to invite listeners to hear the RealAudio file, then use existing Internet technology — Chat and WebChat, or perhaps the MBONE itself — to discuss the program in question. This use isn't an MBONE use, but because it combines multimedia and real-time communication, the effect is much the same.

The MBONE is more than capable of handling radio broadcasts. In fact, because of the lack of a video feed, it can support radio much better than videoconferencing and provide several additional scheduled sessions. The problem is that radio, unlike television, tends to be a local phenomenon these days, so how radio programmers make use of the MBONE, as it becomes increasingly available, remains to be seen. In all likelihood, we'll hear short broadcasts of events not readily available elsewhere on our radio dials, and some material may be more promotional than informative.

Games

If one area exists where stand-alone computers have been far more successful than Internet-connected machines, that area is games. You can buy hordes of multimedia extravaganzas for your stand-alone PC or Mac, some of which are superb as both games and spectacles, and most of which incorporate audio, video, animation, and smooth interfaces. A few games support multi-player capabilities, but the vast majority are designed to be played by one person at a time.

By contrast, games on the Internet (or commercial services such as the ImagiNation Network) are designed for multi-player use, but in doing so they tend to sacrifice most multimedia features. What they gain, however, is the possibility of global, simultaneous game-play among large numbers of players. In other words, the Internet has the potential of bringing the "social" back into gaming.

The primary gaming technology on the Internet today is the MUD, or Multi-User Dungeon. Initially designed to offer multi-player, fantasy- or science-fiction-text adventure games along the lines of the famous Zork, today's MUDs are used for games and education (the latter in the form of MOOs or MUSHes). Although MUDs have a large following and can be extremely enjoyable to play, these games are still missing one important ingredient — multimedia. When playing a MUD, you see text and only text, although some MUD designers are working to incorporate MUDs with the Web to offer visual representations of the places you visit in the game. For more on MUDs, see `http://draco.centerline.com:8080/~franl/mud.html`, which links you to several MUD sites.

Other Internet games, such as the famous Netrek, offer real-time multi-player capabilities with a graphical component. Figure 7-7 shows an important Netrek information page, complete with a screen shot of the game in action. This 16-player arcade-style simulation is basically a computer game with multiple players, and it has enjoyed such success that some businesses and schools have banned it from their computers because it uses up too many resources. Despite its success, however, it pales beside most multimedia computer games (from a purely aesthetic perspective), and it barely scratches the surface of what can be done with Internet gaming.

Figure 7-7: Netrek Home Page, with links to information archives about the game (http://factoryx.factoryx.com/).

Whether the MBONE will become large enough (from a bandwidth sense) to support long gaming sessions is uncertain. If it does, however, the gaming possibilities are endless. Consider the role-playing game, for example, made famous in the late 1970s (the days before home computers) by Dungeons and Dragons. In this game, one person (the gamesmaster) put together a "world" and a set of plot lines; the other players — usually about six — played the role of characters in that world, attempting to solve the plot. At its worst, D&D was, and still is, an exercise in juvenile stupidity. At its best, though, this type of game truly became interactive storytelling. To date, no computer role-playing game has come anywhere close to similar success at the storytelling level.

Games conducted over the MBONE may well offer a global version of that kind of gaming, perhaps with dozens of players and more than one gamesmaster. With real-time collaboration, whiteboarding, graphical maps, and all sorts of other paraphernalia, these games would bring a social element to computer gaming that it currently lacks in most cases, and in the process could conceivably develop an important new art form. This capability does not lie in the near future, but it is something to aim for. The problem is overload: game players tend to forget about things such as how long they've been online, and the MBONE has limited resources. But the potential is enormous.

Other types of games are possible as well, from checkers to Trivial Pursuit and Pictionary to even Charades. For many people, getting players into the same house to play a game is next to impossible; the MBONE can potentially solve that problem, and change the entire concept of social gaming in the process.

The MBONE and Education

One of the great ironies of this century is that television was originally seen to be an exclusively educational medium. Indeed, we've now educated ourselves in the vagaries of Beverly Hills lifestyles, how to fight bad guys without losing our cowboy hats, and all kinds of other life-enhancing details, but television hasn't exactly fulfilled its educational promise. And yet, at its best, TV can be (and has been) supremely educational. The shock of the Kennedy assassinations, the glory of the moon landings, the horror of Vietnam, the terror of Tiananmen Square, the tragedy of the Challenger shuttle explosion, the tearing down of the Berlin Wall, and the end of the Soviet Union have all provided great, educational TV experiences. As far as educational programming goes, however, the provisions have been sporadic and deal only with *popular* education.

Most education, of course, isn't popular. It is challenging, demanding, often boring, and sometimes almost exclusively solitary. Broadcast the moon walk on TV and you'd get an audience; broadcast the physics conferences and lab experiments that led to the building of the Eagle, and you'd have almost no viewers. Sesame Street may be popular with young children, but once they mature past the early years, education is work, not play, and TV doesn't seem to go well with work.

The MBONE, on the other hand, will. Because it was designed as a medium for broadcasting to very specific audiences rather than mass audiences, the MBONE can be used for educational purposes. The next section examines three possibilities for using the MBONE for educational purposes: distance education, special projects, and conferences. All three areas are vital components to the field of education, and the MBONE provides applications for each one.

Distance education

Videoconferencing already has a place in *distance education*, which is defined here as taking courses without being on campus. But most distance education remains based in the older style of listening to audio tapes and reading lecture notes, then working by yourself to get through the course. Many people receive degrees through distance education, but almost all comment that they would have liked the interaction of being on campus. The fact that most students on campus don't actually participate in lectures or classes doesn't matter; distance students feel isolated from the group, and the MBONE potentially can help eliminate part of this feeling.

Ideally, an MBONE-based distance education course would be combined with an on-campus class. The instructor would conduct an interaction-based session (as opposed to a straight lecture, which could be handled just as easily with videotape), and would accept questions and discussion from MBONE-connected students as well as in-class students. Sessions of this type need not last longer than 45 minutes to be effective, as long as they are well-organized. Whereas on-campus classes can meander to a certain degree, an MBONE-connected session must not (at least for now) waste any time. The organization and protocol of the session must be established and adhered to by the instructor, the on-campus students, and the distance students alike.

The potential for a greatly enriched learning experience for distance students is partially in place, but large barriers to it still remain. Because this technology is so expensive, the only viable possibility is to have distance students meet at assigned locations that have workstations with MBONE connections in place. This fact creates a built-in discriminating factor against truly isolated students in favor of those students in the larger population areas, but those who want to use the MBONE this way will have to work around the problem. In spite of its flaws, however, the idea remains a powerful one.

Special projects

The prototype for special educational projects on the Internet is surely NASA's JASON Project (http://seawifs.gsfc.nasa.gov/scripts/JASON.html). Introduced by Dr. Robert Ballard, the same person who found the sunken Titanic, the JASON Project is an annual, two-week expedition to a remote part of the world that is broadcast/multicast in real-time to "a network of educational, research, and cultural institutions in the United States, Canada, Bermuda, and the United Kingdom." One of the technologies in use is the MBONE.

The 1995 expedition, Island Earth, examined the volcanoes of Hawaii. Basically, the MBONE let students from around the world view the event and participate in it in real time. The pedagogical value of such a multicast is clear, and you can just imagine the vast range of activities that would benefit from such a setup. With sufficient funding, MBONE multicasts could form the basis of a kind of collaborative learning we have not yet experienced.

The key to the success of such a venture is planning and organization. Teachers and students must be prepared to be a part of such a session, the equipment must be readied and tested, and parents must be informed. In other words, the project must be as fully developed as any other classroom project. But when you consider the MBONE's potential for enabling students to reach beyond the classroom and learn alongside students from around the world, the amount of preparation seems worthwhile. There are problems with this format, of course — skeptical teachers, underfunded schools, less-than-caring students, parents who don't believe in technologically assisted learning — but these problems are the same ones encountered in many education situations. The point is that the MBONE can provide the basis for special learning projects, and that it is already doing so.

Conferences

Scholarship and research rely on the publication of results. Formal publication takes place in journals or technical reports, which remain paper-based for the most part, but initial publication often takes place at academic or research conferences. The problem with conferences is that you have to travel to them, and with the funding cuts that universities and research institutes are experiencing, travel has become difficult for many researchers and impossible for some.

Another problem exists in deciding which conferences to attend. Even with unlimited travel funding, taking in all applicable conferences would be impossible; as a result, important research relevant to your particular area may be missed or overlooked until it is too late.

Papers delivered at a conference are sometimes published in a book called "Proceedings." But you cannot engage in a question-and-answer session with a book of proceedings, and the talks that rely on visual or audio demonstrations become rather lifeless in the book format. Reading the proceedings is not an easy task either, whereas if you're attending a conference, you're more likely to listen simply because you're there.

An important initial role of the MBONE will be to help disseminate research information through conferences. Conference sessions (including keynote addresses) could be multicast live along the lines of a full videoconference. Viewers could sign up for the sessions, pay the conference fee, and have the resources to participate fully, using speech, whiteboards, and other tools. The major difference here is that the MBONE eliminates the associated travel and accommodation costs. An added benefit could be an increased desire by users to participate and learn.

In fact, conferences are already being conducted across the MBONE to some extent. One example is the Workshop on Computer Based Tools to Assist in Air Quality Modeling (http://www.iceis.mcnc.org/conference/state-workshop-3-22-95/index.html), conducted on March 22, 1995. As Figure 7-8 shows, the conference was available via the MBONE, and the participants were encouraged to communicate with others at the conference through the MBONE as well. Another example is the IEEE Infocom '95 conference. This conference offered MBONE sessions for non-traveling participants. The following is an excerpt from the conference instructions for MBONE users:

MBONE communications are multi-way. During question periods, we will solicit questions from remote participants, and try to interleave them with questions from the local audience. Please wait to ask your question until the chair explicitly asks for questions from MBONE/Internet listeners. The person sitting in front of the workstation which is doing the MBONE transmission, whom we call the "MBONE moderator," will act as your stand-in in the conference hall, and collaborate with the chair to handle incoming questions smoothly. To avoid everyone politely waiting for everybody else, please jot a short note (like simply your name) on the current whiteboard page. The MBONE moderator will then explicitly ask you to proceed with your question by announcing your name and location. At that point, you should start speaking, beginning your question by stating your name, affiliation, and geographical location. If your audio sounds badly broken up, it may be best to simply type the question on the whiteboard rather than trying to use the microphone.

Figure 7-8: The MBONE information page from the 1995 Air Quality workshop.

In reality, these instructions differ little from the standard conference protocol. You wait your turn, you are acknowledged, and you ask your question. Because you can put your question on the whiteboard, however, you may have an even greater chance of being answered than a member of the physical audience would. The point is that conferences can be conducted over the MBONE, and that some conferences have already used this format with success.

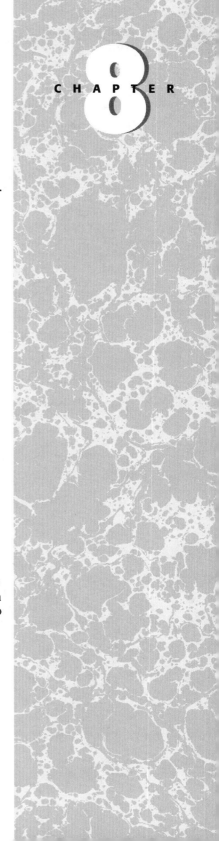

CHAPTER 8

Research Applications

The following article is reprinted with permission of its authors and of *IEEE Computer* magazine. We gratefully acknowledge the cooperation of these parties in bringing you this information.

MBONE Provides Audio and Video Across the Internet

Michael R. Macedonia and Donald P. Brutzman

Naval Postgraduate School

Reprinted with permission of the authors and *IEEE Computer* magazine.

Donald P. Brutaman and Michael R. Macedonia, "MBONE Provides Audio and Video Across the Internet," *IEEE Computer* 27 (April 1994): 30-36

The joy of science is in the discovery. In March 1993, our group at the Naval Postgraduate School heard that the Jason Project, an underwater exploration and educational program supported by Woods Hole Oceanographic Institution in Massachusetts, was showing live video over the Internet from an underwater robot in waters off Baja, Mexico. We worked furiously to figure out how to receive that video signal, laboring diligently to gather the right equipment, contact the appropriate network managers, and obtain hardware permissions from local bureaucrats. After several days of effort, we learned that a satellite antenna uplink cable on the Jason support ship had become flooded with seawater a few hours before we became operational.

Despite this disappointment, we remained enthusiastic because, during our efforts, we discovered how to use the Internet's most unique network, MBONE. Short for Multicast Backbone [1], MBONE is a virtual network that has been in existence since early 1992. It was named by Steve Casner [1] of the University of Southern California Information Sciences Institute and originated from an effort to multicast audio and video from meetings of the Internet Engineering Task Force. Today, hundreds of researchers use MBONE to develop protocols and applications for group communication. Multicast provides one-to-many and many-to-many network delivery services for applications such as videoconferencing and audio where several hosts need to communicate simultaneously.

This article describes the network concepts underlying MBONE, the importance of bandwidth considerations, various application tools, MBONE events, interesting MBONE uses (see the two sidebars), and provides guidance on how to connect your Internet site to the MBONE.

Multicast networks

Multicasting has existed for several years on local area networks such as Ethernet and Fiber Distributed Data Interface. However, with Internet Protocol multicast addressing at the network layer, group communication can be established across the Internet. IP multicast addressing [2] is an Internet standard (Request For Comment 1112) developed by Steve Deering [3] of the Xerox Palo Alto Research Center and is supported by numerous workstation vendors, including Sun, Silicon Graphics, Digital Equipment Corporation, and Hewlett-Packard. Categorized officially as an IP Class D address, an IP multicast address is mapped to the underlying hardware multicast services of a LAN. Two things make multicasting feasible on a worldwide scale:

1. Installation of high bandwidth Internet backbone connections.

2. Widespread availability of workstations with adequate processing power and built-in audio capability.

The reason MBONE became a virtual network is that it shares the same physical media as the Internet. It uses a network of routers (mrouters) that can support multicast. These mrouters are either upgraded commercial routers, or dedicated workstations running with modified kernels in parallel with standard routers.

MBONE is augmented by "tunneling," a scheme to forward multicast packets among the islands of MBONE subnets through Internet IP routers that (typically) do not support IP multicast. This is done by encapsulating the multicast packets inside regular IP packets. As installed commercial hardware is upgraded to support multicast traffic, this mixed system of specially dedicated mrouters and tunnels will no longer be necessary. We expect that most commercial routers will support multicast in the near future, eliminating the inefficiencies and management headaches of duplicate routers and tunnels.

Bandwidth constraints

The key to understanding the constraints of MBONE is thinking about bandwidth. The reason a multicast stream is bandwidth-efficient is that one packet can touch all workstations on a network. Thus, a 128-kilobit per second video stream (typically 1-4 frames per second) uses the same bandwidth whether it is received by one workstation or 20. That is good. However, that same multicast packet is ordinarily prevented from crossing network boundaries such as routers. The reasons for this current restriction are religious and obvious from a networking standpoint. If a multicast stream that can touch every workstation could jump from network to network without controls, the entire Internet would quickly become saturated by such streams. That would be disastrous! Therefore, controls are necessary.

MBONE can control multicast packet distribution across the Internet in two ways:

1. It can limit the lifetime of multicast packets.

2. It can use sophisticated pruning algorithms to adaptively restrict multicast transmission. This is being tested.

Responsible daily use of the MBONE network consists merely of making sure you don't overload your local or regional bandwidth capacity. MBONE protocol developers are experimenting with automatically pruning and grafting subtrees, but for the most part MBONE uses thresholds to truncate broadcasts to the leaf routers. The truncation is based on the setting for the time-to-live (ttl) field in a packet that is decremented each time the packet passes though an mrouter. A ttl value of 16 would limit multicast to a campus, as opposed to values of 127 or 255, which might send a multicast stream to every subnet on the MBONE (currently about 13 countries). A ttl field is sometimes decremented by large values under a global thresholding scheme provided to limit multicasts to sites and regions if desired.

These issues can have a major impact on network performance. For example, a default video stream consumes about 128 Kbps of bandwidth, or nearly 10 percent of a T1 line (a common site-to-site link on the Internet). Several simultaneous high-bandwidth sessions might easily saturate network links and routers. This problem is compounded by the fact that general-purpose workstation routers that MBONE typically uses are normally not as fast or robust as the dedicated hardware routers used in most of the Internet.

Networking details

When a host on an MBONE-equipped subnet establishes or joins a common shared session, it announces that event via the Internet Group Management Protocol. The mrouter on the subnet forwards that announcement to the other mrouters in the network. Groups are disbanded when everyone leaves, freeing up the IP multicast address for reuse. The routers occasionally poll hosts on the subnets to determine if any are still group members. If there is no reply by a host, the router stops advertising that host's group membership to the other multicast routers. MBONE routing protocols are still immature, and their ongoing design is a central part of this network experiment. Most MBONE routers use the Distance Vector Multicast Routing Protocol, which some network researchers commonly consider inadequate for rapidly changing network topologies because routing information propagates too slowly [4]. The Open Shortest Path Working Group [5] has proposed a Multicast extension to the Open Shortest Path link-state protocol that addresses this issue using an algorithm developed by Deering [5]. With both protocols, mrouters must dynamically compute a source tree for each participant in a multicast group.

MBONE is small enough that this technique is not a problem. However, some researchers speculate that, for a larger network with frequently changing group memberships, these routing techniques will be computationally inefficient. Research efforts on these issues are ongoing, since every bottleneck conquered results in a new bottleneck revealed.

Topology and event scheduling

The MBONE community must manage the MBONE topology and the scheduling of multicast sessions to minimize congestion. By the beginning of 1994, some 750 subnets were already connected worldwide. Topology changes for new nodes are added by consensus: A new site announces itself to the MBONE mail list, and the nearest potential providers decide who can establish the most logical connection path to minimize regional Internet loading.

Scheduling MBONE events is handled similarly. Special programs are announced in advance on an MBONE event electronic mail list; for example, rem-conf-request@ es.net for subscription requests and rem-conf@es.net for messages (see Tables 1 and 2). Advance announcements usually prevent overloaded scheduling of Internet-wide events and alert potential participants.

Cooperation is key. Many people are surprised to learn that no single person or entity is "in charge" of either local topology changes or event scheduling.

Protocols

The magic of MBONE is that teleconferencing can be done in the hostile world of the Internet where variable packet delivery delays and limited bandwidth play havoc with applications that require some real-time guarantees. Limited experiments demonstrated the feasibility of audio over the ARPAnet as early as 1973. However, only a few years ago, transmitting video across the Internet was considered impossible. Development of effective multicast protocols disproved that widespread opinion. In this respect, MBONE is like the proverbial talking dog: It's not so much what the dog has to say that is amazing, it's more that the dog can talk at all!

The key network concepts that make MBONE possible are IP multicast and real-time stream delivery via adaptive receivers. For example, in addition to the multicast protocols, many MBONE applications are using the draft Real-Time Protocol on top of the User Datagram Protocol and Internet Protocol. RTP [6], being developed by the Audio-Video Transport Working Group of the Internet Engineering Task Force, provides timing and sequencing services, permitting the application to adapt and smooth out network-induced latencies and errors.

Related real-time delivery schemes are also being evaluated. The end result is that even with a time-critical application such as an audio tool, participants normally perceive conversations as if they are in real time. This is because there is actually a small buffering delay to synchronize and resequence the arriving voice packets. Protocol development continues. Although operation is usually acceptable in practice, many aspects of MBONE are still considered experimental.

Data compression

Other aspects of this research include the related needs to compress a variety of media and optionally provide privacy through encryption. Several techniques to reduce bandwidth include Joint Photographic Experts Group compression, wavelet-based encoding, and the ISO standard H.261 for video. Visually, this translates to "velocity compression"; rapidly changing screen blocks are updated much more frequently than slowly changing blocks.

Encodings for audio include Pulse Coded Modulation and Group Speciale Mobile (the name of the standardization group for the European digital cellular telephony standard). Besides concerns for real-time delivery, audio is a difficult media for both MBONE and teleconferencing in general. This is because of the need to balance signal levels for all parties, who may have different audio processing hardware (for example, different microphones and amplifiers). Audio also generates lots of relatively small packets, which are the bane of network routers.

Application tools

Besides basic networking technology, MBONE researchers are developing new applications that typify many of the goals associated with the information superhighway. Session availability is dynamically announced using a tool called sd (session directory), which displays active multicast groups (see Figure 8-1). The sd tool also launches multicast applications and automatically selects unused addresses for any new groups. Steve McCanne and Van Jacobson of the University of California Lawrence Berkeley Laboratory developed sd.

Video, audio, and a shared drawing whiteboard are the principal MBONE applications, provided by software packages called nv (net video), vat (visual audio tool), and wb (whiteboard). The principal authors of these tools are Ron Frederick of Xerox Palo

Alto Research Center for nv, and McCanne and Jacobson for vat and wb. Each program is available in executable form without charge from various anonymous File-Transfer Protocol sites on the Internet. Working versions are available for Sun, Silicon Graphics, DEC, and Hewlett-Packard architectures, with ports in progress for Macintosh. No DOS, OS-2, Amiga, or Windows versions are available, although ported tools can be found for 386 boxes running the (free) 386BSD UNIX. Pointers to all public application tools are included in the Frequently Asked Questions (FAQ) document [1]. Mirror FTP sites are available overseas.

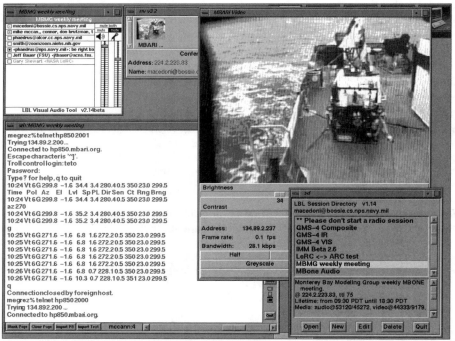

Figure 8-1: MBONE session at the Monterey Bay Aquarium Research Institute showing application tools nv (network video), vat (visual audio tool), wb (whiteboard), and sd (session directory). (Courtesy of the JASON project.)

Additional tools are also available or under development. Winston Dang of the University of Hawaii has created imm (Image Multicaster Client), a low-bandwidth image server. It typically provides live images of Earth from various geostationary satellites at half-hour intervals in either visible or infrared spectra. Henning Schulzrinne of AT&T/Bell Laboratories developed nevot, a network voice terminal providing multiple party conferences with a choice of transport protocols. Eve Schooler of the Information Sciences Institute is part of a team developing mmcc, a session orchestration tool and multimedia conference control program. Mike Macedonia of the Naval Postgraduate School, coauthor of this article, has created a multicast version of NPSNET [7], a 3D distributed virtual environment that uses the IEEE Distributed Interactive Simulation (DIS) application protocol [8]. Stephen Lau of SRI International is experimenting with using graphics workstation windows as image drivers. Kurt Lidl of UUnet Technologies, Falls Church, Virginia, is working on a network news distribution application that uses multicast to reduce overall Internet loading and expedite news delivery. (Their goal is 120 ms total propagation coast to coast — which is amazing, since light takes about 16 ms to make that trip.)

Events

Many of the most exciting events on the Internet appear on MBONE first. Perhaps the most popular is NASA Select, the in-house cable channel broadcast during space shuttle missions. It's exciting seeing an astronaut positioning another astronaut by the boots to repair a satellite — live on your desktop from 150 miles above the surface of the planet.

Conferences on supercomputing, the Internet Engineering Task Force, scientific visualization, and many other topics have appeared — often accompanied by directions on how to download PostScript copies of presented papers and slides from anonymous FTP sites. Radio Free VAT is a community radio station whose DJs sign up for air time via an automated server (vat-radio-request@elxr.jpl.nasa.gov). Xerox PARC occasionally broadcasts lectures by distinguished speakers. Internet Talk Radio (Carl Malamud, info@radio.com) has presented talks by US Vice President Al Gore, talk-show host Larry King, and others. Another new area is remote learning, which can use MBONE to bring expertise over long distances and multiply training benefits. Finally, default MBONE audio and video channels are provided so that new users can experiment and get advice from more experienced users.

Groupwork on groupware

The MBONE community is active and open. Work on tools, protocols, standards, applications, and events is very much a cooperative and international effort. Feedback and suggestions are often relayed to the entire MBONE electronic mail list. (As an example, the article you are reading was previewed by that group.)

Cooperation is essential due to the limited bandwidth of many networks — in particular, transoceanic links. So far, no hierarchical scheme has been necessary for resolving potentially contentious issues such as topology changes or event scheduling. Interestingly, distributed problem solving and decision making has worked on a human level just as successfully as on the network protocol level. We hope this decentralized approach will continue to be successful, even with the rapid addition of new users.

Cost of admission

The cost of equipment is often relatively low, but to get on MBONE, you need the willingness to study and learn how to use these new and fast-moving tools, you need bandwidth, and you need some hardware. NPS runs MBONE tools on workstations connected via Ethernet (10 Mbps). Off-campus links are via T1 lines (1.5 Mbps).

We found that bandwidth capacities lower than T1 are generally unsuitable for MBONE video, although some users — sometimes entire countries! — on specially configured networks have managed to make the tools work at 56 and 64 Kbps.

Given adequate network bandwidth, you next need a designated MBONE network administrator. Working part-time, it typically takes one to three weeks for a network-knowledgeable person to establish MBONE at a new site. Setup is not for the faint of heart, but all the tools are documented, and help is available from the MBONE list.

You should read the Frequently Asked Questions a few times, ensure that software tools and multicast-compatible kernels are available for your target workstations, and subscribe to the mail list in advance to enable you to ask questions and receive answers. Table 1 shows the various worldwide MBONE list subscription request addresses. After subscribing, review the FAQ.

These tools can also work in isolation between workstations on a single LAN without an mrouter. We recommend that you test the application tools locally in advance (before going through the dedicated mrouter effort) to see if they are compatible with your system and match your expectations.

To receive multicast packets on your LAN, you will need to configure an mrouter. This can be either a single workstation on a LAN, or a host dedicated as a parallel mrouter. A nondedicated single workstation can receive and pass multicast to its LAN neighbors, but this arrangement can place double MBONE traffic on that LAN.

A more practical approach is to dedicate an old unused workstation as an mrouter and equip it with two Ethernet cards, which are needed so this mrouter can act independently and in parallel with your standard IP router. (NPS uses both approaches.) After deciding on your mrouter configuration, obtain and load the application software tools. You are now ready to put multicast on your LAN.

Once connected, you should pass along any lessons learned to the tool authors or the MBONE list. When the opportunity presents itself, show your overall network site administrator something spectacular on MBONE (such as a live space walk) and make sure your site is budgeting funds to increase your network bandwidth.

Demands on network bandwidth are significant and getting more critical. You might consider Tengdin's First (and Only) Law of Telecommunications: "The jump from zero to whatever baud rate is the most important jump you can make. After that, everyone always wants to go straight to the speed of light."

Caveats aplenty

Problems still exist, and a lot of work is in progress. The audio interface takes coaching and practice. Leaving your microphone on by mistake can disrupt a session, since typically only one person can be understood at a time. You will need a video capture board in your workstation to transmit video, but no special hardware is needed to receive video. One-to-four frames per second video seems pretty slow (standard video is 30 frames per second), but in practice it is surprisingly effective when combined with phone-quality voice. There is one big danger: One user blasting a high-bandwidth video signal (greater than 128 Kbps) can cause severe and widespread network problems. Controls on access to tools are rudimentary, and security is minimal; for example, a local user might figure out how to listen through your workstation mike (unless you unplug it). Audio broadcast preparations are often overlooked but can be just as involved as video broadcast preparations. Network monitoring tools are not yet convenient to use. There is no guaranteed delivery: Lost packets stay lost. Internet bandwidth is still inadequate for MBONE in many countries.

On one occasion, an unusual topology change at NPS caused a feedback loop that overrode the NASA Select audio track. Although plenty of people were willing to point out the symptoms of our error, it was not possible for the rest of the network to cut off the offending workstation cleanly. More situations will undoubtedly occur as MBONE developers and users learn more. Unpleasant surprises usually trigger a flurry of discussion and a corresponding improvement in the tools.

Expect to spend some time if you want to be an MBONE user. It is time-consuming because learning and fixing are involved, and because it is lots of fun!

It is not every day that someone says to you, "Here is a multimedia television station that you can use to broadcast from your desktop to the world." These are powerful concepts and powerful tools that extend our ability to communicate and collaborate tremendously. They have already changed the way people work and interact on the net.

MBONE and Distance Learning at the Naval Postgraduate School

Mike McCann, Naval Postgraduate School Visualization Laboratory

In March 1993, the W.R. Church Computer Center at the Naval Postgraduate School dedicated a Sun Sparcstation 2 to act as a Multicast Backbone (MBONE) router for the campus and the Monterey Bay research community. This router and an IP-encapsulated tunnel from Stanford University provides the NPS backbone with real-time audio, video, and other MBONE data feeds.

The MBONE is an excellent tool for those doing research in networks and video teleconferencing technology. Although it is not generally thought of as "ready for prime time" (audio dropouts may be frequent and video, at best, is only 3 frames per second over the Internet), NPS successfully used it to provide training in Cray Fortran optimization from the National Center for Atmospheric Research in Boulder, Colorado.

Five people who would not have been able to afford to travel to Boulder remotely "attended" the three-day training course at the NPS Computer Center's Visualization Laboratory. For the session, students — including myself — enjoyed two-way audio and video between the classroom at NCAR and the lab at NPS, and could ask questions of the NCAR instructor over the network. Advance preparation, good audio, and a camera operator in the NCAR classroom gave us a real feeling of presence in Boulder. "It was just like being there," one of my classmates said.

Paul Hyder of NCAR was instrumental in helping set up a direct "backup" tunnel between NPS and NCAR, where the slowest link is the T1 line between NPS and Stanford. During the course, there was only one 30-minute period of broken-up audio. We later determined that this interruption was caused by congestion on NCAR's Ethernet LAN. For much of 1993, the NPS Visualization Lab loaned a Sun Sparcstation 10 to the Monterey Bay Aquarium Research Institute for testing and incorporation into the live audio/video link to the research vessel Point Lobos and the remotely operated vehicle Ventana that explore the Monterey submarine canyon each day (see Figure 8-1). Local researchers in oceanography, virtual reality, and autonomous underwater vehicles continue to take advantage of the collaboration opportunities that this technology makes possible.

It might not be too long before MBONE enables us to videoconference with a classroom or a colleague half way around the world — directly from our desktop workstations.

The figure shows the sd (session directory) of MBONE events. (Courtesy of the JASON project.)

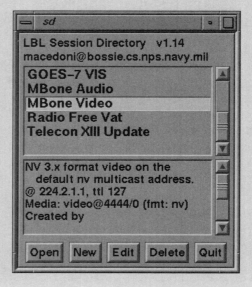

Remote Science over the MBONE during the Jason Project

Andy Maffei, Woods Hole Oceanographic Institution

Jason/Medea is a remotely operated, dual-vehicle system developed by the Woods Hole Oceanographic Institution for underwater science and exploration. The Jason Foundation for Education uses this system as part of an annual Jason Project expedition.

During 1993, more than 600,000 K-12 students were involved in the project via live satellite transmissions. While prime broadcast hours of the expedition focused on the project's educational mission, an intense science program was conducted on a concurrent round-the-clock basis. The EDS Corporation and the University of Texas at Dallas provided a 56 Kbps data circuit for the project. Running on a Sun Workstation, MorningStar PPP software established the Internet connection with research vessel Laney Chouest, from which the vehicles were deployed. This Internet connection made a transparent link with the multicast IP-based MBONE. Although the lab experimented with multicast video conferencing tools such as nv and vat, our primary interest in using the MBONE was to transmit experimental data and to support shore-based models that depicted the positions and movement of the Laney Chouest and the two Jason/Medea vehicles. This technology was used by several investigators collaborating on Jason science projects at different locations throughout the US.

Both 2D and 3D models were developed at the Deep Submergence Laboratory for use on Sun and Silicon Graphics workstations. Software packages to access these models, along with real-time MBONE data, were available to anyone on the MBONE who wanted to try them out. As sonar surveys progressed during the expedition, data was transmitted back to shore, and the detailed models were updated and then distributed over the Internet.

A workstation on board the Laney Chouest generated multicast packets containing navigation and attitude information for the three vehicles. These packets were distributed in real time over the MBONE so users running the modeling software could watch a graphic display of Jason prowling real seafloor features as scientists investigated seamounts, thermal plumes, and the area's unique ecology. In addition to vehicle information, experimental data variables (such as temperatures) were multicast on the MBONE. Scientists and other interested users could write programs to read these experimental values, watch the models evolve, and get immediate feedback on progress being made during different experiments.

From the accounts of participating researchers, MBONE use enhanced the science carried out during the cruise. However, since we spent a lot of time supporting specific experiments, we were unable to spend much time helping other interested MBONE users get models up and running at their own sites. This was the first time we used multicast IP during an experiment, but we nevertheless learned a great deal. Such unique experiments demonstrate the value of other science-based tools, in addition to more generic videoconferencing applications.

For additional information, contact Andy Maffei at Woods Hole Oceanographic Institution, Deep Submergence Laboratory, Woods Hole, MA 02543.

Table 8-1
E-mail Addresses for Requesting Addition
to the MBONE Mail Lists

Mail List	Mailing List for Subscription Requests	Region
mbone-eu	mbone-eu-request@sics.se	Europe
mbone-jp	mbone-jp-request@wide.ad.jp	Japan
mbone-korea	mbone-korea-request@mani.kaist.ac.kr	Korea
mbone-na	mbone-na-request@isi.edu	North America
mbone-nz	mbone-nz-request@waikato.ac.nz	New Zealand
mbone-oz	mbone-oz-request@internode.com.au	Australia
mbone-sg	mbone-sg-request@lincoln.technet.sg	Singapore
mbone	mbone-request@isi.edu	Others
rem-conf	rem-conf-request@es.net	Worldwide

Table 8-2
Electronic Mail Addresses for Putting
Messages on the Mailing Lists

Mail List	Mailing List for Posting Messages	Purpose
Mbone	mbone@isi.edu	Network configuration and tool development
rem-conf	rem-conf@es.net	Conference announce-ments and general discussion

References

1. Casner, "Frequently Asked Questions (FAQ) on the Multicast Backbone," May 6, 1993, ftp://venera.isi.edu/mbone/faq.txt.

2. D. E. Comer, *Internetworking with TCP/IP*, Vol. 1, Prentice Hall, Englewood Cliffs, N.J., 1991.

3. S. Deering, "Host Extensions for IP Multicasting," Request For Comment 1112, Aug. 1989, ftp://nic.ddn.mil/rfc/rfc1112.txt.

4. R. Perlman, *Interconnections: Bridges and Routers*, Addison-Wesley, New York, 1993, p. 258.

5. J. Moy, "Multicast Extensions to OSPF," Internet Engineering Task Force Draft, July 1993, `ftp://nic.ddn.mil/internet-drafts/draft-ietf-mospf-multicast-04.txt`.

6. H. Schulzrinne and S. Casner, "RTP: A Transport Protocol for Real-Time Applications," Internet Engineering Task Force Draft, Oct. 20, 1993, `ftp://nic.ddn.mil/internet-drafts/draft-ietf-avt-rtp-04.ps`.

7. D. R. Pratt, M. J. Zyda, et al., NPSNET Annual Lab Review, Dec. 1993, available at `ftp://taurus.cs.nps.navy.mil/pub/npsnet/npsnet.annual.report.ps`.

8. IEEE Standard for Information Technology — Protocols for Distributed Interactive Simulation Applications, Version 2.0, Univ. of Central Florida, Inst. for Simulation and Training, Orlando, Florida, May 28, 1993.

Further reading

Baker, S., "Multicasting for Sound and Video," *UNIX Review*, Feb. 1994, pp. 23-29.

Casner, S., and S. Deering, "First IETF Internet Audiocast," *ACM SIGComm Computer Communications Review*, July 1992, pp. 92–97; also at `ftp://venera.isi.edu/pub/ietf-audiocast.article.ps`.

Curtis, P., MBONE map, available via anonymous FTP from `ftp://parcftp.xerox.com/pub/net-research/mbone-map-big.ps`.

Deering, S., "MBONE: The Multicast Backbone," CERFnet Seminar, Mar. 3, 1993, `ftp://parcftp.xerox.com/pub/net-research/cerfnet-seminar-slides.ps`.

Acknowledgments

We thank the originators of the MBONE tools and dozens of MBONE users who provided essential contributions to this article.

About the authors

Michael R. Macedonia, PhD, is Vice President of Fraunhofer Center for Research in Computer Graphics, Inc., which is located in Providence, RI. He may be reached at `mmacedon@crcg.edu`.

Don Brutzman, PhD, is an Assistant Professor at the Naval Postgraduate School in Monterey, CA. He may be reached at `brutzman@nps.navy.mil` or via his Web page, `http://www.stl.nps.navy.mil/~brutzman`.

FTP availability

This article is available electronically via anonymous FTP to `taurus.cs.nps.navy.mil` in subdirectory pub/i3la as mbone.ps; in Uniform Resource Locator (URL) format used above, this anonymous FTP request corresponds to `ftp:/ /taurus.cs.nps.navy.mil/pub/i3la/mbone.ps`.

Text and hypertext versions of this article are available at

`ftp://taurus.cs.nps.navy.mil/pub/i3la/mbone.txt`

`ftp://taurus.cs.nps.navy.mil/pub/i3la/mbone.html`

This article was published in *IEEE Computer* magazine, pp. 30–36, April 1994.

Making the MBONE Connection

P A R T

In This Part

◆   ◆   ◆   ◆

What You Need — Hardware and Software

The MBONE, being a somewhat sophisticated service, requires a no less complex infrastructure for it to work as expected. It is probably the Internet service that consumes the greatest amount of network bandwidth per user. A few items are required before you can really enjoy what makes the Internet not only a giant distributed database but also a place to meet people, to share projects, and to transmit knowledge to others by a person and not by a lifeless document. These requirements include MBONE hardware, network bandwidth, multicast capability, an MBONE feed, and any platform-specific items.

Hardware

Here is a question that a lot of people have: How much will it cost in new hardware to be able to participate in the MBONE?

There are two answers to that question: nothing, and a few hundred dollars. It really depends on the degree of participation that you desire.

To receive MBONE events, an ordinary UNIX workstation, a PC running Windows, or a Mac will do. This is the "nothing" part of the answer. No special hardware is required to receive MBONE sessions.

To send audio, a microphone is required, along with sound hardware. Sound hardware is already included with most UNIX workstations and Macs. It's possible to buy very cheap sound hardware for the PC, and one brand that comes to mind is the de facto industry standard Sound Blaster card.

Sending video data becomes a little more expensive. A frame grabber card and a camera are required. For example, on Sun workstations, the VideoPix card is already used to send video to the MBONE. Other frame grabber brands include Parallax and J300, to name a couple.

Multicast

Another prerequisite to profit from the MBONE is the ability to handle multicast traffic appropriately. The traffic that runs over most of the Internet is unicast traffic. Unicast means that for a single source, there is one single destination. Multicast traffic is traffic with one single source but multiple destinations.

Most UNIX platforms require patches to enable multicast. Proper multicast is native to Solaris 2.x for Sun workstations. SGI workstations also come with multicast. Patches are required for the other UNIX flavors, such as SunOS 4.x, AIX 3.x, and so on. See Appendix C for instructions on how to get these patches.

PCs can talk multicast with only certain versions of networking software.

Macs can handle multicast with a recent version of Mac-TCP. Unfortunately, there aren't any native MBONE tools for the Mac yet, but we will see later how to get around this limitation.

This level of multicast handling is called *host multicast*.

Another level of multicast handling, *multicast routing*, is required to get MBONE traffic. Routing means to switch from one network to another until the final destination is reached. It's easy to send multicast traffic onto the local network, and if the multicast traffic is used on the local network only, then there is no problem. If multicast traffic has to be sent to other locations on the Internet, then you must work around a current limitation of the Internet. On the Internet (or rather, most of it), only unicast traffic is routed. To send multicast traffic to other networks, you must fool the Internet routers into thinking that you are sending them unicast traffic.

The most common method of fooling the Internet routers is to use a small program called mrouted. mrouted grabs the multicast traffic from the local network and disguises it as unicast traffic before sending it to the Internet. The multicast packets are put in unicast packets, which is called *encapsulating*. At the other end, another mrouted program takes this "multicast traffic in disguise" and turns it back into real multicast traffic. This becomes a virtual multicast-in-disguise link between your mrouted program and the destination's mrouted program. These virtual links are called *tunnels*. To receive MBONE traffic, you have to set up a tunnel between you and your network provider or any other site willing to give you an MBONE feed.

Not all platforms can run mrouted. The capability to route multicast traffic (via tunnels or not) requires special talents that are native in very few platforms. The operating system FreeBSD is one example. Solaris 2.x and SunOS 4.x can run mrouted, but they require that their kernel be patched to do it. See Appendix C for a list of platforms suitable for running Mrouted.

Ideally, your mrouted machine should be a separate machine so that other applications running on the machine does not influence the quality of the routing. However, I have done it the other way, too. At one time, I provided an MBONE feed for five sites on a Sun SPARC IPX running Solaris 2.3. This machine was also my backup machine. The poor IPX was nearly overloaded, but it worked.

Not only UNIX platforms can route multicast traffic. With special software, Proteon and Cisco routers can route multicast traffic, too. If you think this is the way you want to go, you should contact your vendor to find out more about it. However, you should know that the updates for Proteon and Cisco router software do not arrive nearly as fast as the UNIX mrouted updates hit the Internet. This means that if you go for a Proteon router, for example, it may become outdated and incompatible with the rest of the MBONE for a period of time. Because the router may become outdated, I recommend going with a UNIX multicast routing machine. CPU cycles are much cheaper on a UNIX machine than on a router, anyway.

Network Bandwidth

A certain amount of network bandwidth is required to receive MBONE broadcasts. Although there is no definite minimum, I'll try to establish guidelines so that you easily can determine the approximate amount of bandwidth that you need to watch or participate in a conference.

First, whatever amount of bandwidth you have, you always should run a version of the multicast routing software that supports pruning. This requirement is especially true with low bandwidth links such as ISDN. When your multicast routing software supports pruning, it will only receive the traffic that is required. The required traffic is determined by which events are joined by the people who profit from the MBONE traffic you receive. You will only receive the traffic for those events. Without pruning, you will always receive the whole MBONE traffic. For pruning to work properly, not only must you support pruning, but your feed must support it as well. If only one of you supports pruning, you will again receive the whole MBONE traffic, whether the events are watched by your people or not. Another setup in which you would receive all this traffic is if you feed a site that doesn't support pruning. This site would ask for the whole MBONE traffic, causing your site to receive it all as well.

The people who developed the MBONE have estimated that the total bandwidth consumption of the MBONE should be around a maximum of 500 Kbps. Limiting the amount of data (video, audio, whiteboard, images, and so on) to the value of 128 Kbps for video is also a common practice. However, users tend to use less than this upper limit by limiting their frame rate or by choosing lower bandwidth audio/video encoding schemes. Audio streams almost invariably take up 64 Kbps. These two rules have remained pretty constant, even though the various tools have greatly evolved over time.

A video stream from an NV (an MBONE video tool) format produces between 25 Kbps and 120 Kbps at roughly 1-15 frames per second. VIC, another MBONE tool that can handle a very effective video compression scheme called H.261, is used more and more. This video compression algorithm allows VIC to take up less bandwidth than does NV. However, to be able to compress an H.261 stream, much more CPU is required, and unless you can afford a very powerful machine, you will produce a lower frame rate with VIC than with NV.

An uncompressed (u-law format) audio stream uses 64 Kbps, which becomes 78 Kbps on the network because of overhead packets. Software compression of the audio stream will lower the 78 Kbps. There are multiple audio compression schemes that can be used. Some schemes even permit sending audio data that uses as little as 5 Kbps of your bandwidth, the quality of the audio being proportional to the amount of bandwidth used.

If a site's network link is a T1 (1.5 Mbps), the site can fully participate in MBONE events. A T1 link is probably the minimum link to have if full participation is desired. Full participation is defined as the capability to create any number of simultaneous events and to join any number of existing events. The creation of events will, of course, have to remain within the MBONE constraints. These constraints are easy to understand; the MBONE has been designed with a total capacity of 500 Kbps. This amount of bandwidth must be shared between all the MBONE users in the world. This sharing of bandwidth suggests that a single user cannot send enormous amounts of data onto the MBONE without being noticed and flamed. A mailing list exists to announce future MBONE events. Announcing an event on this list eliminates any conflict that may occur for the scheduling of events.

If a site has a fractional T1 or a lesser link, the site is not automatically disqualified for MBONE enjoyment. One of the most frequent questions that comes up is related to the new popularity of ISDN links, which offer a good price/bandwidth ratio. Can a site take advantage of its ISDN link for participating in MBONE events? The answer is yes, under certain conditions.

The first condition, one we already discussed, is that you, your feed, and the people you feed need to support pruning. Because the MBONE is designed to operate at a maximum 500 Kbps, receiving all the MBONE traffic would prevent you from being able to participate in a single session.

Someone with an ISDN link could receive an MBONE event if the total bandwidth of the event is lower than that of the ISDN link. Given the numbers presented earlier, you can easily imagine that events that match this criteria are not too numerous.

One trick is to watch part of an event. Some events are created as many separate events, one for video, one for audio, and one for the whiteboard. You can select video only, sound only, or both video and sound. In many cases, however, the priority of the MBONE traffic gives you good sound but problematic video. The shortcoming is in the design of the multicast routing software. The various kinds of MBONE traffic are categorized and given different priorities. Audio data has the highest priority because it is the most important. It is very difficult to follow a speech if you receive only 60 percent (for example) of the data due to packet loss. The whiteboard has a medium priority and video a low priority.

If your site is linked to the outside world via an ISDN link, which is the link through which all your users access FTP, e-mail, news, and so on, than you should forget about watching the MBONE via that link. A big FTP transfer or a user downloading a Web page can easily disrupt the MBONE events you are watching.

However, sites with a low bandwidth link to the outside world are far from being prevented from taking advantage of these tools and the remote conferences. It is possible to create a session that uses lower-quality video and audio. The result still will be enjoyable, and you will be able to get the information.

It is also perfectly feasible to use the MBONE internally. Imagine a company that installs MBONE tools on all the machines so that employees can use them on the internal network. Users could remotely talk to colleagues four floors below without having to leave the office and miss an important phone call. The company could also pipe a satellite feed into the local MBONE so that everyone receives a special event without having to gather in a huge room equipped with a giant screen TV. Applications of the MBONE, local or global, are very easy to find.

A site with an ISDN link could free the link from time to time to receive a special conference from the larger MBONE. This solution may seem a bit impractical, but it is a small sacrifice to make when the executive staff wants to use the MBONE to inform employees of a new policy. You also can arrange for your network provider to send you a maximum amount of MBONE data so that regular traffic never falls victim to a flood from the MBONE and the amount of MBONE traffic you receive never exceeds the capacity of your link, which would create problems in all the MBONE media you receive.

MBONE Feed

This requirement seems obvious, but it may not be that easy to obtain. If you want to receive MBONE traffic, you must have an MBONE feed to your site. The question is: Who will provide you with a feed, and why?

Normally, your network provider provides the feed for you, if it has chosen to participate in the MBONE. To reach your provider, send mail to the generic
`mbone@network.provider`. The response you receive will give you a good indication
of their level of participation. For example, if you send mail to `mbone@mci.net` or
`mbone@jvnc.net`, the message is picked up from a mailbox by the person who takes
care of MBONE feeds at this provider. If the message bounces back with a "user
unknown" error message, chances are good that your network provider does not
participate in the MBONE. However, you really should give them a phone call, just in
case they are planning to participate or they just didn't set up that generic e-mail
address. They also could be planning to join the MBONE and to begin offering feeds
and don't have anything official set up yet.

If your network provider does participate, then setting up a feed with it will be easy.

What if your network provider does not participate? It is always possible to set up a
feed with another site, but you should seek approval from your network provider
before proceeding. Normally, your provider should not have a problem with this. In
fact, it's best for the provider if it participated, but giving you approval at least allows
it to know where you get your link and to advise you if the planned feed is not optimal.

It is better for a network provider to participate in the MBONE because it can then
have some control over the feeds that run over its network. Nothing is more disrup-
tive to a network than 15 unsynchronized sites all setting up their own feeds to the
MBONE. Fifteen times the maximum MBONE bandwidth would cross the same wires,
a problem that a single feed to the network provider could avoid.

The source of your MBONE feed is a very important aspect of setting up a feed. For
example, at McGill University in Montreal (Canada), it's easy to get a feed from
best.net in California. However, this setup would be suboptimal. McGill currently gets
its feed from jvnc.net, which is relatively close to the New York Network Access Point,
where traffic from one network provider switches to other network providers. Some
people argue that it's better for McGill to get a feed from CA*net instead of MCI.
Currently, McGill is the main feed for Canada. Getting a link from CA*net would indeed
be one of the best solutions if the CA*net feed was an entity other than ourselves. The
best solution is to get a link from RISQ (our regional network provider), which would
set up their feed with CA*net.

CA*net's network provider is MCI, and at the time McGill's MBONE feed was set up,
MCI was not officially providing links. So, McGill set up a feed with jvnc, which is still a
pretty optimal situation. McGill should probably move the link to MCI now that it
supports MBONE.

This discussion about Canadian feeds and network infrastructure may seem uninter-
esting, but it's necessary to illustrate a simple idea. When setting up an MBONE
feed, the most important thing to keep in mind is avoiding redundant feeds over
network links.

I may have given you the impression that to set up an MBONE feed, you must know how the Internet is arranged. This is not the case. A mailing list exists for such matters. This mailing list is subdivided in smaller mailing lists corresponding to various areas of the planet. Sending mail to the appropriate mailing list assures you that you will get an answer from a competent person who is in a good network position to give you an MBONE feed. See Appendix D for a list of these useful mailing lists.

MBONE Tools for UNIX

Video, audio, and a shared whiteboard are the principal MBONE applications, but a variety of programs are available for fulfilling these functions. Each program is available as ready-to-run executable programs, or as source code from various anonymous FTP sites.

IP Multicast extensions

If your workstation only knows how to handle unicast packets, you'll have to add special software to its kernel before it can handle multicasting. IP multicast extensions are available as kernel patches for a variety of flavors of UNIX. Depending on your system, you may be able to find precompiled multicast additions; if not, you'll get to experience the joys of compiling them in yourself. Think of it as a character building experience.

You can find IP multicast extensions for UNIX via FTP at `ftp.parcftp.xerox.com` under `/pub/net-research/ipmulti3.5-*.tar.Z`. Other sites where you can find the multicast extensions include: `louie.udel.edu:/pub/people/ajit/ ipmulti3.5-*.tar.gz` and `ftp.adelaide.edu.au:/pub/av/multicast/ ipmulti3.5-*.tar.gz`.

The distribution includes kernel modifications for SunOS 4.1.3, SunOS 4.1.3_U1B, and SunOS 4.1.4, as well as the mroute daemon and various supporting binaries.

Once your workstation knows how to send and receive multicast packets, you'll need to get the software tools to make use of the MBONE. A wide variety of software is available — the major packages for MBONE multimedia are covered next. The standard multimedia setup for conferencing on the MBONE includes whiteboard (wb), the visual audio tool (vat), and session directory (sd). Make sure that you pick up these three essential tools.

nv: network video

The network video package, nv, was developed at Xerox Palo Alto research Center. nv is a videoconferencing tool that uses a default bandwidth of 128 Kbps and offers video rates of 3 to 5 frames per second. Versions are available for Sun, Silicon Graphics, DEC, and Hewlett-Packard systems. We've heard from the grapevine that programmers are working on a version for the Macintosh, one of the earliest signs that multicasting tools will soon be available to "the rest of us." Currently, however, no DOS, OS/2, or Windows versions are available, although a PC running Linux or 386BSD UNIX can use nv.

The following excerpt is from the nv main page:

```
nv allows users to transmit and receive slow frame rate video via
UDP/IP across an internet. Video streams can be either sent point
to point, or sent to several destinations simultaneously using IP
multicast. Receivers need no special hardware - just an X dis-
play. Transmitters need some sort of frame capture hardware.
Several different boards are supported so far, with more to come
in future releases.
By default, the video transmitted is a 320x240 image for NTSC, or
384x288 for PAL. It can be sent either as 8-bit greyscale, or
24-bit YUV 4:2:2 color. Other sizes (both smaller and larger) can
also be selected. It will be displayed at the receiver using a
24-bit color visual if one is available. If not, it will be
dithered using whatever the default visual is. The frame rate
varies with the amount of motion and the bandwidth available.
Frame rates of 3-5 frames/second are typical for the default
bandwidth of 128 Kbps. Some systems will support higher frame
rates if the bandwidth is raised or smaller images are sent.
```

You can get nv via FTP from ftp://parcftp.xerox.com/net-research/nv*

wb: whiteboard

The whiteboard tool, called simply wb, creates a shared, virtual whiteboard on your computer screen. wb is frequently used as a visual aid to accompany MBONE video lectures — and occasionally for Friday afternoon doodling. Besides offering standard drawing tools (likes, circles, and so on), wb can also be used to share PostScript files — speakers can show PostScript "slides" on wb to accompany live video images sent using nv.

The following excerpt is from the wb README file:

```
If you simply want a shared "whiteboard" drawing surface, you
don't need to do anything but install wb. But wb can also be used
to export, view and annotate arbitrary PostScript files. If you
```

```
want to include PostScript images in your wb conference, either
your X server has to support Display PostScript (the DEC & SGI X
servers do) or wb has to be able to exec the public domain post-
script renderer 'GhostScript'. If you want to render postscript
with Ghostscript, it has to be installed on your machine and has
to be in your shell search path with the name "gs". (If you don't
have Ghostscript it can be ftp'd from prep.ai.mit.edu, file pub/
gnu/ghostscript-*.tar.Z.).
```

Versions of wb are available for Linux, Sun, Silicon Graphics, DEC, and Hewlett-Packard systems, with ports in progress for Macintosh. You can find them via FTP at `ftp://ftp.ee.lbl.gov/conferencing/wb`.

vat: visual audio tool

The visual audio tool, or vat, was developed at Lawrence Berkeley Laboratories in California. Vat is a program for sending and receiving audio via the MBONE. "vat" is a bit of a misnomer because although its interface is visual (that is, graphical), vat does only sound, not video.

vat enables private communications between two hosts (well, as private as anything zipping unencrypted over the Internet can be), as well as public audioconferencing. vat provides a variety of compression formats, allowing it to interoperate with several platforms and programs. vat will even let you chat with users on Windows or Macintosh PCs, assuming that they have audioconferencing software on their end, too.

vat provides conference hosts a list of all the other hosts that are currently tuned in to a multicast session — a nifty way to tell how many others (and who) are listening to your lecture, diatribe, or ad-hoc Internet Radio show. Ready-to-run versions of vat are available for Sun, Silicon Graphics, DEC, Linux, and Hewlett-Packard platforms, with ports in progress for Macintosh. On most architectures, no special hardware other than a microphone is required — sound I/O is provided via the built-in audio hardware.

You can get vat via FTP from `ftp://ftp.ee.lbl.gov` in the conferencing/vat* directory.

NeVoT

Developed at the University of Massachusetts, NeVoT, which stands for "network voice terminal", is another program that provides multiperson audioconferencing. It supports a wide variety of audio protocols, including 16-bit linear encoding, 64 Kbps mu-law PCM, 32 Kbps ADPCM, 32 Kbps Intel/DVI ADPCM, GSM, and others.

You can receive NeVot via FTP from `ftp://gaia.cs.umass.edu/pub/hgschulz/nevot` or `ftp://ftp.fokus.gmd.de/pub/minos/nevot`. Precompiled versions are available for SPARCstations, Hewlett-Packard 9000 running HP-UX, SGI running Irix 5.2, DEC Alpha running OSF 1.0, DECstation running Ultrix, IBM workstations running AIX, and Linux workstations.

ivs

The INRIA Videoconferencing System (ivs) is an audio and videoconferencing package for FreeBSD, DEC, SunOS, Linux, other platforms. ivs is frequently used for participation in MICE (Multimedia Integrated Conferencing for Europe) seminars. It provides a video resolution of 320x200 pixels, in 256 or millions of colors, and provides a respectable 20:1 compression ratio. Only minimal hardware upgrades are required to a machine commonly found on the desk of an engineer: a video camera and a frame grabber.

ivs is available by anonymous FTP from `zenon.inria.fr:rodeo/ivs/last_version`. For more information about ivs, visit the ivs home page at `http://www.inria.fr/rodeo/ivs.html`.

sd: session directory

The sd — which stands for session directory — tool is sort of the "TV Guide" of the MBONE. Session directory displays a window showing current and planned MBONE sessions. The sd tool provides a straightforward interface to the Internet Group Management Protocol, which allows users to use their workstations to join and leave multicast groups. A user can click on a session name for information about the multicast (such as the planned time and date). The user can see, hear, or participate in a current session by double-clicking on a session name, which automatically launches the appropriate tool — nv, vat, wb, or whatever.

Sd is available precompiled for Sun, SGI, Linux, DEC, and other operating systems. You can get it via FTP from `ftp://ftp.ee.lbl.gov/conferencing/sd`.

CU-SeeMe Reflector for Macs

There are no MBONE applications for the Macintosh yet. But this platform can still profit from the MBONE. If the MBONE events are to be watched on Macs, another piece of software, a CU-SeeMe reflector, is required.

A very popular audio/video application on the Mac, called CU-SeeMe, enables Mac users to watch certain MBONE events. The conditions for using it are numerous, but because this is the only kind of MBONE connectivity that Mac users can get, it is surely better than nothing. Mac MBONE tools are in the works, though.

The CU-SeeMe reflector does not get all the MBONE traffic. The reflector has to be configured to receive traffic from a certain MBONE event so that it allows CU-SeeMe users to connect to it and receive this MBONE traffic. The MBONE event must meet two conditions. First, the video sent to the MBONE must be encoded in CU-SeeMe format at the source, and second, the audio must be encoded in DVI format.

Next, you will need a CU-SeeMe client on the Mac. When the reflector is up and running, getting MBONE traffic is as simple as connecting to the CU-SeeMe reflector. The greatest inconvenience of this CU-SeeMe way of getting MBONE events is that events with the proper format of video and audio are very rare. Future versions of the reflector will try to implement real-time conversion of video and audio so that all the other MBONE events can be watched by CU-SeeMe users. Another inconvenience is that one reflector has to be set up for each event that you want to join simultaneously. If you want to watch only one event at a time, you have to reconfigure the reflector so that it "points" to the other event. Also note that unless you use multiple Macs, watching more than one event is not possible because only one copy of the CU-SeeMe software can run on a particular Mac.

See Appendix F for pointers on where to get the CU-SeeMe reflector software and the CU-SeeMe client software.

If you've got the hardware and the bandwidth, and if you've coerced your network administrator to set up an extra workstation as an mrouter, then you're ready to download some client software from the Internet and see for yourself what's on the MBONE.

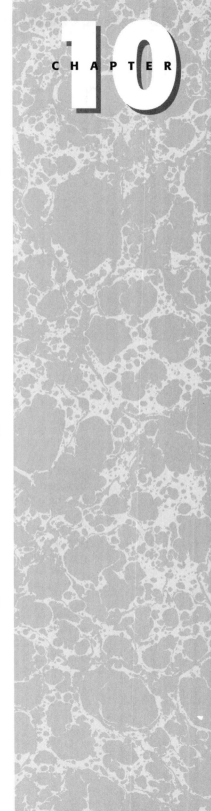

Bandwidth and Storage

In this chapter, we talk in more detail about bandwidth and storage requirements. We will also discuss in detail the ins and outs of multicast router configuration. We already discussed some bandwidth requirements in Chapter 9, summarized in a few key points:

✦ A T1 (1.54 Mbps) link allows you to fully participate in the MBONE experiment.

✦ MBONE via an ISDN (Integrated Services Digital Network) link is possible, but video will be problematic.

✦ Even with a slow link to the Internet, the MBONE can still be used internally at its full potential.

✦ Pruning is a mandatory feature to support if you don't want to waste your bandwidth with unnecessary traffic.

Before we can talk more about bandwidth, it is important to understand what multicast traffic is and why it saves us bandwidth. One question everybody asks themselves is: What is it about the way the MBONE works that makes it so special?

The answer is the use of multicast traffic. Ordinary IP traffic is called unicast, which means that for one source you have one destination. When a source sends unicast packets to a series of networks, as shown in Figure 10-1, this traffic travels through a variety of routing nodes to finally arrive at its destination. Except for routing the traffic, only the destination node will grab and keep the packets.

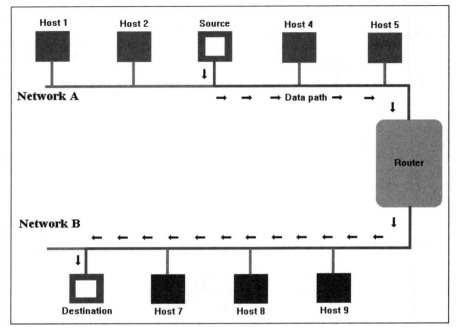

Figure 10-1: Sample path of a unicast packet.

Another type of traffic is called broadcast traffic (see Figure 10-2). For one given source, the destination is everybody who is on the local network. Broadcast traffic is already a way to send a packet to more than one destination. The problem is that destinations that do not want the packet will still receive it and process it. Since broadcast packets are not allowed to pass through routers, they are confined to the local network and cannot be used for the MBONE. This is a fortunate feature of broadcast packets. Imagine the havoc that could be created on the Internet by a person flooding it with broadcast packets. Even a user on a PPP link would get the packet, and if the broadcast packets would be numerous enough, the user's PPP connection would be seriously disrupted. With a sufficient number of people, any kind of link could be disrupted this way.

Multicast traffic is a better way to send packets to multiple destinations. When a source sends a packet to a complex network (see Figure 10-3), the routers that support multicast routing compare the intended destination in the packet to their own member list and forward the packet to the members in the intended destination group. Therefore, a single packet is able to reach multiple hosts around the world. That is real bandwidth economy! Only the people who want the packet will receive it. Now, there is one more notion to this to understand.

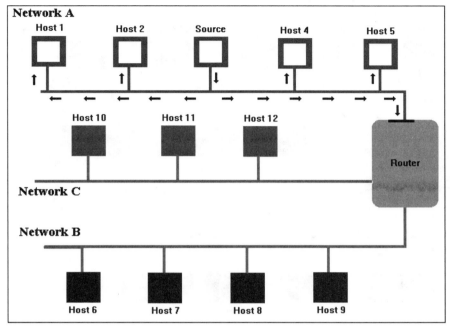

Figure 10-2: Sample path of a broadcast packet.

Because the multicast packet does not have a precise destination, it never reaches one. Imagine that you are driving in a car on a trip to no particular place, and you decide along the way who you are going to visit before continuing the trip. You could go on like this for a very long time. At some point you could even go back to your point of origin, but only to continue your trip via the same roads you already used. Now imagine that there are thousands and thousands of cars on the same kind of trip. For regular people who are in a hurry to get to their destination, the roads would rapidly get too crowded for anybody to drive on them. The solution to this dilemma is called Time-To-Live (TTL). It can be compared to the gas tank of the car.

Every time a multicast packet goes through a multicast router, the packet's TTL value is decreased by one. So, if you have a packet with a TTL value of 4, the packet only goes through four multicast routers before dying. Using a small TTL, you can actually send all the multicast traffic you want, and the traffic does not burden network links that should not be burdened with that traffic.

To summarize in one sentence, the MBONE uses multicast traffic because no other way of sending packets to multiple destinations provides us with these two features:

1. The possiblity to reach everyone on the Internet

2. The bandwidth savings when multiple destinations are involved

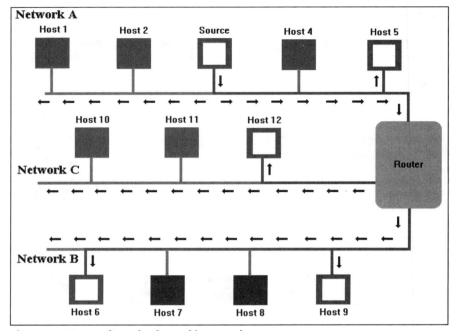

Figure 10-3: Sample path of a multicast packet.

Now, what if you are an Internet provider who wants to be a feed for customers? Or you are a commercial site that wants to provide MBONE connectivity to many areas of your business?

If your network does not support native multicast routing, then you will have to proceed with tunnels. Native multicast routing is the ability for routers to route multicast traffic. A few brands of routers can do this already (Cisco, Proteon) with special versions of the software that runs on them. More brands will certainly do it in the future. This is the best way to save bandwidth because the traffic destined to a multicast group will go through a particular link only once, whatever the number of participants.

If your network does not support native multicast routing, a program called mrouted allows you to work around this limitation, but the price to pay is more bandwidth consumption for the local network to which the machine that runs mrouted is connected.

This mrouted program runs on a variety of UNIX platforms, and it works by encapsulating multicast packets inside regular unicast packets. Two multicast routers that both encapsulate multicast packets and talk to each together are said to communicate via a tunnel.

If your network provider does not support native multicast routing, it will send you the MBONE traffic via a tunnel. And if you choose to feed customers or sites, you will feed them via a tunnel. Along with tunnels, mrouted also supports physical interfaces. A physical interface is basically the Ethernet adaptor on your machine. Now you're going to ask, "But what will I do with a physical interface?" I am glad you asked, because a physical interface is the main way to provide MBONE connectivity to all the machines that sit on a network. Defining a physical interface simply instructs mrouted to send multicast traffic to the physical interface. If you remember the travel in a car example, by being sent to the physical interface, MBONE traffic becomes available to all the machines that share the physical network attached to this particular physical interface.

The mrouted program learns about the tunnels and physical interfaces it has to maintain through the use of a configuration file. This file is normally named `mrouted.conf` and resides in `/etc` (see Figure 10-4).

At the beginning of the template configuration file that comes with the program, you can see the general syntax of the phyint and tunnel lines. The syntax here is not quite up-to-date because my configuration file is pretty old. However, the manual pages that accompany the software describe all the possible options, which are the following:

✦ **phyint.** This option is used to specify a non-default metric for the interface or to disable multicast forwarding for the interface. In my configuration file, I have set the metric to 1 (which is the default anyway).

✦ **tunnel.** This option is used to specify tunnels. It has your multicast router IP address followed by the other end's IP address. Note that for mrouted there is no difference between a site you feed and a site from which you are fed. In fact, the notion of feeding is always relative to the location from which the traffic is coming.

The phyint and tunnel arguments that I use are the following:

✦ **metric.** This argument sets a metric value for the interface or tunnel. The metric in networking represents a "cost" of sending traffic down that link. The higher the metric, the higher the cost. It is used mainly for influencing the choice of routes. It means that you could feed two sites with two different paths, and with the metric you could decide which path is the main one and which path is the backup path.

✦ **threshold.** If you remember the car example, you will also remember the fuel tank and the TTL (Time-To-Live). TTL interacts very closely with the threshold. How they come together allows you to decide which MBONE event you create will remain local and which one will be received by the region, the country, or the world.

Figure 10-4 shows my own mrouted configuration file (it is authentic except that IP addresses and names have been changed):

```
# $Id: mrouted.conf,v 1.3 1993/05/30 02:10:11 deering Exp $
#
#    This is the configuration file for "mrouted", an IP multicast
#       router.
#    mrouted looks for it in "/etc/mrouted.conf".
#
#    Command formats:
#
#        phyint <local-addr> [disable] [metric <m>] [threshold <t>]
#        tunnel <local-addr> <remote-addr> [srcrt] [metric <m>]
#        [threshold <t>]
#
#    any phyint commands MUST precede any tunnel commands
#
phyint  123.456.78.90 metric 1 threshold 1

# Department of Algorythms
tunnel 123.456.78.90 123.456.3.4 metric 1 threshold 8

# Faculty of Harmonies
tunnel   123.456.78.90 123.456.141.16 metric 1 threshold 8

# Department of Finding New Ways to Fly
tunnel   123.456.78.90 123.456.186.10 metric 1 threshold 8

# Department of Having a Look Inside Human Bodies
tunnel   123.456.78.90 123.456.101.182 metric 1 threshold 8

# A very collaborative site
tunnel   123.456.78.90 123.456.210.1 metric 1 threshold 16

# University of The Other Side of the City
tunnel   123.456.78.90 123.457.90.90 metric 1 threshold 16

# University of Far To the East
tunnel   123.456.78.90 124.222.4.3 metric 1 threshold 32

#University of Good Ole Earth
tunnel   123.456.78.90 129.111.3.18 metric 1 threshold 32

# My Feed from which I get the MBONE Traffic
tunnel   123.456.78.90 130.130.130.130 metric 1 threshold 64
```

Figure 10-4: mrouted configuration file.

The threshold is a numeric value of which I specify the minimum TTL required to allow the packet to go through. For example, if you create an MBONE event with a TTL of 20, and you have the exact same configuration file I do, then all sites at the other of my tunnels with thresholds of 8 and 16 can receive it, as well as my physical interface. The sites at the other of my tunnels with thresholds of 32 and 64 would not be able to receive my event. Why did I do it this way? To better answer this, I should tell you what reasons prompted me to organize my thresholds as I did.

Figure 10-5 shows an example of an assymmetric tunnel configuration.

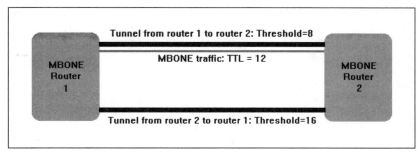

Figure 10-5: An assymmetric tunnel configuration.

My tunnels with thresholds of 8 are all at my own site. My tunnels with a threshold of 16 are all in the province of Quebec. My tunnels with a threshold of 32 are inter-province tunnels. Finally, my tunnel with a threshold of 64 is my MBONE feed to the United States.

This configuration allows me to have a pretty fine granularity for choosing the scope of my MBONE events. If I want to create an event relevant for McGill people only, I would choose a TTL of 7 or less. The event would not pass through tunnels with a threshold of 16 and thus would not flood the links to other universities. The same principle applies to events that I want to remain within the city of Montreal or in Canada. Only for those events that I want to send to the whole world would I choose a threshold of 64 and more. In this way you can use the MBONE internally if you have a slow link to the outside.

Something else to know is that thresholds must be symmetric. If you configure a tunnel with a threshold of 8, then the other end of the tunnel must configure the tunnel with the same threshold. The reason for this is that if you create an event and a user at the other end of the tunnel wants to participate in the event, one of you will not be able to receive the other user's data, which could be a bit annoying. For example, you could talk all you wanted and the other person would not hear you.

In Figure 10-4, one end has the tunnel configured with a threshold of 8 and the other end has it with a threshold of 16. The event was created by you with a TTL of 12. Because the TTL is 12 and the threshold on your end is 8, you will be able to talk and send video and the other end will receive it perfectly. However, because the threshold on their end is 16, a TTL of 12 is not enough to pass through the tunnel, and they will never be able to send you any data. The fix to this would of course be for them to set the threshold to 8.

✦ **rate limit.** Rate limit is used to reserve an amount of bandwidth so that multicast traffic that passes through that tunnel never exceeds the value specifed with this argument. If you have an ISDN link and you want to be sure that multicast traffic will never exceed the capacity of your link, then set rate limit at around 120 Kbps. Rate limit can also be used as an argument for the tunnel to your upfeed so that none of your users will be able to flood the MBONE (and disrupt it) with an exaggerated amount of data.

Tunnels must be carefully engineered to avoid duplicate tunnels over the same physical link. Ideally, no more than one or two tunnels should go through a T1 link.

You can see from my configuration file that I have nine tunnels and one physical interface. For each packet I receive, I duplicate this packet nine times: once for the physical interface and eight times for the eight tunnels from which the packet did not come. The packet has to be encapsulated and sent out for each one of these tunnels.

Now imagine that my router does that for the whole MBONE traffic. It would receive 500 Kbps from one tunnel and send it back to eight other tunnels and one physical interface. 500 Kbps of bandwidth is taken up for receiving the traffic, and because I duplicate it nine times and send it out to one local network (tunnels go through that physical network before they reach the router), this physical network will endure 10 times the traffic I receive, which is 5000 Kbps (or 5 Mbps). With these kinds of numbers, saturating an Ethernet is easy, and in fact, my multicast router is alone on its Ethernet. If my multicast router shared its Ethernet with other machines, the traffic from the other machines would disrupt the MBONE here, and vice-versa. And that traffic doesn't take into consideration the packets sent by the sites I feed.

A solution to this would be to have multiple Ethernet adapters on my multicast router. In fact, I do have two Ethernet adapters, but the second one is not yet in use and is destined to feed my own department. Later, a third Ethernet adapter will be used to feed the engineering buildings. Of course, you will need a corresponding number of Ethernet networks to which you connect your interfaces. Because routers are expensive and the number of ports on them is limited, running a big MBONE router could easily become expensive.

Fortunately, the current situation is not yet this drastic.That a combination of all my downfeeds corresponds to a participation to all the events is very rare. Remember that mrouted does support pruning and that this alone almost guarantees that I will never have to route all the traffic.

Storage and CPU

What do you need in terms of storage and CPU for a machine to participate in the MBONE? It depends, but in all cases the amount of storage needed is low.

In terms of memory, there is no absolute number. My multicast router runs FreeBSD on a dedicated 90 MHz pentium machine with 20 megabytes of memory and seems to work fine. Because the MBONE is based on multicast UDP (User Datagram Protocol) traffic, and UDP has been designed to be unreliable, a packet that does not make it to the dest-ination is not retransmitted and thus not stored for later retransmission. If the MBONE was based on TCP and the physical link over which a tunnel would go experienced problems, then the packet would be stored for later retransmission (up to the maximum size of the network buffers) and a lot of memory would be taken up this way.

Now you're probably asking, "What, the MBONE is unreliable?" The answer is yes. It is and it has to be, except for the text medium (mumble), which hopefully will be based on RMP (Reliable Multicast Protocol) in future versions. The MBONE for the other media has to be unreliable because we don't want an audio packet, for example, to be retransmitted when there is a problem with the original transmission. A packet that is missed cannot be retrieved; it will just make a hole in the speech you're listening to. After a packet has been missed, the rest of the speech continues to flow, and if a retransmitted packet arrives in the middle of a word three seconds after the word it was originally part of, the result could easily be an unintelligible speech.

What is probably more important than memory is the CPU power of your machine. When I first heard about the MBONE, I decided to try it using my own workstation and was able to have mrouted run on a Sun IPX. The tunnel I had was destined to feed my machine only, which was working fine. That same machine was my personal worksta-tion, and I was running all my processes on that machine, including X Windows and the MBONE applications, so any Pentium PC would do fine for a single user. You could even afford having a few tunnels to friends who are willing to try the MBONE. You would want no more than one or two tunnels, however, if you plan to continue working on that machine.

In terms of disk storage, you don't need much, except for running UNIX. My multicast router has a 1GB disk, which is more than enough since most of the machine's activity consists of receiving, duplicating, and sending network packets.

More important than disk space and memory is the speed of the bus and the perfor-mance of the network adapters. Fast adapters on a PCI bus will do a very good job.

More on Bandwidth

SDR introduces a new concept, administrative scopes. This new concept is a much more user-friendly way to specify a scope for a conference.

In SD, we used TTLs to specify the area within which an MBONE event would be constrained. Not only do the default TTL values in SD not necessarily correspond to the threshold values for the various tunnels in multicast routers around your site, but you also have to actually know these threshold values so that you can decide a good TTL value to use. It can rapidly become confusing for the novice users who are just given permission to use the MBONE. One of the drawbacks of the MBONE is the grief caused by users who are improperly informed of the proper procedures; they have in their hands very powerful tools that can send an awful lot of traffic to the Internet.

Administrative scopes will solve a big part of this particular problem, even if the primary reason for their existence was not this. Administrative scopes will be handled by the multicast router using the multicast address of the conference rather than using the TTL field in a multicast packet.

In multicast routers, an administratively scoped region will be defined using the "boundary" argument to the tunnel or phyint options in the mrouted.conf file. Here are the tunnels from my own mrouted.conf file, and I have set boundaries as if I had already set up these administratively scoped regions. Of course, the addresses I use are fake because the IANA (Internet Assigned Numbers Authority) will be assigning them, and I have not gone through this process yet (see Appendix E on how to contact the IANA).

```
# First, let's name our boundaries.
# The syntax is IP address/mask. In the Montreal Example,
# all addresses from 239.124.0.0 to 239.124.255.255 will be part
# of that administratively scoped region (See below for more
#      details).
name CC 239.123.0.0/16
name Montreal 239.124.0.0/16
name Canada 239.125.0.0/16
name McGill 239.126.0.0/16

phyint  132.216.30.10 metric 1 threshold 1

# Department of Algorythms
tunnel 123.456.78.90 123.456.3.4 metric 1 threshold 8 boundary CC

# Faculty of Harmonies
tunnel  123.456.78.90 123.456.141.16 metric 1 threshold 8
boundary CC

# Department of Finding New Ways to Fly
tunnel  123.456.78.90 123.456.186.10 metric 1 threshold 8
boundary CC
```

```
# Department of Having a Look Inside Human Bodies
tunnel  123.456.78.90 123.456.101.182 metric 1 threshold 8
boundary CC

# University of The Other Side of the City
tunnel  123.456.78.90 123.457.90.90 metric 1 threshold 16
boundary CC
boundary McGill

# A very collaborative site
tunnel  123.456.78.90 123.456.210.1 metric 1 threshold 16
boundary CC
boundary McGill

# University of Far To the East
tunnel  123.456.78.90 124.222.4.3 metric 1 threshold 32 boundary
Montreal boundary McGill boundary CC

# My Feed from which I get the MBONE Traffic
tunnel  123.456.78.90 130.130.130.130 metric 1 threshold 64
boundary Canada boundary Montreal boundary McGill boundary CC
```

Figure 10-6: mrouted configuration file with administrative scopes.

To scope a region, all you have to do is put a boundary on every link leaving the region you want to scope. The traffic that will be within the address range of that administrative scope will *not* be sent onto that link. In Figure 10-6, we can have a look at the tunnel to JVNC. If someone in Canada creates an MBONE session that uses "Canada" for an administrative scope, the address is automatically set by SDR so that it is within the range of addresses for that scope. The traffic of that session is not sent down to JVNC. This is valid in both directions, meaning that the address range that I use for the "Canada" scoped region could be reused elsewhere because it would not be in conflict. However, that address range could only be used outside of Canada. Another example of this address reuse is every other department at my site reusing the same address range that I use for my CC boundary. All I have to do is add a "boundary <department>" argument to the tunnel line for that department. Because the traffic from a department that would have created a session using the scope for their own department does not leave the department, no conflict of addresses occurs and every other departement could have a session local to them using the same address range.

The only problem so far with administrative scopes is that SDR currently has no way to automatically know about the various scoped region names, which have to be configured for each user. This is done with SDR's configuration file. This file lives in your home directory on the UNIX machine and is called .sd.tcl. In this file you have to put a series of commands to tell your SDR that it will now know and care about your local administrative scopes. Here is a sample .sd.tcl file:

```
add_admin Canada 239.125.255.255 1234 239.125.0.0 16 63
add_admin Montreal 239.124.255.255 1235 239.125.0.0 16 31
add_admin McGill 239.126.255.255 1236 239.126.0.0 16 15
add_admin CC 239.123.255.255 1237 239.123.0.0 16 7
```

In the preceding example, we can see that the syntax for the add_admin command is

```
add_admin <scope name> <announcement address> <annoucement port>
          <scope band base address> <netmask> <ttl>
```

Where the following conditions apply:

✦ scope name is the name of the scope as defined in your mrouted.conf file.

✦ announcement address is the address used for announcing your MBONE sessions for that scope.

✦ announcement port is the port used for announcing your MBONE sessions for that scope. Note that the port number must be unique for each scope and all SDRs that will use that scope must use the same port number, else the SDR's that don't use the same port will not see announcements from other SDRs.

✦ scope band base address is the lower address of your address range for that scope.

✦ netmask is a value in number of bits for the netmask. This will depend on the size of your address range.

✦ ttl is a default TTL for that scope. In the example, I've set it to the max value I would have set it if I was still using the old TTL scopes. So, for Canada, I've put it to 63 because the threshold value of my tunnel to the United States is 64 and a TTL of 63 would not go through that tunnel. If I had set this TTL to 2, for example, and I wanted to create a session scoped for Canada, it would have been unlikely that I would have reached everyone I wanted to. This is because the TTL values in multicast packets are still decreased by one for every multicast router the packet goes through, even if we use administrative scopes.

The next major release of SDR will include two improvements:

✦ A better way to configure administrative scope. Editing a file and adding commands to that file are not very elegant tasks, and a new mechanism will replace the existing one.

✦ A simplified method for creating sessions. The actual create window is very complex because it is very powerful. However, a lot of MBONE users don't, and don't want to, care about all the things they have to know in order to create a session. The simplified method will hide more things (for example, choosing a protocol for the media) from the user.

Do not forget that SDR is totally new and the version that is available at this moment is an alpha release (which, nevertheless, is very usable). The author of that application (Mark Handley at UCL) has done a great job, and I am sure that he will give us more things in SDR to amaze us.

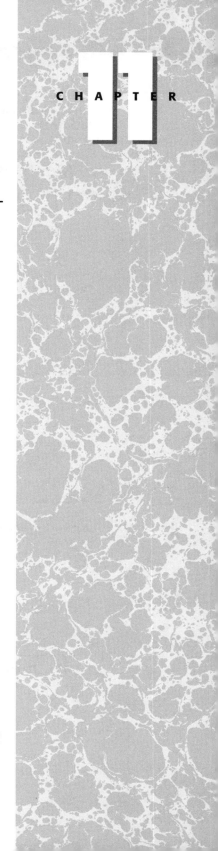

Accounting and Debugging Issues

The MBONE has many users, and more and more people are beginning to use it every day. As the number of MBONE users increases, an important question comes to mind — in the end, who pays for all of this new technology?

To answer that question, you first have to understand what the MBONE is. The MBONE is a research project. All research is funded by entities like governments, universities, and private corporations, and the MBONE is no exception. This research includes the protocols that are used on the MBONE, the tools and applications that have been developed for the MBONE, and everything in the global MBONE virtual network (multicasting, encapsulation, and so on).

The funding also comes from the MBONE end users in one form or another. Users (which may consist of an entire site full of computer operators) pay an Internet provider for access to a number of services, which may include an MBONE tunnel or multicast routing. This Internet provider, in turn, pays a network provider for the use of its physical links. These physical links most often belong to telecommunications companies such as Sprint or MCI. A very small number of Internet providers own their physical links, but in the end, they still have to pay to have access to other sites on physical links that belong to the tele-communications companies.

Telecommunications companies seem to be the big winners in this scenario, but these companies have to spend a fortune to install all the cabling that goes from one end of the country to the other end. They certainly make a profit by owning this equipment, but because the Internet is constantly expanding, they also have to keep upgrading these links, and the mainte-nance it takes to perform this task is very expensive. (So no one really wins, except perhaps the governments who tax a packet of data traveling the networks several times before it reaches its destination. Such is the case in Canada, because the government taxes these services there.)

So, if you are paying for the Internet and MBONE, you may want to know how much your users access the MBONE so that you can charge the costs back to them and become part of this virtual food chain.

There are two ways that your users can conveniently use the MBONE:

1. You can give them a multicast feed to enable them to participate in the sessions they choose.

2. Using a feed that enters your site, all your internal users or departments participate in the sessions they want.

With a multicast feed, you receive a feed from somewhere and provide feeds to other entities, such as departments, faculties, and so on.

People in these other entities use the feed that you provide to participate in all the sessions that they want. However, the number of sessions in which they are able to participate depends heavily on the bandwidth constraints that you impose on the feed. For example, in a tunnel line in the mrouted.conf file, the maximum bandwidth that a link is restricted to, by default, is 512 Kbps (see the rate column in Table 11-1). This bandwidth can be changed with the rate_limit option on the tunnel line, so you can use that option to implement various levels of service.

How do you know what sessions users participated in or how much data they sent? A partial answer can be obtained by using UNIX utilities. UNIX comes with a great deal of networking utilities, and some of them are useful for getting networking statistics on multicast traffic. First, take a look at netstat.

netstat is a utility that can provide you with unicast statistics. It can show you the routing tables on your machine, for example, or it can show you the usage of your network memory buffers. On some platforms (FreeBSD is one of them), netstat can give you multicast statistics as well. The netstat -g command (as shown in Table 11-1) gives you all kind of useful information.

Table 11-1			Output of the netstat-g Command			
			Virtual Interface Table			
Vif	*Thresh*	*Rate*	*Local-Address*	*Remote-Address*	*Pkts-In*	*Pkts-Out*
0	1	0	123.456.78.90	0	0	
1	16	512	123.456.78.90	123.456.210.1	12406	112515353
2	8	512	123.456.78.90	123.456.3.4	5596	44642609
3	8	512	123.456.78.90	123.456.141.16	6	56865205

Vif	Thresh	Rate	Local-Address	Remote-Address	Pkts-In	Pkts-Out
4	8	512	123.456.78.90	123.456.186.10	0	9664355
5	16	512	123.456.78.90	123.457.90.90	0	0
6	64	512	123.456.78.90	130.130.130.130	117148123	183497
7	8	512	123.456.78.90	123.456.101.182	0	0
8	32	512	123.456.78.90	124.222.4.3	149934	15749310
9	32	512	123.456.78.90	129.111.3.18	23821	5056246

Multicast Forwarding Cache

Origin	Group	Packets	In-Vif	Out-Vifs:Ttls
130.240.3.81	224.2.195.52	39771	6	1:16 4:8
130.240.3.76	224.2.213.97	32600	6	1:16 3:8 4:8
192.153.117.35	224.2.252.231	357	6	1:16 4:8
128.138.213.1	224.2.0.1	75657	6	1:16 4:8
198.93.139.41	224.2.252.231	50856	6	1:16 4:8
128.55.192.227	224.2.143.24	56682	6	1:16 3:8 4:8
128.232.0.49	224.0.1.1	7747	6	1:16 3:8 4:8 9:32
146.88.1.106	224.2.245.77	716	6	1:16 4:8
128.40.64.5	224.2.244.129	72840	6	1:16 4:8
130.240.12.79	224.2.187.164	8381	6	1:16 4:8
130.199.130.175	224.2.0.1	11	6	1:16 4:8
192.16.123.88	224.2.213.97	98957	6	1:16 3:8 4:8
128.100.197.178	224.0.1.1	1	1	4:8 6:64
171.69.58.88	224.2.231.173	45701	6	1:16 3:8 4:8
131.188.34.89	224.2.0.1	81533	6	1:16 4:8
171.69.58.92	224.2.143.24	14998	6	1:16 3:8 4:8
204.188.121.18	224.2.127.255	11	6	1:16 4:8
128.3.112.2	224.2.0.1	63309	6	1:16 4:8
129.89.9.110	224.2.187.164	14420	6	1:16 2:8 3:8 4:8 9:32
129.240.200.196	224.2.236.244	80710	6	1:16 4:8

(continued)

Multicast Forwarding Cache *(continued)*

Origin	Group	Packets	In-Vif	Out-Vifs:Ttls
128.4.1.1	224.0.1.1	5513	6	1:16 3:8 4:8
204.62.246.98	224.2.248.110	131170	6	1:16 4:8
193.60.11.44	224.2.143.24	191421	6	1:16 3:8 4:8
128.84.247.156	224.2.0.1	58315	6	1:16 3:8 4:8
128.3.112.2	224.2.127.255	15	6	1:16 4:8
204.62.246.73	224.2.143.24	6814956	6	1:16 3:8 4:8
131.225.220.147	224.2.0.1	98359	6	1:16 3:8 4:8
131.225.220.147	224.2.231.173	299682	6	1:16 3:8 4:8
130.199.130.175	224.2.1.1	10651	6	1:16 4:8
130.240.3.81	224.2.219.172	66366	6	1:16 3:8 4:8
130.240.3.81	224.2.177.132	16363	6	1:16 4:8
199.104.80.5	224.2.248.110	1199	6	1:16 4:8
128.232.0.56	224.0.1.1	8709	6	1:16 3:8 4:8 9:32
18.77.1.243	224.2.251.237	197837	6	1:16 4:8
192.6.28.26	224.2.0.1	26537	6	1:16 4:8
129.242.6.80	224.2.189.16	73074	6	1:16 3:8 4:8
171.69.60.189	224.2.231.173	30666	6	1:16 3:8 4:8
13.2.116.196	224.2.127.255	153	6	1:16 3:8 4:8 8:32 9:32
130.199.130.175	224.2.187.164	4	6	1:16 4:8
130.240.3.38	224.2.213.97	32596	6	1:16 3:8 4:8
163.221.196.12	224.2.0.1	98133	6	1:16 4:8
171.68.225.139	224.2.0.1	120	6	1:16 4:8
150.83.68.41	224.2.143.24	75111	6	1:16 4:8
130.240.3.81	224.2.236.244	39975	6	1:16 3:8 4:8
171.69.129.220	224.2.0.1	14937	6	1:16 3:8 4:8
130.240.3.81	224.2.189.16	25754	6	1:16 4:8
171.69.60.152	224.2.231.173	45353	6	1:16 3:8 4:8
156.40.113.11	224.2.143.24	210	6	1:16 2:8 3:8 4:8 8:32 9:32
171.69.129.220	224.2.231.173	45548	6	1:16 3:8 4:8

Origin	Group	Packets	In-Vif	Out-Vifs:Ttls
129.242.6.80	224.2.177.132	37541	6	1:16 3:8 4:8
171.69.58.81	224.2.231.173	45643	6	1:16 3:8 4:8
171.69.58.81	224.2.0.1	15031	6	1:16 3:8 4:8
204.62.246.68	224.2.127.255	3787	6	1:16 4:8
198.93.139.41	224.2.187.164	50838	6	1:16 4:8
192.80.13.56	224.2.0.1	1880	6	1:16 3:84:8
128.182.61.159	224.2.0.1	138180	6	1:16 4:8
204.188.121.18	224.2.187.164	7050	6	1:16 4:8
128.4.1.24	224.0.1.1	21169	6	1:16 3:8 4:8
192.58.206.100	224.2.0.1	112335	6	1:16 3:8 4:8
204.62.246.76	224.2.245.77	1142781	6	1:16 4:8
204.160.73.10	224.2.231.173	2	6	1:16 4:8 9:32

In Table 11-1, the first part of the output titled "Virtual Interface Table," shows multicast traffic statistics for each virtual interface on your multicast router, where a virtual interface can be a physical interface or a tunnel. You can use this output to find out how much traffic was received and sent by each of your down feeds. The Virtual Interface (VIF) 0 in Table 11-1 is the physical interface of the machine; because it doesn't send any multicast traffic to the local network, the number of packets that go in and out on it are zero.

The number of packets in for the VIF 6 is much higher than for the other VIFs, because VIF 6 is the feed that I use to receive all MBONE traffic from the rest of the world. You can also see that the number of packets out to VIF 6 is pretty low, at approximately 183 K-packets. What this means is that not very much traffic has been sent out of Canada; rather, the biggest part of the traffic has been sent within the Montreal area.

You will notice that for VIF 1, the number of packets out is almost as high as the number of packets in for VIF 6. The reason behind this is that the other end of this tunnel feeds a number of sites, of which one is an mrouted version 2.2 that doesn't support pruning (see Chapter 10 for a discussion on the importance of pruning).

As you can see, netstat can give you a fairly accurate picture of the MBONE usage of each of your feeds. There are drawbacks to using this method to check your feed stats though:

✦ Because this method only provides information in terms of the number of packets, obtaining accurate numbers in terms of bytes is difficult.

✦ You can reset the counters for the packets in and out only by a machine reboot.

✦ To calculate MBONE usage for each feed, you need to take regular snapshots of these counters, parse the output, and compare values with previous snapshots — a difficult and time-consuming process.

✦ This method doesn't give you a per-session means of doing accounting.

These drawbacks are not major ones, but they are significant enough to make the accounting tasks a little more difficult to perform because they require that you employ human resources to develop the accounting tools that will fit your needs.

The fourth drawback is important here because it means that you cannot monitor how MBONE is used on an individual basis. For example, suppose that you are willing to let your customers use the MBONE for free except when they use it for events that are not related to work (such as musical events, radio, world news, and so on). netstat does not provide you with the level of granularity needed to discern between work-related uses and personal uses. You could use the second part of the netstat output shown in Table 11-1 for this purpose (the part titled "Multicast Forwarding Cache"), but this method also has major drawbacks:

✦ Because it is a cache, you have no guarantee that it lists all the hosts that sent packets out to MBONE events.

✦ Because the groups are listed as multicast IP addresses, you have to listen for all the SD or SDR advertisements to find these groups in the list and then decide whether the session is chargeable based on criteria X. This would be fairly difficult to do, assuming that you don't want to have a person employed full-time simply to check SD or SDR advertisements and categorize the various MBONE events.

The multicast forwarding cache is simply a who's who list of who sends packets to what multicast group. It can give you an indication of where the traffic originated and to which VIF location your multicast router should send it. Only the most active senders appear in this list, however, which makes the cache ineffective for monitoring all MBONE activity.

Netstat is also an inadequate tool to use if you receive a single MBONE feed that will be used by all your internal users. Imagine a corporation placing the MBONE that is available to its employees in various departments. The problem with such a setup is that although you will be able to monitor the amount of data flowing in or out of your site, you will not be able to determine the individual sessions in which the traffic was sent or received. Again, this restriction presents a problem if you want to charge for MBONE usage.

The tool that comes to the rescue in these situations is called *mlisten*. The mlisten tool is part of a package that also includes mprocess.

mlisten listens to the control port of a specific multicast address and records the IP addresses of all the participants for that session. This tool uses a parameter file containing a few settings that influence the way that mlisten collects data.

mprocess takes the output produced by mlisten and creates a new output file in another form. This new output file contains four columns of summary information about the session that mlisten monitored. These four columns contain the following information:

✦ An offset in seconds since the start of the measurement

✦ The average number of listeners during the last measurement interval

✦ The number of participants who joined the MBONE event during the last measurement interval

✦ The number of participants who left the MBONE event during the last measurement interval

This mprocess output file can be fed to a plot-generation program so that you can get a graphic representation of your audience.

Another tool that may be of use to you is traceroute (and its multicast equivalent, mtrace). You can't use this utility for doing accounting tasks per se, but it will help you establish policies at your site regarding who gets a feed from you and who doesn't, or who you get a feed from. This task is more important than you might think, because if you set up your network in a chaotic way, multiple MBONE feeds may end up crossing your network provider's physical links, costing you money. traceroute shows the route that a packet takes from your host to a destination host that you specified (see Figure 11-1). This trace will be useful to you if, for example, you are a network provider and a site requests an MBONE feed from you. By doing a traceroute to the site, you can determine whether you would be the best person to provide them with a feed.

Figure 11-1 and 11-2 show two examples of traceroute in action. Suppose that both sites in the examples requested an MBONE link from me, an Internet service provider. traceroute clearly shows me that I could give the first site a feed if they want one, but giving a feed to the second site would be out of the question.

```
traceroute to mix.net (198.168.73.2), 30 hops max, 40 byte pack-
        ets
   1   Therouter.CC.McGill.CA (123.456.78.9)  1.566 ms  1.367 ms
        1.359 ms
   2   McGill-gate.Provider.Net (123.456.79.1)  2.343 ms  1.747 ms
        1.700 ms
   3   192.77.58.10 (192.77.58.10)  1.601 ms  1.443 ms  1.507 ms
   4   MIX.NET (198.168.73.2)  38.857 ms  43.820 ms  39.798 ms
```

Figure 11-1: The traceroute output to the first site.

```
traceroute to cam.org (198.168.100.5), 30 hops max, 40 byte packets
   1   Therouter.CC.McGill.CA (123.456.78.9)  1.742 ms  1.456 ms  1.694 ms
   2   McGill-gate.RISQ.Net (123.456.79.1)  1.628 ms  2.258 ms  2.140 ms
   3   psp.qc.canet.ca (192.68.56.5)  57.032 ms  19.398 ms  5.093 ms
   4   psp.ny.canet.ca (205.207.238.154)  8.557 ms  11.782 ms  11.525 ms
   5   border4-hssi1-0.Boston.mci.net (204.70.23.5)  13.494 ms  14.662 ms
        20.854 ms
   6   core-fddi-1.Boston.mci.net (204.70.3.33)  12.987 ms  13.102 ms
        12.707 ms
   7   core-hssi-2.NewYork.mci.net (204.70.1.1)  21.413 ms  17.191 ms
        16.772 ms
   8   border2-fddi-0.NewYork.mci.net (204.70.3.18)  16.663 ms  15.848 ms
        16.102 ms
   9   sprint-nap.NewYork.mci.net (204.70.45.6)  19.688 ms  22.025 ms
        21.864 ms
  10   fd-0.enss218.t3.ans.net (192.157.69.4)  24.534 ms  23.664 ms
        20.710 ms
  11   t3-3.cnss32.New-York.t3.ans.net (140.222.32.4)  26.026 ms  25.305
        ms 24.435 ms
  12   cnss40.New-York.t3.ans.net (204.149.4.8)  27.959 ms  28.373 ms
        29.114 ms
  13   t3.New-York-Mtl.t3.ans.net (198.168.57.25)  38.749 ms  37.864 ms
        36.716 ms
  14   Hydro.CAM.ORG (198.168.73.132)  53.998 ms  40.718 ms  44.047 ms
  15   * Ocean.CAM.ORG (198.168.100.5)  64.561 ms  *
```

Figure 11-2: A traceroute output for the second site.

The second site in Figure 11-2 should probably request a link either from ANS or MCI.

The multicast equivalent of traceroute is mtrace. It will show you the multicast route that a packet will use to go from point A to point B. This information not only enables you to determine whether giving a feed to a requesting party is appropriate for you, but also enables you to direct them to a more appropriate site for requesting a feed if you are unable to provide the feed.

Figure 11-3 shows an example of an mtrace output. I had to get some help from friends for this example because mtrace has to be supported by multicast routers for it to work. Because no mtrace path exists in Canada that is longer than 2 hops, and 2 hops is inadequate for providing a good example, here is an mtrace from MFSDatanet.com to uunet.net .

```
Mtrace from 137.39.246.98 to 150.225.14.20 via group 224.2.0.1
      Querying full reverse path... * switching to hop-by-hop:
 0 tacostand.MFSDatanet.COM (150.225.14.20)
 -1 comet.MFSDatanet.COM (150.225.14.11) DVMRP thresh^ 1
 -2 wdcmon.MFSDatanet.COM (150.225.20.36) DVMRP thresh^ 1
 -3 * mae-bone.psi.net (192.41.177.247) DVMRP thresh^ 64
 -4 * MBONE1.UU.NET (137.39.43.34) DVMRP thresh^ 64
 -5 * MBONE2.UU.NET (137.39.246.98) DVMRP thresh^ 64
 -6 MBONE2.UU.NET (137.39.246.98)
Round trip time 156 ms
Waiting to accumulate statistics... Results after 10 seconds:
 Source Response Dest Packet Statistics For Only For Traffic
137.39.246.98 224.0.1.32 All Multicast Traffic From 137.39.246.98
 v __/ rtt 152 ms Lost/Sent = Pct Rate To 224.2.0.1
137.39.246.98 MBONE2.UU.NET
 v ^ ttl 64 -1/62 = -1% 6 pps 0/0 = —% 0
pps
137.39.43.34 MBONE1.UU.NET
 v ^ ttl 65 -1/381 = 0% 38 pps 0/0 = —% 0
pps
192.41.177.247 mae-bone.psi.net
 v ^ ttl 66 2/469 = 0% 46 pps 0/0 = —% 0
pps
192.41.177.25
150.225.20.36 wdcmon.MFSDatanet.COM
 v ^ ttl 67 0/21 = 0% 2 pps 0/0 = —% 0
pps
150.225.14.11 comet.MFSDatanet.COM
 v \__ ttl 68 2 0 pps 0 0
pps
150.225.14.20 150.225.14.20
 Receiver Query Source
```

Figure 11-3: An example of an mtrace output.

The first part of the mtrace output shows the multicast route used by the packets to get from the source host to the destination. Here we can see the thresholds for each hop on the path; this information is useful for determining the TTL value that you should use when you want to create an MBONE event and make sure that it reaches every location to which you want it to go.

The second part provides statistics about the path itself. This data includes the percentage of packet loss incurred along the routing path. You can use this information to locate the source of the problem when you are receiving traffic from an MBONE event and experiencing a high percentage of data loss.

I said earlier that all the multicast routers between the source host and the destination host have to support mtrace for mtrace to work. You can verify if a particular router supports mtrace by using the mrinfo utility. Figure 11-4 shows an example of an mrinfo output.

```
127.0.0.1 (localhost.CC.McGill.CA) [version
    3.8,prune,genid,mtrace]:
  123.456.78.90 -> 0.0.0.0 (local) [1/1/querier/leaf]
  123.456.78.90 -> 123.456.210.1 (MBONE.Collaboration.CA) [1/16/
    tunnel/leaf]
  123.456.78.90 -> 123.456.3.4 (deadbeef.Algo.McGill.CA) [1/8/
    tunnel/leaf]
  123.456.78.90 -> 123.456.141.16 (LoveNotes.Harmo.McGill.CA) [1/
    8/tunnel/leaf]
  123.456.78.90 -> 123.456.186.10 (crash.WaysToFly.mcgill.ca) [1/
    8/tunnel/leaf]
  123.456.78.90 -> 123.457.90.90 (MBONE.UOtherSideCity.CA) [1/16/
    tunnel/down/leaf]
  123.456.78.90 -> 130.130.130.130 (mbonehost.jvnc.net) [1/64/
    tunnel/leaf]
  123.456.78.90 -> 123.456.101.182 (123.456.101.182) [1/8/tunnel/
    down/leaf]
  123.456.78.90 -> 124.222.4.3 (MBONE.cs.FarEast.ca) [1/32/
    tunnel/leaf]
  123.456.78.90 -> 129.111.3.18 (cythera.GOE.ca) [1/32/tunnel]
```

Figure 11-4: An example of an mrinfo output.

To generate the mrinfo output in Figure 11-4, I simply issued the mrinfo command without arguments; this gave me the mrinfo for my localhost. Issuing the mrinfo command with the name of the multicast router as an argument would give you the mrinfo for that router. In Figure 11-4, the first line shows that my localhost supports mtrace and also supports pruning. mrinfo also shows which tunnel is down, and it (the remote host) is a leaf in the tree for mtrace. The output also shows every link with their metric and threshold. Doing an mrinfo on each of these nodes would tell me whether or not the thresholds are symmetric; if they aren't, I could then contact the remote site and have them change the thresholds.

These various tools can help you perform accounting tasks on your MBONE usage, as well as assist you in debugging your MBONE setup. These tools comprise a limited toolkit, however, and some people may say that the tools are not very user friendly, either. If you are willing to put in some supplementary programming effort, however, you'll find these tools to be very flexible in how you can use them and what they can provide for you.

The future will undoubtedly provide us with even more of these tools for working with the MBONE. And keep in mind that the MBONE is still a research project; as such, the structure of the MBONE itself will continue to change, and so too will the tools for managing it.

The Future of the MBONE

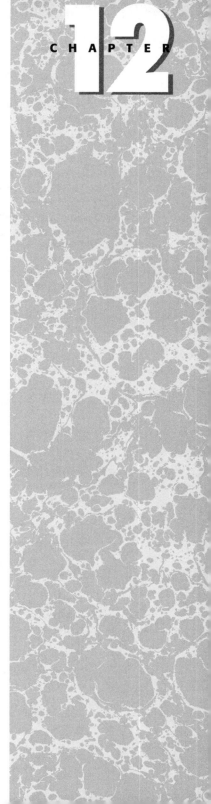

The MBONE is a wonderful way to the use the Internet, but it doesn't come without problems. Some problems are caused by the growing popularity of the MBONE, and others can be blamed on the fact that the technology is not quite able to fully support it.

Current Problems and Possible Solutions

The first problem, and also the most obvious one, is that IP multicast is still not supported everywhere. This fact places restrictions on spontaneously using the MBONE to send information to sites that *do* support IP multicast. Sites without true support for multicasting must utilize IP tunneling to work around this lack of support. Using these tunnels requires human intervention at both ends, and sometimes, weeks or months can pass between the moment a site decides to get on the MBONE and the moment the site can effectively use it. The MBONE certainly isn't "plug-and-play."

Over time, more and more sites will begin routing multicast packets in their native fashion, with true mrouters. As more sites gain experience with this task, the number of sites using IP tunneling will decrease. IP tunneling using mrouted is a clever hack — but compared to true multicasting, it is a relatively inefficient system.

Another problem arises from this transition away from mrouted: by using mrouted, we've grown accustomed to its advanced features, such as the support for mtrace and pruning. Currently, most native multicast routers do not support these features. Although multicast routers will eventually incorporate these features if they are to take over for mrouted, this is not the case today; as a result, the deployment of native multicast routing has been slow.

The next biggest problem deals with the bandwidth of the Internet. The MBONE was designed to use 500 Kbps to transmit multicasts, which is an adequate maximum bandwidth for now. As the MBONE becomes more popular, however, the 500 Kbps maximum bandwidth will not be sufficient for handling the increased demands placed on it. Not only will the number of events that conflict with each other increase, but the needs of the people using MBONE will also grow. One day users will certainly want to transmit full-motion, full-screen video via the MBONE, and this capability will require lots of bandwidth — more than the 500 Kbps limit imposed on the MBONE today.

This last problem is relatively easy to solve — the simple solution is to give it time. Five years ago, the links that existed between the provinces of Canada consisted of 56-Kbps links. At that time, the United States had begun working with T1 links. Today, the links that exist between the Canadian provinces have been upgraded to 45-Mbps ATM (*asynchronous transfer mode*) links. The United States also uses ATM links, multiple T3 links, and now, interstate fiber-optic links. Also five years ago, an individual could connect to the Internet from his or her home at a speed of 9600 bps; today, that same individual can connect to the Internet with an ISDN link (128 Kbps) for about the same price. As time passes, the capacity of the links is increasing; conversely, the cost of these links is decreasing. At some point in time, bandwidth may cease to be a problem altogether.

Phone companies already have plans to bring video into the home, but the problem is trying to find an efficient way to get it there. One solution is to run fiber into the home, but currently, the cost of carrying out this particular solution would be astronomical. Another solution is to bring fiber-optic links to distribution centers (one per neighborhood or area) and share this link over the service area.

Whatever solution is adopted, real-time home video will one day be a reality. At that point, the MBONE technology will be so deeply integrated in our everyday lives that the MBONE will cease to exist as a separate entity from the Internet itself.

Another big problem with using the MBONE is of a more technical nature. Currently, the Internet's network protocols do not provide the necessary support needed for real-time service. This means that the MBONE cannot work as well as it should. Real-time traffic requires minimal delays between the transmitter and the receiver and low-packet loss rates. The Internet currently doesn't have the capabilities to ensure that real-time traffic will be delivered with minimal delays and low loss rates. Packet loss rates strongly influence the quality of service that you can get from the MBONE.

A partial solution to this problem is called *IPng*, or *IPV6*. IPng (Internet Protocol, Next Generation) is the next version of the IP protocol, and its principles have already been adopted. The transition to the new IP protocol is expected to take place over the next ten years. This new protocol will provide the MBONE with the provisions that it needs to support real-time traffic. To do this, the new IP protocol will be able to determine the real-time traffic's needs and then take that into consideration when routing the various kinds of traffic. Time-dependant traffic (such as a real-time multicast) can be routed quickly; less time-dependant traffic (like an e-mail message to a friend) can take the slow boat to its destination.

Another part of the solution is still to come, however. In the meantime, networking research is being done on the important issues that still plague our real-time traffic capabilities, and IETF (Internet Engineering Task Force) workgroups have been formed to develop standard protocols that would support real-time services on the Internet. In the future, we can expect these workgroups to solve problems related to such topics as admission control (refusing a request if the currently available re-sources are not sufficient) to packet classification and queuing (scheduling each packet for routing in the appropriate order of priority).

Another related problem is that the tools for managing a huge structure such as the MBONE are still being developed. Although some MBONE management tools are available, they do yet not form an entire MBONE management package. You can obtain these tools from a variety of sources, but you make have to go through a great deal of work to retrieve everything that you need to properly manage your MBONE site.

Again, this problem will be solved over time. The management tools will continue to evolve and become integrated with the MBONE infrastructure.

Summary

The MBONE does have some problems today, but as the Internet and MBONE con-tinue to evolve, these problems will (hopefully) fade away. Currently, the MBONE is a useful means of communicating with people in remote locations. The MBONE enables humans to communicate like never before. Until someone invents teleportation, the MBONE will probably remain the best means for bringing people together who would otherwise be separated by thousands of miles.

Technical Reference

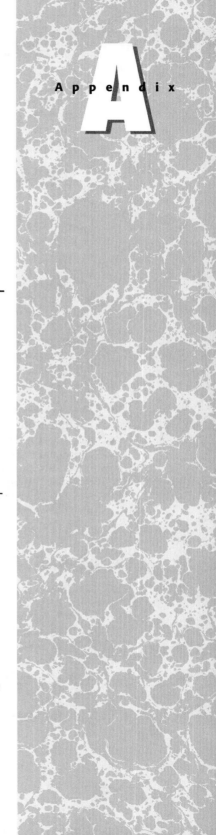

Host Extensions for IP Multicasting: RFC 1112

Network Working Group   S. Deering

Request for Comments: 1112   Stanford University

Obsoletes: RFCs 988, 1054   August 1989

1. Status Of This Memo

This memo specifies the extensions required of a host implementation of the Internet Protocol (IP) to support multicasting. It is the recommended standard for IP multicasting in the Internet. Distribution of this memo is unlimited.

2. Introduction

IP multicasting is the transmission of an IP datagram to a "host group," a set of zero or more hosts identified by a single IP destination address. A multicast datagram is delivered to all members of its destination host group with the same "best-efforts" reliability as regular unicast IP datagrams, i.e., the datagram is not guaranteed to arrive intact at all members of the destination group or in the same order relative to other datagrams.

The membership of a host group is dynamic; that is, hosts may join and leave groups at any time. There is no restriction on the location or number of members in a host group. A host may be a member of more than one group at a time. A host need not be a member of a group to send datagrams to it.

A host group may be permanent or transient. A permanent group has a well-known, administratively assigned IP address. It is the address, not the membership of the group, that is permanent; at any time a permanent group may have any number of members, even zero. Those IP multicast addresses that are not reserved for permanent groups are available for dynamic assignment to transient groups that exist only as long as they have members.

Internetwork forwarding of IP multicast datagrams is handled by "multicast routers," which may be co-resident with, or separate from, Internet gateways. A host transmits an IP multicast datagram as a local network multicast that reaches all immediately-neighboring members of the destination host group. If the datagram has an IP time-to-live greater than 1, the multicast router(s) attached to the local network take responsibility for forwarding it towards all other networks that have members of the destination group. On those other member networks that are reachable within the IP time-to-live, an attached multicast router completes delivery by transmitting the datagram as a local multicast.

This memo specifies the extensions required of a host IP implementation to support IP multicasting, where a "host" is any Internet host or gateway other than those acting as multicast routers. The algorithms and protocols used within and between multicast routers are transparent to hosts and will be specified in separate documents. This memo also does not specify how local network multicasting is accomplished for all types of network, although it does specify the required service interface to an arbitrary local network and gives an Ethernet specification as an example. Specifications for other types of network will be the subject of future memos.

3. Levels Of Conformance

There are three levels of conformance to this specification:

✦ **Level 0: no support for IP multicasting.** There is, at this time, no requirement that all IP implementations support IP multicasting. Level 0 hosts will, in general, be unaffected by multicast activity. The only exception arises on some types of local network, where the presence of level 1 or 2 hosts may cause misdelivery of multicast IP datagrams to level 0 hosts. Such datagrams can easily be identified by the presence of a class D IP address in their destination address field; they should be quietly discarded by hosts that do not support IP multicasting. Class D addresses are described in section 4 of this memo.

✦ **Level 1: support for sending but not receiving multicast IP datagrams.** Level 1 allows a host to partake of some multicast-based services, such as resource location or status reporting, but it does not allow a host to join any host groups. An IP implementation may be upgraded from level 0 to level 1 very easily and with little new code. Only sections 4, 5, and 6 of this memo are applicable to level 1 implementations.

✦ **Level 2: full support for IP multicasting.** Level 2 allows a host to join and leave host groups, as well as send IP datagrams to host groups. It requires implementation of the Internet Group Management Protocol (IGMP) and extension of the IP and local network service interfaces within the host. All of the following sections of this memo are applicable to level 2 implementations.

4. Host Group Addresses

Host groups are identified by class D IP addresses, i.e., those with "1110" as their high-order four bits. Class E IP addresses, i.e., those with "1111" as their high-order four bits, are reserved for future addressing modes.

In Internet standard "dotted decimal" notation, host group addresses range from 224.0.0.0 to 239.255.255.255. The address 224.0.0.0 is guaranteed not to be assigned to any group, and 224.0.0.1 is assigned to the permanent group of all IP hosts (including gateways). This is used to address all multicast hosts on the directly connected network. There is no multicast address (or any other IP address) for all hosts on the total Internet. The addresses of other well-known, permanent groups are to be published in "Assigned Numbers."

Appendix II contains some background discussion of several issues related to host group addresses.

5. Model of a Host IP Implementation

The multicast extensions to a host IP implementation are specified in terms of the layered model illustrated in Figure A-1. In this model, ICMP and (for level 2 hosts) IGMP are considered to be implemented within the IP module, and the mapping of IP addresses to local network addresses is considered to be the responsibility of local network modules. This model is for expository purposes only, and should not be construed as constraining an actual implementation.

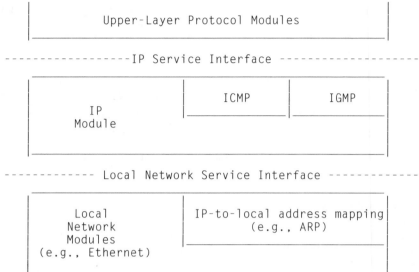

Figure A-1: Multicast extensions to a host IP implementation.

To provide level 1 multicasting, a host IP implementation must support the transmission of multicast IP datagrams. To provide level 2 multicasting, a host must also support the reception of multicast IP datagrams. Each of these two new services is described in a separate section, to follow. For each service, extensions are specified for the IP service interface, the IP module, the local network service interface, and an Ethernet local network module. Extensions to local network modules other than Ethernet are mentioned briefly but are not specified in detail.

6. Sending Multicast IP Datagrams

6.1. Extensions to the IP service interface

Multicast IP datagrams are sent using the same "Send IP" operation used to send unicast IP datagrams; an upper-layer protocol module merely specifies an IP host group address, rather than an individual IP address, as the destination. However, a number of extensions may be necessary or desirable.

First, the service interface should provide a way for the upper-layer protocol to specify the IP time-to-live of an outgoing multicast datagram, if such a capability does not already exist. If the upper-layer protocol chooses not to specify a time-to-live, it should default to 1 for all multicast IP datagrams, so that an explicit choice is required to multicast beyond a single network.

Second, for hosts that may be attached to more than one network, the service interface should provide a way for the upper-layer protocol to identify which network interface is to be used for the multicast transmission. Only one interface is used for the initial transmission; multicast routers are responsible for forwarding to any other networks, if necessary. If the upper-layer protocol chooses not to identify an outgoing interface, a default interface should be used, preferably under the control of system management.

Third (level 2 implementations only), for the case in which the host is itself a member of a group to which a datagram is being sent, the service interface should provide a way for the upper-layer protocol to inhibit local delivery of the datagram; by default, a copy of the datagram is looped back. This is a performance optimization for upper-layer protocols that restrict the membership of a group to one process per host (such as a routing protocol) or that handle loopback of group communication at a higher layer (such as a multicast transport protocol).

6.2. Extensions to the IP module

To support the sending of multicast IP datagrams, the IP module must be extended to recognize IP host group addresses when routing outgoing datagrams. Most IP implementations include the following logic:

```
if IP-destination is on the same local network,
    send datagram locally to IP-destination
else
    send datagram locally to GatewayTo( IP-destination )
```

To allow multicast transmissions, the routing logic must be changed to

```
if IP-destination is on the same local network
or IP-destination is a host group,
    send datagram locally to IP-destination
else
    send datagram locally to GatewayTo( IP-destination )
```

If the sending host is itself a member of the destination group on the outgoing interface, a copy of the outgoing datagram must be looped back for local delivery, unless inhibited by the sender (level 2 implementations only).

The IP source address of the outgoing datagram must be one of the individual addresses corresponding to the outgoing interface.

A host group address must never be placed in the source address field or anywhere in a source route or record route option of an outgoing IP datagram.

6.3. Extensions to the local network service interface

No change to the local network service interface is required to support the sending of multicast IP datagrams. The IP module merely specifies an IP host group destination, rather than an individual IP destination, when it invokes the existing "Send Local" operation.

6.4. Extensions to an Ethernet local network module

The Ethernet directly supports the sending of local multicast packets by allowing multicast addresses in the destination field of Ethernet packets. All that is needed to support the sending of multicast IP datagrams is a procedure for mapping IP host group addresses to Ethernet multicast addresses.

An IP host group address is mapped to an Ethernet multicast address by placing the low-order 23-bits of the IP address into the low-order 23 bits of the Ethernet multicast address 01-00-5E-00-00-00 (hex). Because there are 28 significant bits in an IP host group address, more than one host group address may map to the same Ethernet multicast address.

6.5. Extensions to local network modules other than Ethernet

Other networks that directly support multicasting, such as rings or buses conforming to the IEEE 802.2 standard, may be handled the same way as Ethernet for the purpose of sending multicast IP datagrams. For a network that supports broadcast but not multicast, such as the Experimental Ethernet, all IP host group addresses may be mapped to a single local broadcast address (at the cost of increased overhead on all local hosts). For a point-to-point link joining two hosts (or a host and a multicast router), multicasts should be transmitted exactly like unicasts. For a store-and-forward network like the ARPANET or a public X.25 network, all IP host group addresses might be mapped to the well-known local address of an IP multicast router; a router on such a network would take responsibility for completing multicast delivery within the network as well as among networks.

7. Receiving Multicast IP Datagrams

7.1. Extensions to the IP service interface

Incoming multicast IP datagrams are received by upper-layer protocol modules using the same "Receive IP" operation as normal, unicast datagrams. Selection of a destination upper-layer protocol is based on the protocol field in the IP header, regardless of the destination IP address. However, before any datagrams destined to a particular group can be received, an upper-layer protocol must ask the IP module to join that group. Thus, the IP service interface must be extended to provide two new operations:

> JoinHostGroup (group-address, interface)

> LeaveHostGroup (group-address, interface)

The JoinHostGroup operation requests that this host become a member of the host group identified by "group-address" on the given network interface. The LeaveGroup operation requests that this host give up its membership in the host group identified by "group-address" on the given network interface. The interface argument may be omitted on hosts that support only one interface. For hosts that may be attached to more than one network, the upper-layer protocol may choose to leave the interface unspecified, in which case the request will apply to the default interface for sending multicast datagrams (see section 6.1).

It is permissible to join the same group on more than one interface, in which case duplicate multicast datagrams may be received. It is also permissible for more than one upper-layer protocol to request membership in the same group.

Both operations should return immediately (i.e., they are non-blocking operations), indicating success or failure. Either operation may fail due to an invalid group address or interface identifier. JoinHostGroup may fail due to lack of local resources. LeaveHostGroup may fail because the host does not belong to the given group on the given interface. LeaveHostGroup may succeed, but the membership persist, if more than one upper-layer protocol has requested membership in the same group.

7.2. Extensions to the IP module

To support the reception of multicast IP datagrams, the IP module must be extended to maintain a list of host group memberships associated with each network interface. An incoming datagram destined to one of those groups is processed exactly the same way as datagrams destined to one of the host's individual addresses.

Incoming datagrams destined to groups to which the host does not belong are discarded without generating any error report or log entry. On hosts with more than one network interface, if a datagram arrives via one interface, destined for a group to which the host belongs only on a different interface, the datagram is quietly discarded. (These cases should occur only as a result of inadequate multicast address filtering in a local network module.)

An incoming datagram is not rejected for having an IP time-to-live of 1 (i.e., the time-to-live should not automatically be decremented on arriving datagrams that are not being forwarded). An incoming datagram with an IP host group address in its source address field is quietly discarded. An ICMP error message (Destination Unreachable, Time Exceeded, Parameter Problem, Source Quench, or Redirect) is never generated in response to a datagram destined to an IP host group.

The list of host group memberships is updated in response to JoinHostGroup and LeaveHostGroup requests from upper-layer protocols. Each membership should have an associated reference count or similar mechanism to handle multiple requests to join and leave the same group. On the first request to join and the last request to leave a group on a given interface, the local network module for that interface is notified, so that it may update its multicast reception filter (see section 7.3).

The IP module must also be extended to implement the IGMP protocol, specified in Appendix I. IGMP is used to keep neighboring multicast routers informed of the host group memberships present on a particular local network. To support IGMP, every level 2 host must join the "all-hosts" group (address 224.0.0.1) on each network interface at initialization time and must remain a member for as long as the host is active.

(Datagrams addressed to the all-hosts group are recognized as a special case by the multicast routers and are never forwarded beyond a single network, regardless of their time-to-live. Thus, the all-hosts address may not be used as an Internet-wide broadcast address. For the purpose of IGMP, membership in the all-hosts group is really necessary only while the host belongs to at least one other group. However, it is specified that the host shall remain a member of the all-hosts group at all times because (1) it is simpler, (2) the frequency of reception of unnecessary IGMP queries should be low enough that overhead is negligible, and (3) the all-hosts address may serve other routing-oriented purposes, such as advertising the presence of gateways or resolving local addresses.)

7.3. Extensions to the local network service interface

Incoming local network multicast packets are delivered to the IP module using the same "Receive Local" operation as local network unicast packets. To allow the IP module to tell the local network module which multicast packets to accept, the local network service interface is extended to provide two new operations:

JoinLocalGroup (group-address)

LeaveLocalGroup (group-address)

where "group-address" is an IP host group address. The JoinLocalGroup operation requests the local network module to accept and deliver up subsequently arriving packets destined to the given IP host group address. The LeaveLocalGroup operation requests the local network module to stop delivering up packets destined to the given IP host group address. The local network module is expected to map the IP host group addresses to local network addresses as required to update its multicast reception filter. Any local network module is free to ignore LeaveLocalGroup requests, and may deliver up packets destined to more addresses than just those specified in JoinLocalGroup requests, if it is unable to filter incoming packets adequately.

The local network module must not deliver up any multicast packets that were transmitted from that module; loopback of multicasts is handled at the IP layer or higher.

7.4. Extensions to an Ethernet local network module

To support the reception of multicast IP datagrams, an Ethernet module must be able to receive packets addressed to the Ethernet multicast addresses that correspond to the host's IP host group addresses. It is highly desirable to take advantage of any address filtering capabilities that the Ethernet hardware interface may have, so that the host receives only those packets that are destined to it.

Unfortunately, many current Ethernet interfaces have a small limit on the number of addresses that the hardware can be configured to recognize. Nevertheless, an implementation must be capable of listening on an arbitrary number of Ethernet multicast addresses, which may mean "opening up" the address filter to accept all multicast packets during those periods when the number of addresses exceeds the limit of the filter.

For interfaces with inadequate hardware address filtering, it may be desirable (for performance reasons) to perform Ethernet address filtering within the software of the Ethernet module. This is not mandatory, however, because the IP module performs its own filtering based on IP destination addresses.

7.5. Extensions to local network modules other than Ethernet

Other multicast networks, such as IEEE 802.2 networks, can be handled the same way as Ethernet for the purpose of receiving multicast IP datagrams. For pure broadcast networks, such as the Experimental Ethernet, all incoming broadcast packets can be accepted and passed to the IP module for IP-level filtering. On point-to-point or store-and-forward networks, multicast IP datagrams will arrive as local network unicasts, so no change to the local network module should be necessary.

Appendix I: Internet Group Management Protocol (IGMP)

The Internet Group Management Protocol (IGMP) is used by IP hosts to report their host group memberships to any immediately-neighboring multicast routers. IGMP is an asymmetric protocol and is specified here from the point of view of a host, rather than a multicast router. (IGMP may also be used, symmetrically or asymmetrically, between multicast routers. Such use is not specified here.)

Like ICMP, IGMP is an integral part of IP. It is required to be implemented by all hosts conforming to level 2 of the IP multicasting specification. IGMP messages are encapsulated in IP datagrams, with an IP protocol number of 2. All IGMP messages of concern to hosts have the format shown in Figure A-2.

```
 0                   1                   2                   3
 0 1 2 3 4 5 6 7 8 9 0 1 2 3 4 5 6 7 8 9 0 1 2 3 4 5 6 7 8 9 0 1
+-+-+-+-+-+-+-+-+-+-+-+-+-+-+-+-+-+-+-+-+-+-+-+-+-+-+-+-+-+-+-+-+
|Version| Type  |    Unused     |           Checksum            |
+-+-+-+-+-+-+-+-+-+-+-+-+-+-+-+-+-+-+-+-+-+-+-+-+-+-+-+-+-+-+-+-+
|                       Group Address                           |
+-+-+-+-+-+-+-+-+-+-+-+-+-+-+-+-+-+-+-+-+-+-+-+-+-+-+-+-+-+-+-+-+
```

Figure A-2: All IGMP messages of concern to hosts have this format.

Version

This memo specifies version 1 of IGMP. Version 0 is specified in RFC-988 and is now obsolete.

Type

There are two types of IGMP messages of concern to hosts:

Host Membership Query is equal to the host group address being reported, and with an IP time-to-live of 1, so that other members of the same group on the same network can overhear the Report. If a host hears a **Report** for a group to which it belongs on that network, the host stops its own timer for that group and does not generate a Report for that group. Thus, in the normal case, only one Report will be generated for each group present on the network, by the member host whose delay timer expires first. Note that the multicast routers receive all IP multicast datagrams, and therefore need not be addressed explicitly. Further note that the routers need not know which hosts belong to a group, only that at least one host belongs to a group on a particular network.

There are two exceptions to the behavior described above. First, if a report delay timer is already running for a group membership when a Query is received, that timer is not reset to a new random value, but rather allowed to continue running with its current value. Second, a report delay timer is never set for a host's membership in the all-hosts group (224.0.0.1), and that membership is never reported.

If a host uses a pseudo-random number generator to compute the reporting delays, one of the host's own individual IP address should be used as part of the seed for the generator, to reduce the chance of multiple hosts generating the same sequence of delays.

A host should confirm that a received Report has the same IP host group address in its IP destination field and its IGMP group address field, to ensure that the host's own Report is not canceled by an erroneous received Report. A host should quietly discard any IGMP message of type other than Host Membership Query or Host Membership Report.

Multicast routers send Queries periodically to refresh their knowledge of memberships present on a particular network. If no Reports are received for a particular group after some number of Queries, the routers assume that that group has no local members and that they need not forward remotely-originated multicasts for that group onto the local network. Queries are normally sent infrequently (no more than once a minute) so as to keep the IGMP overhead on hosts and networks very low. However, when a multicast router starts up, it may issue several closely-spaced Queries in order to build up its knowledge of local memberships quickly.

When a host joins a new group, it should immediately transmit a Report for that group, rather than waiting for a Query, in case it is the first member of that group on the network. To cover the possibility of the initial Report being lost or damaged, it is recommended that it be repeated once or twice after short delays. (A simple way to accomplish this is to act as if a Query had been received for that group only, setting the group's random report delay timer. The state transition diagram, Figure A-3, illustrates this approach.)

Note that on a network with no multicast routers present, the only IGMP traffic is the one or more Reports sent whenever a host joins a new group.

State transition diagram

IGMP behavior is more formally specified by the state transition diagram. A host may be in one of three possible states, with respect to any single IP host group on any single network interface:

1. **Non-Member state,** when the host does not belong to the group on the interface. This is the initial state for all memberships on all network interfaces; it requires no storage in the host.

2. **Delaying Member state,** when the host belongs to the group on the interface and has a report delay timer running for that membership.

3. **Idle Member state,** when the host belongs to the group on the interface and does not have a report delay timer running for that membership.

There are five significant events that can cause IGMP state transitions:

1. **Join group** occurs when the host decides to join the group on the interface. It may occur only in the Non-Member state.

2. **Leave group** occurs when the host decides to leave the group on the interface. It may occur only in the Delaying Member and Idle Member states.

3. **Query received** occurs when the host receives a valid IGMP Host Membership Query message. To be valid, the Query message must be at least eight octets long, have a correct IGMP checksum, and have an IP destination address of 224.0.0.1. A single Query applies to all memberships on the interface from which the Query is received. It is ignored for memberships in the Non-Member or Delaying Member state.

4. **Report received** occurs when the host receives a valid IGMP Host Membership Report message. To be valid, the Report message must be at least eight octets long, have a correct IGMP checksum, and contain the same IP host group address in its IP destination field and its IGMP group address field. A Report applies only to the membership in the group identified by the Report, on the interface from which the Report is received. It is ignored for memberships in the Non-Member or Idle Member state.

5. **Timer expired** occurs when the report delay timer for the group on the interface expires. It may occur only in the Delaying Member state.

All other events, such as receiving invalid IGMP messages, or IGMP messages other than Query or Report, are ignored in all states.

There are three possible actions that may be taken in response to the listed earlier events:

1. **Send report** for the group on the interface.
2. **Start timer** for the group on the interface, using a random delay value between 0 and D seconds.
3. **Stop timer** for the group on the interface.

In Figure A-3, each state transition arc is labeled with the event that causes the transition, and, in parentheses, any actions taken during the transition.

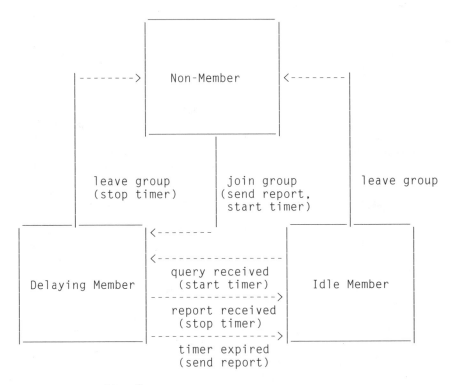

Figure A-3: A state transition diagram.

The all-hosts group (address 224.0.0.1) is handled as a special case. The host starts in Idle Member state for that group on every interface, never transitions to another state, and never sends a report for that group.

Protocol parameters

The maximum report delay, D, is 10 seconds.

Appendix II: Host Group Address Issues

This appendix is not part of the IP multicasting specification but provides background discussion of several issues related to IP host group addresses.

Group address binding

The binding of IP host group addresses to physical hosts may be considered a generalization of the binding of IP unicast addresses. An IP unicast address is statically bound to a single local network interface on a single IP network. An IP host group address is dynamically bound to a set of local network interfaces on a set of IP networks.

It is important to understand that an IP host group address is NOT bound to a set of IP unicast addresses. The multicast routers do not need to maintain a list of individual members of each host group. For example, a multicast router attached to an Ethernet need associate only a single Ethernet multicast address with each host group having local members, rather than a list of the members' individual IP or Ethernet addresses.

Allocation of transient host group addresses

This memo does not specify how transient group address are allocated. It is anticipated that different portions of the IP transient host group address space will be allocated using different techniques. For example, there may be a number of servers that can be contacted to acquire a new transient group address. Some higher-level protocols (such as VMTP, specified in RFC-1045) may generate higher-level transient "process group" or "entity group" addresses that are then algorithmically mapped to a subset of the IP transient host group addresses, similar to the way that IP host group addresses are mapped to Ethernet multicast addresses. A portion of the IP group address space may be set aside for random allocation by applications that can tolerate occasional collisions with other multicast users, perhaps generating new addresses until a suitably "quiet" one is found.

In general, a host cannot assume that datagrams sent to any host group address will reach only the intended hosts, or that datagrams received as a member of a transient host group are intended for the recipient. Misdelivery must be detected at a level above IP, using higher-level identifiers or authentication tokens. Information transmitted to a host group address should be encrypted or governed by administrative routing controls if the sender is concerned about unwanted listeners.

Author's Address

Steve Deering
Stanford University
Computer Science Department
Stanford, CA 94305-2140
Phone: (415) 723-9427

Requirements for Multicast Protocols: RFC 1458

Network Working Group

Request for Comments: 1458

TASC

May 1993

R. Braudes

S. Zabele

Status of This Memo

Summary

Multicast protocols have been developed over the past several years to address issues of group communication. Experience has demonstrated that current protocols do not address all of the requirements of multicast applications. This memo discusses some of these unresolved issues and provides a high-level design for a new multicast transport protocol, group address and membership authority, and modifications to existing routing protocols.

Table of Contents

1. Introduction

Multicast protocols have been developed to support group communications. These protocols use a one-to-many paradigm for transmission, typically using class D Internet Protocol (IP) addresses to specify specific multicast groups. While designing network services for reliable transmission of very large imagery as part of the DARPA-sponsored ImNet program, we have reviewed existing multicast protocols and have determined that none meet all of the requirements of image communications [3]. This RFC reviews the current state of multicast protocols, highlights the missing features, and motivates the design and development of an enhanced multicast protocol.

First, the requirements for network services and underlying protocols related to image communications are presented. Existing protocols are then reviewed, and an analysis of each protocol against the requirements is presented. The analyses identify the need for a new multicast protocol. Finally, the features of an ideal, reliable multicast protocol that adapts to network congestion in the transmission of large data volumes are presented. Additional network components needed to fully support the new protocol, including a Multicast Group Authority and modifications to existing routing protocols, are also introduced.

2. The Image Communications Problem

2.1 Scope

Image management and communications systems are evolving from film-based systems toward an all-digital environment where imagery is acquired, transmitted, analyzed, and stored using digital computer and communications technologies. The throughput required for communicating large numbers of very large images is extremely large, consisting of thousands of terabytes of imagery per day. Temporal requirements for capture and dissemination of single images are stringent, ranging from seconds to, at most, several minutes. Imagery will be viewed by hundreds of geographically distributed users who will require on-demand, interactive access to the data.

Traditional imaging applications involve images on the order of 512×512 pixels. In contrast, a single image used for remote sensing can have tens of thousands of pixels on a side. Multiplying the data volume associated with remotely sensed images by even a small number of users clearly motivates moving beyond the current suite of reliable protocols.

Basic image-communication applications involve the distribution of individual images to multiple users for both individual and collaborative analyses, and network efficiency requires the use of multicast protocols. Areas where multicasting offers significant advantages include real-time image acquisition and dissemination, distribution of annotated image-based reports, and image conferencing. Images are viewed on a heterogeneous set of workstations with differing processing and display capabilities, traveling over a heterogeneous network with bandwidths varying by up to six orders of magnitude between the initial down link and the slowest end user.

2.2 Requirements

Multicast protocols used for image communications must address several requirements. Setting up a multicast group first requires assigning a multicast group address. All multicast traffic is then delivered to this address, which implies that all members of the group must be listening for traffic with this address.

Within an image communications architecture, such as that used for the ImNet program, diversity and adaptability can be accommodated by trading quality of service (i.e., image quality) with speed of transmission. Multicast support for quality-speed trades can be realized either through the use of different multicast groups, where each group receives a different image quality, or through the use of a single hierarchical stream with routers (or users) extracting relevant portions.

Due to the current inability of routers to support selective transmission of partial streams, a multiple stream approach is being used within ImNet. Efficient operation using a multiple stream approach requires that users be able to switch streams very quickly, and that streams with no listeners not be disseminated. Consequently, rapid configuration of multicast groups and rapid switching between multicast groups is essential.

Inevitably, network congestion or buffer overruns result in packet loss. A full range of transport reliability is required within an image communications framework. For some applications such as image conferencing, packet loss does not present a problem, as dropped mouse movements can be discarded with no meaningful degradation in utility. However, for functions such as image archiving or detailed image analysis, transport must be completely reliable, where any dropped packets must be retransmitted by the sender. Additionally, several hierarchical image compression methods can provide useful, albeit degraded, imagery using a semireliable service, where higher-level data is transmitted reliably and the lower level data is transmitted unreliably.

In support of reliable transport, image communications services must also support adaptation to network congestion using flow control mechanisms. Flow control regulates the quantity of data placed on the network per unit time interval, thereby increasing network efficiency by reducing the number of dropped packets and avoiding the need for large numbers of retransmissions.

3. Review of Existing Multicast Protocols

Several existing protocols provide varying levels of support for multicasting, including IP/Multicast[5], the Xpress Transfer Protocol (XTP)[11], and Experimental Internet Stream Protocol Version 2 (ST-II)[10]. Although the Versatile Message Transaction Protocol (VMTP)[4] also supports multicast, it has been designed to support the transfer of small packets and so is not appropriate for large image communications. Additionally, a specification exists for the Multicast Transport Protocol (MTP)[2].

The image communication requirements for a multicast protocol include multicast group address assignment, group setup, membership maintenance (i.e., join, drop, and switch membership), group teardown, error recovery, and flow control, as presented earlier. The remainder of this section discusses how well each of the existing protocols meets these requirements.

3.1 IP/Multicast

IP/Multicast is an extension to the standard IP network-level protocol that supports multicast traffic. IP/Multicast has no address allocation mechanism, with addresses assigned either by an outside authority or by each application. This has the potential for address contention among multiple applications, which would result in the traffic from the different groups becoming commingled.

There is no true setup processing for IP/Multicast; once an address is determined, the sender simply transmits packets to that address with routers determining the path(s) taken by the data. The receiver side is only slightly more complex, as an application must issue an add membership request for IP to listen to traffic destined to the desired address. If this is the first member of a group, IP multicasts the request to routers on the local network using the Internet Group Multicast Protocol (IGMP) for inclusion in routing tables. Multicast packets are then routed like all other IP packets, with receivers accepting traffic addressed to joined groups in addition to the normal host address.

A major problem with the IP/Multicast setup approach is informing hosts of multicast group addresses. If addresses are dynamically allocated, then a mechanism must be established for informing receivers which addresses have been assigned to which groups. This requires a minimum of one round trip, with an address requested from a server and then returned to the receiver.

Dropping membership in a group involves issuing a request to the local IP, which decrements the count of members in the IP tables. However, no special action is taken when group membership goes to zero. Instead, a heartbeat mechanism is used, in which hosts are periodically polled for active groups, and routers stop forwarding group traffic to a network only after several polls receive no activity requests for that group, to ensure that a membership report is not lost or corrupted in transit. This causes the problem of unneeded traffic being transmitted, due to a long periodicity for the heartbeat (minimum of one minute between polls); consequently, there is no method for quickly dropping a group over a given path, impeding attempts to react to network congestion in real-time.

Finally, there is no transport level protocol compatible with IP/Multicast that is both reliable and implements a flow control mechanism.

3.2 XTP

XTP is a combined network and transport level protocol that offers significant support for multicast transfers. As with IP/Multicast, XTP offers no inherent address management scheme, so that an outside authority is required.

XTP is also similar to IP/Multicast as there is no explicit setup processing between the sender and the receivers prior to the establishment of group communications. Although there is implicit processing in key management, an external mechanism is required for passing the multicast group address to the receivers. The receivers must have established "filters" for the address prior to transmission in order to receive the data, and suffers the same problems as IP/Multicast.

In contrast to IP/Multicast, XTP does require explicit handshaking between the sender and receivers that wish to join an existing group; however, there is no parallel communication for receivers dropping out of groups, and the only mechanism for a sender to know if there are any receivers is the polling scheme used for error control and recovery. This causes the same problems with sending traffic to groups without members discussed under IP/Multicast.

The XTP specification does not address how routers distribute a multicast stream among different connected networks; however, it does include a discussion of the optional bucket, damping, slotting, and cloning algorithms to reduce duplicate multicast traffic within a local network.

The specification allows the user to determine whether multicast transfers are unreliable or semireliable, where semireliable transfers are defined to provide a "high-probability of success" [9] of delivery to all receivers. Reliability cannot be guaranteed due to the fact that XTP does not maintain the cardinality of the receiver set, and so cannot know that the data has been received by all hosts.

XTP recovers from errors using a go-back-n approach (assuming that the bucket algorithm has been implemented) by retransmitting dropped packets to all members of the multicast group, as group members are unknown. This has the potential of flooding the network if only a single receiver dropped a packet.

3.3 ST-II

ST-II is another network protocol that provides support for multicast communications. Similar to IP/Multicast and XTP, ST-II requires a separate application-specific protocol for assigning and communicating multicast group addresses.

Although ST-II is a network level protocol, it guarantees end-to-end bandwidth and delay, and so obviates the need for many of the functions of a transport protocol. The guarantee is provided by requiring bandwidth reservations for all connections, which are made at setup time, and ensuring that the requested bandwidth is available throughout the lifetime of the connection. The enforcement policy ensures that the same path is followed for all transmissions, and prohibits new connections over the network unless there is sufficient bandwidth to accommodate the expected traffic. This is accomplished by maintaining the state of all connections in the network routers, trading the overhead of this connection setup for the performance guarantees.

Connection setup involves negotiation of the bandwidth and delay parameters and path between the sender, intermediate routers, and receivers. If the requested resources cannot be made available, the sender is given the option of either accepting what is available or canceling the connection request.

To add a new user to an existing group, the new receiver must first communicate directly with the sender using a different protocol to exchange relevant information, such as the group address. The sender then requests ST-II to add the new receiver, with the basic connection setup processing invoked as before with the new connection completed only if there is sufficient bandwidth to process the user.

Although the resource guarantee system imposed by ST-II tries to prevent network congestion from occurring, there are situations where priority traffic must be introduced into the network. ST-II makes this very expensive, as the resource requirements for existing connections must be adjusted, which can only be accomplished by the origin of each stream. This must be completed prior to the connection setup for the priority stream, introducing a large delay before the important data can be transmitted.

ST-II connections can be closed by either the sender or the receiver. When the last receiver along a path has been removed, the resources allocated over that path are released. When all receivers have been removed, the sender is informed and has the option of either adding a new receiver or tearing down the group.

3.4 MTP

MTP is a transport level protocol designed to support efficient, reliable multicast transmissions on top of existing network protocols such as IP/Multicast. It is based on the notion of a multicast "master" that controls all aspects of group communications.

Allocation of a specific group address, or network service access point, is not considered part of MTP, and as with the other multicast protocols, requires the use of an outside addressing authority. The MTP specification does require the master to make a "robust effort"[2] to ensure that the address selected is not already in use by trying to join an existing group at that address, but the problems described earlier remain.

Once the address is established, receivers issue a request to join the existing group using a unique connection identifier that is preassigned. The MTP specification addresses neither how the identifier is allocated nor how the receivers learn its value, but is assumed to be handled through an external protocol. The join request specifies whether the receiver wishes to be a producer of information or only a receiver, whether the connection should be reliable or best effort, whether the receiver is able to accept multiple senders of information, the minimum throughput desired, and the maximum data packet size. If the request can be granted, then the master replies with an ACK with a multicast connection identifier; otherwise, a NAK is returned.

Dropping membership in a group is coordinated through the master. The specification does not address what action the master should take when the group is reduced to a single member, but a logical action would be to stop distributing transmit tokens if there are no active receivers.

One of the major features in MTP is the ordering of received data. The master distributes transmit tokens to data producers in the group, which allow data to be provided at a specified rate. Rate control provides flow control within the protocol, with members that cannot maintain a minimum flow requested to leave the group.

Error recovery utilizes a NAK-based selective retransmission scheme. Senders are required to maintain data for a time period specified by the master, and to be able to retransmit this data when requested by members of the group. These retransmissions are multicast to the entire group, requiring receivers to be able to cope with duplicate packets. If a retransmission request arrives after the data has been released, the sender must NAK the request.

A potential problem with MTP is the significant amount of overhead associated with the protocol, with virtually all control traffic flowing through the master. The extra delay and congestion makes MTP inappropriate for the image dissemination applications.

3.5 Summary

Our analysis has determined that there are significant problems with all of the major multicast protocols for the reliable, adaptive multicast transport of large data items. The problems include inadequate address management, excessive processing of control information, poor response to network congestion, inability to handle high-priority traffic, and suboptimal error recovery and retransmission procedures. We have developed a high-level notion of the requirements for a service that addresses these issues, which we now discuss.

4. Protocol Suite for Reliable, Adaptive Multicast

We present an integrated set of three basic components required to provide a reliable multicast service: the Multicast Group Authority (MGA); the Reliable, Adaptive Multicast Protocol (RAMP); and modified routing algorithms. These components are designed to be compatible with, and take full advantage of, reservation systems such as RSVP [12].

In this discussion, we have broadened the definition of the term "Quality of Service (QOS)." There are many applications where the information content of the underlying data can be reduced through data compression techniques. For example, a $1,024 \times 1,024$ pixel image can be sub-sampled down to 512×512 pixels. This degradation results in a lower quality of service for the end user, while reducing the traditional network QOS requirements for the transfer.

4.1 The Multicast Group Authority

The Multicast Group Authority (MGA) provides services related to managing the multicast address space and high-level management support to existing multicast groups. The MGA has three primary responsibilities: address management, service registration, and group membership maintenance.

The MGA is hierarchical in nature, similar to the Internet Domain Name System (DNS)[7]. Requests for service are directed to an MGA agent on the local workstation, which are propagated upwards as required.

4.1.1 Address management

The MGA is responsible for the allocation and deallocation of addresses within the Internet Class D address space. Address requests received from application processes or other MGA nodes result in a block of addresses being assigned to the requesting MGA node. The size of the address block allocated is dependent on the position of the requester in the MGA hierarchy, to reduce the number of address requests propagated through the MGA tree.

Figure B-1 can be used to show what happens when an application requests a multicast address from the authority at node 1.1.1. Assuming that this is the first request from this branch of the MGA, node 1.1.1 issues a request to its parent, node 1.1, which propagates the request to node 1. Node 1 passes this request to the root, which issues a block of, say, 30 class D addresses. Of these 30, ten are returned to node 1.1, with the remaining 20 reserved for requests from node 1's other children. Similarly, node 1.1 passes three addresses to node 1.1.1, reserving the other seven for future requests. Finally, node 1.1.1 answers the applications request for an address, keeping the remaining two addresses for future use.

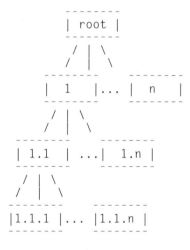

Figure B-1: Sample MGA hierarchy.

When the root exhausts the address space, a request is made to the children for reclamation of unused addresses. This request propagates down the tree, with unused addresses passed back through the hierarchy and returned to the address pool. If the entire address space is in use, then requests for additional addresses are not honored.

When an application no longer requires an address, it is returned to the local MGA node, which keeps it until either it is requested by another application, it is requested by its parent, or the node is terminated. At node termination, all available addresses are returned to the parent. Parents periodically send heartbeat requests to their children to ensure connectivity, and local nodes similarly poll applications, with addresses recalled if the queries are not answered.

4.1.2 Service registration, requests, release, and group membership maintenance

The MGA maintains the state of all registered multicast services and receivers. State information includes the number of members associated with each group by requested QOS reliability, which is updated as services are offered or rescinded and as members join or leave a group. The state information is used to ensure that there is at least one group member listening to each multicast transfer.

Servers register the availability of service, specifying whether reliable service is available (Section 4.2.2) and, optionally, the number of qualities of service offered (Section 4.2.1). A multicast group address is allocated from the address pool and the service is assigned an identifier as required. If a reservation protocol that requires information from the server (such as RSVP) is in use, then the MGA notifies the reservation system of the service with any required parameters. The service registration is propagated through the MGA, so that potential clients can discover service availability. However, servers do not begin data transfers until directed to do so by the MGA.

Client requests for service are also processed through the MGA. Service requests specify a service, a desired quality of service, and a reliability indication. If the request is for a service that has been registered, then the routing support is directed to add a route for the new user (Section 4.3.1). If necessary, the MGA also notifies the reservation protocol. If either the requested QOS is not being provided or it is provided unreliably and the request is for reliable transport, then the service provider is also notified. If the service has not yet been registered, an identifier for the service is assigned and the request is queued for when the service is registered. In either case, a response is sent to the requester.

Requests for termination of group membership are also sent to the MGA. If the request originates at a client, the MGA notifies the routing function and reservation protocol of the termination in case the route should be released (Section 4.3.2). If termination results in a given QOS no longer having any recipients, the service provider is notified that the QOS is no longer required and should not be transmitted. Server-directed group terminations follow a similar procedure, with all clients of the group notified, and the service offering is removed from the MGA state tables.

4.2 The Reliable Adaptive Multicast Protocol (RAMP)

RAMP is a transport level protocol designed to provide reliable multicast service on top of a network protocol such as IP/Multicast, with unreliable transport also available. RAMP is built on the premise that applications can request one quality of service (using our extended definition), but only require reliable transmission at a lower level of quality. For example, consider the transmission of hierarchical image data, in which a base spatial resolution is transmitted, followed by higher resolution data. An application may require the base data to be sent reliably, but can tolerate dropped packets for the higher resolution by using interpolation or pixel replication from the base level to approximate the missing data. Similar methods can be applied to other data types, such as audio or video.

4.2.1 Quality of service levels

RAMP allows a multicast service to be provided at multiple qualities of service, with all or some of these levels transmitted reliably. These QOS can be distributed across different groups using different class D addresses, or in the simplest case, be transmitted in individual groups. Single packets can be used for either a single QOS, or they may be applicable to multiple qualities of service.

When a data packet is transmitted, a header field indicates the QOS level(s) associated with that packet. In the old IP implementations, the Type of Service field can be used as a bit field with one bit for each applicable QOS, although this is incompatible with RFC 1349 [1]. If a packet is required for multiple QOS, then multiple values are encoded in the field. The RAMP host receiver protocol only accepts those packets addressed to a group in which an application has requested membership and that has a QOS value that is in the set of values requested by the receivers.

The quality of service requested within a flow can be modified during the life of the flow. QOS modification requests are forwarded to the MGA, which reduces the number of receivers in the original QOS group and increments the count for the requested QOS. These changes are propagated through the MGA hierarchy, with the server notified if either the original QOS has no remaining receivers or if the new QOS is not currently being served; similarly, the routers are notified if routing changes are required.

4.2.2 Error Recovery

Sequence numbers are used in RAMP to determine the ordering of packets within a multicast group. Mechanisms for ordering packets transmitted from different senders is a current research topic (2, 6), and an appropriate sequencing algorithm will be incorporated within the protocol.

Applications exist that do not require in-order delivery of data; for example, some image servers include position identification information in each packet. To enhance the efficiency of such schemes, RAMP includes an option to allow out-of-order delivery of packets to a receiver.

A NAK-based selective retransmission scheme is used in RAMP to minimize the protocol overhead associated with ACK-based schemes. When a receiver notices that one or more packets have not been received, and the transmission is reliable, a request is sent to the sender for the span of packets that are missing.

RAMP at the sender aggregates retransmission requests for the time specified by the retransmission hold timer (Section 4.2.3). After this time, the requests are evaluated to determine if sufficient receivers dropped a given packet to make multicasting the retransmission worthwhile by comparing it to a threshold value. All packets that have received a number of retransmission requests greater than the threshold are multicast to the group address, with other packets unicast to the individual requesters. The proposed retransmission scheme is a compromise between the extremes of multicasting and unicasting all retransmissions. The rationale is that multicasting a request issued by a single sender unnecessarily floods networks that had no packet loss, whereas unicasting to a large number of receivers floods the entire network. The optimal approach, dynamically constructing a new multicast group for each dropped packet, is currently too costly in terms of group setup time.

For those cases where the service provider is unable to retransmit the data due to released or overwritten buffers, the protocol delivers NAK responses using either multicast or unicast based on the number of retransmission requests received.

4.2.3 Flow control

RAMP utilizes a rate-based flow control mechanism that derives rate reductions from requests for retransmission or router back-off requests (i.e., ICMP source quench messages), and derives rate increases from the number of packets transmitted without retransmission requests. When a retransmission request is received, the protocol uses the number of packets requested to compute a rate reduction factor. Similarly, a different reduction factor is computed upon receipt of a router-generated squelch request. The rate reduction factors are then used to compute a reduced rate of transmission.

When a given number of packets have been transmitted without packet loss, the rate of transmission is incrementally increased. The size of the increase will always be smaller than the size of the smallest rate decrease, in order to minimize throttling.

The retransmission hold timer is modified according to both application requests and network state. As the number of retransmission requests rises, the hold timer is incremented to minimize the number of duplicate retransmissions. Similarly, the timer is decremented as the number of retransmission requests drops.

RAMP allows for priority traffic, which is marked in the packet header. The protocol transmits a variable number of packets from each sending process in proportion to the priority of the flow.

4.3 Routing support

The protocol suite requires routing support for four functions: path setup, path tear-down, forwarding based on QOS values, and prioritized packet loss due to congestion. The support must be integrated into routers and network-level protocols in a similar fashion to IGMP[8].

Partial support comes as a direct consequence of using reservation protocols such as RSVP. This RFC does not mandate the means of implementing the required functions, and the specified protocols are compatible with known reservation protocols.

The routers state tables must maintain both the multicast group address and the QOS level(s) requested for each group on each outbound interface in order to make appropriate routing decisions (Section 4.3.3). Therefore, the router state tables are updated whenever group membership changes, including QOS changes.

4.3.1 Path setup

Routers receive path setup requests from the MGA as required when new members join a multicast group, which specifies the incoming and outgoing interfaces, the group address, and the QOS associated with the request. When the message is received, the router establishes a path between the server and the receiver, and subsequently updates the multicast group state table. The mechanism used to discern the network interfaces is not specified but may take advantage of other protocols such as the RSVP path and reservation mechanism.

4.3.2 Path tear-down

Path tear-down requests are also propagated through the routers by the MGA when group membership changes or QOS changes no longer require data to be sent over a given route. These are used to inform routers of both deletions of QOS for a given path and deletions of entire paths. The purpose of the message is to explicitly remove route table entries in order to minimize the time required to stop forwarding multicast data across networks once the path is no longer required.

4.3.3 Multicast routing based on quality of service

Traditional multicast routing formulates route/don't route decisions based on the destination address in the packet header, with packets duplicated as necessary to reach all destinations. In the proposed new protocol suite, routers also consult the QOS field for each packet as different paths may have requested different qualities of service. Packets are only forwarded if the group address has been requested and the quality of service specified in the header is requested in the state table entry for a given interface.

4.3.4 Quality of service based on packet loss

Network congestion causes router queues to overflow, and as a result, packet loss occurs. The QOS and priority indications in the packet headers can be used to prioritize the order in which packets are dropped. First, packets with the priority field set in the header are dropped last. Within packets of equal priority, packets are dropped in order of QOS, with the highest QOS packets dropped first. The rationale is that other packets with lower QOS may be usable by receivers, whereas packets with high QOS may not be usable without the lower QOS data.

5. Interactions among the Components: An Example

The MGA, RAMP, and routing support functions all cooperate in the multicast process. As an example, assume that a network exists with a single server (S), three routers (R1, R2, and R3), and two clients (C1 and C2). The path between S and C1 goes through R1 and R2, whereas the path between S and C2 goes through R1, R2, and R3. The network is shown in Figure B-2.

```
S ------- R1 ------- R2 ------- R3
           |         |
          C1        C2
```

Figure B-2: Sample network configuration.

Service registration

When S is initiated, it registers a service with the MGA node in the local workstation, offering reliable service at two qualities of service, Q1 and Q2. As this is the first multicast offering on the workstation, the local MGA requests a block of multicast addresses from the hierarchy and assigns an address and service identifier to S. If the RSVP reservation protocol is in operation, the local MGA node in S notifies RSVP to send a RpathS message out for the service, which goes through R1, R2, and R3, reaching the RSVP nodes on C1 and C2. The service and its characteristics are propagated throughout the MGA hierarchy, ultimately reaching the MGA nodes resident on C1 and C2. The service is now available throughout the network.

Service request and path setup

The client C1 requests reliable service from S at QOS Q1 by issuing a request to the MGA node in C1. If a reservation protocol is in use, then it is used to reserve bandwidth and establish a path between the sender and receiver, going through R1 and R2; otherwise, the path is established through R1 and R2 by the routing protocol. R1 now forwards all packets from S with QOS Q1 along the path to R2, which routes them to C1. In concert with the path setup, the add membership request is propagated through MGA to the server workstation. The local MGA tables are checked and it is noted that the service is not currently being offered, so the server is notified to begin reliable distribution of the service at Q1.

Initial delivery

The server now begins transmitting Q1 data, which is observed by R1. R1 inspects the header and notes that the packet has QOS Q1. The routing tables specify that QOS Q1 for this address are only forwarded along the interface leading to R2, and R1 acts accordingly. Similarly, R2 routes the packet to C1. When the data arrives at C1, the RAMP node inspects the QOS and destination address fields in the header, accepts the packet, and forwards it to the C1 client process.

Error recovery

During transmission, if the RAMP node in C1 realizes that packets have been dropped, a retransmission request is returned to the server identifying spans of the missing packets. The RAMP node accepts the packet, builds the retransmission packets, and sets the retransmission hold timer. When the timer expires, the number of retransmission requests for each missing packet is compared against the threshold, and the packets are either unicast directly to the requesters or multicast to the entire group. As in this case, there is only requester, the threshold is not exceeded, and the packets are retransmitted to C1U's unicast address.

Group membership addition

Client C2 now joins the group, requesting reliable transmission at QOS Q2. Following the process used for C1, the request propagates through the MGA (and potentially reservation protocol) hierarchy. Upon completion of the request processing, R1 routes packets for QOS Q1 and Q2 to R2, while R2 forwards QOS Q1 packets to C1 and Q2 packets to R3; client C1 only accepts packets marked as Q1, whereas C2 only accepts Q2 packets. The server is notified that it now has clients for Q2 and begins serving that QOS in addition to Q1.

QOS-based routing

First, assume that QOS Q1 data is independent of QOS Q2 data. When the server sends a packet with Q1 marked in the header, the packet is received by R1 and is forwarded to R2. R2 receives the packet and sends it out the interface to C1, but not to R3. Next, the server delivers a packet for Q2. R1 receives the packet and sends it to R2, which forwards it to R3 but not to C1. R3 accepts the packet and forwards it to C2.

Now, assume that either Q2 is a subset of Q1, or that receivers of Q1 data also require Q2 data as in conditional compression schemes. Therefore, all Q2 packets are marked for both Q1 and Q2, whereas the remaining Q1 packets only have Q1 set in the header. Q1-only packets are routed as before, following the path S→ R1→ R2 →C1. However, Q2 packets are now routed from S to R1 to R2, at which point R2 duplicates the packets and sends them to both C1 and R3, with R3 forwarding them to C2. At C1, these packets have Q1 marked, and so are accepted, while at C2, the packet is accepted as the Q2 bit is verified.

Group membership deletion

When C1 issues a drop membership request, the MGA on the client workstation is notified, and the request is propagated through the MGA hierarchy back to the server MGA node. In parallel, the routers are notified to close the path, as it is no longer required, possibly through the reservation protocol. As this is the last client for the Q1 QOS, the server is informed to stop transmitting Q1 data, with Q2 data unaffected. A similar process occurs when C2 drops membership from the group, leaving the server idle. At this point, the server has the option of shutting down and returning the group address to the MGA, or continuing in an idle state until another client requests service.

Acknowledgments

This research was supported in part by the Defense Research Projects Agency (DARPA) under contract number F19618-91-C-0086.

References

1. Almquist, P., "Type of Service in the Internet Protocol Suite," RFC 1349, Consultant, July 1992.

2. Armstrong, S., A. Freier, and K. Marzullo, "Multicast Transport Protocol," RFC 1301, Xerox, Apple, Cornell University, February 1992.

3. Braudes, R., and S. Zabele, "A Reliable, Adaptive Multicast Service for High-Bandwidth Image Dissemination," submitted to ACM SIGCOMM '93.

4. Cheriton, D., "VMTP: Versatile Message Transaction Protocol," RFC 1045, Stanford University, February 1988.

5. Deering, S., "Host Extensions for IP Multicasting," STD 5, RFC 1112, Stanford University, August 1989.

6. Mayer, E., "An Evaluation Framework for Multicast Ordering Protocols," Proceedings ACM SIGCOMM '92, Baltimore, Maryland, pp. 177-187.

7. Mockapetris, P., "Domain Names - Concepts and Facilities," STD 13, RFC 1034, USC/Information Sciences Institute, November 1987.

8. Postel, J., "Internet Control Message Protocol - DARPA Internet Program Protocol Specification," STD 5, RFC 792, USC/Information Sciences Institute, September 1981.

9. Strayer, W., B. Dempsey, and A. Weaver, "XTP: The Xpress Transfer Protocol," Addison-Wesley Publishing Co., Reading, MA, 1992.

10. Topolcic, C., Editor, "Experimental Internet Stream Protocol, Version 2 (ST- II)," RFC 1190, CIP Working Group, October 1990.

11. "XTP Protocol Definition Revision 3.6," Protocol Engines Incorporated, PEI 92-10, Mountain View, CA, 11 January 1992.

12. Zhang, L., S. Deering, D. Estrin, S. Shenker, and D. Zappala, "RSVP: A New Resource ReSerVation Protocol," Work in Progress, March 1993.

Security Considerations

Security issues are not discussed in this memo.

Authors' Addresses

Bob Braudes

TASC

55 Walkers Brook Drive

Reading, MA 01867

Phone: (617) 942-2000

E-mail: rebraudes@tasc.com

Steve Zabele

TASC

55 Walkers Brook Drive

Reading, MA 01867

Phone: (617) 942-2000

E-mail: gszabele@tasc.com

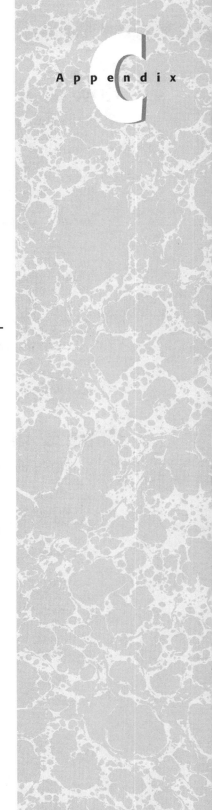

The MBONE FAQ: Frequently Asked Questions about the Multicast Backbone

By Steve Casner, with modifications by Henning Schulzrinne and David M. Kristol. Reprinted with permission.

What is the MBONE?

The MBONE is an outgrowth of the first two IETF "audiocast" experiments in which live audio and video were multicast from the IETF meeting site to destinations around the world. The idea is to construct a semi-permanent IP multicast testbed to carry the IETF transmissions and support continued experimentation between meetings. This is a cooperative, volunteer effort.

The MBONE is a virtual network. It is layered on top of portions of the physical Internet to support routing of IP multicast packets since that function has not yet been integrated into many production routers. The network is composed of islands that can directly support IP multicast, such as multicast LANs like Ethernet, linked by virtual point-to-point links called "tunnels." The tunnel endpoints are typically workstation-class machines having operating system support for IP multicast and running the "mrouted" multicast routing daemon.

How do IP multicast tunnels work?

IP multicast packets are encapsulated for transmission through tunnels so that they look like normal unicast datagrams to intervening routers and subnets. A multicast router that wants to send a multicast packet across a tunnel will prepend another IP header, set the destination address in the new header to be the unicast address of the multicast router at the other end of the tunnel, and set the IP protocol field in the new header to be 4 (which means the next protocol is IP). The multicast router at the other end of the tunnel receives the packet, strips off the encapsulating IP header, and forwards the packet as appropriate.

Previous versions of the IP multicast software (before March 1993) used a different method of encapsulation based on an IP Loose Source and Record Route option. This method remains an option in the new software for backward compatibility with nodes that have not been upgraded. In this mode, the multicast router modifies the packet by appending an IP LSRR option to the packet's IP header. The multicast destination address is moved into the source route, and the unicast address of the router at the far end of the tunnel is placed in the IP Destination Address field. The presence of IP options, including LSRR, may cause modern router hardware to divert the tunnel packets through a slower software processing path, causing poor performance. Therefore, use of the new software and the IP encapsulation method is strongly encouraged.

What is the topology of the MBONE?

We anticipate that within a continent, the MBONE topology will be a combination of mesh and star: the backbone and regional (or mid-level) networks will be linked by a mesh of tunnels among mrouted machines located primarily at interconnection points of the backbones and regionals. Some redundant tunnels may be configured with higher metrics for robustness. Then each regional network will have a star hierarchy hanging off its node of the mesh to fan out and connect to all the customer networks that want to participate.

Between continents there will probably be only one or two tunnels, preferably terminating at the closest point on the MBONE mesh. In the US, this may be on the Ethernets at the two FIXes (Federal Internet eXchanges) in California and Maryland. But because the FIXes are fairly busy, it will be important to minimize the number of tunnels that cross them. This may be accomplished using IP multicast directly (rather than tunnels) to connect several multicast routers on the FIX Ethernet.

How is the MBONE topology going to be set up and coordinated?

The primary reason we set up the MBONE e-mail lists (see below) was to coordinate the top levels of the topology (the mesh of links among the backbones and regionals). This must be a cooperative project combining knowledge distributed among the participants, somewhat like Usenet. The goal is to avoid loading any one individual with the responsibility of designing and managing the whole topology, though perhaps it will be necessary to periodically review the topology to see if corrections are required.

The intent is that when a new regional network wants to join in, they will make a request on the appropriate MBONE list, then the participants at "close" nodes will answer and cooperate in setting up the ends of the appropriate tunnels. To keep fanout down, sometimes this will mean breaking an existing tunnel to inserting a new node, so three sites will have to work together to set up the tunnels.

To know which nodes are "close" will require knowledge of both the MBONE logical map and the underlying physical network topology, for example, the physical T3 NSFnet backbone topology map combined with the network providers' own knowledge of their local topology.

Within a regional network, the network's own staff can independently manage the tunnel fanout hierarchy in conjunction with end-user participants. New end-user networks should contact the network provider directly, rather than the MBONE list, to get connected.

What is the anticipated traffic level?

The traffic anticipated during IETF multicasts is 100-300 kilobits per second, so 500 Kbps seems like a reasonable design bandwidth. Between IETF meetings, most of the time there will probably be no audio or video traffic, though some of the background session/control traffic may be present. A guess at the peak level of experimental use might be 5 simultaneous voice conversations (64 Kbps each). Clearly, with enough simultaneous conversations, we could exceed any bandwidth number, but 500 Kbps seems reasonable for planning.

Typically, audio is carried at 32 or 64 Kbps, video at up to 128 Kbps. Other services such as imm and sd need very small amounts of bandwidth.

Note that the design bandwidth must be multiplied by the number of tunnels passing over any given link since each tunnel carries a separate copy of each packet. This is why the fanout of each mrouted node should be no more than 5-10 and the topology should be designed so that at most 1 or 2 tunnels flow over any T1 line.

While most MBONE nodes should connect with lines of at least T1 speed, it will be possible to carry restricted traffic over slower speed lines. Each tunnel has an associated threshold against which the packet's IP time-to-live (TTL) value is compared. By convention in the IETF multicasts, higher bandwidth sources such as video transmit with a smaller TTL so they can be blocked while lower bandwidth sources such as compressed audio are allowed through.

Why should I (a network provider) participate?

To allow your customers to participate in IETF audiocasts and other experiments in packet audio/video, and to gain experience with IP multicasting for a relatively low cost.

What technical facilities and equipment are required for a network provider to join the MBONE?

Each network-provider participant in the MBONE provides one or more IP multicast routers to connect with tunnels to other participants and to customers. The multicast routers are typically separate from a network's production routers since most production routers don't yet support IP multicast. Most sites use workstations running the mrouted program, but the experimental MOSPF software for Proteon routers is an alternative (see MOSPF question later). It is best if the workstations can be dedicated to the multicast routing function to avoid interference from other activities and so there will be no qualms about installing kernel patches or new code releases on short notice. Since most MBONE nodes other than endpoints will have at least three tunnels, and each tunnel carries a separate (unicast) copy of each packet, it is also useful, though not required, to have multiple network interfaces on the workstation so it can be installed parallel to the unicast router for those sites with configurations like this:

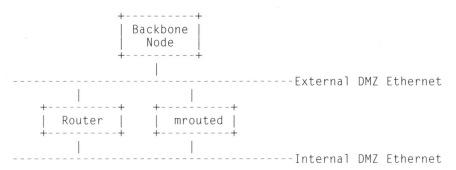

```
                    +----------+
                    | Backbone |
                    |   Node   |
                    +----------+
                         |
    ---------------------------------------------------External DMZ Ethernet
            |                     |
    +----------+          +----------+
    |  Router  |          | mrouted  |
    +----------+          +----------+
            |                     |
    ---------------------------------------------------Internal DMZ Ethernet
```

(The "DMZ" Ethernets borrow that military term to describe their role as interface points between networks and machines controlled by different entities.) This configuration allows the mrouted machine to connect with tunnels to other regional networks over the external DMZ and the physical backbone network, and connect with tunnels to the lower-level mrouted machines over the internal DMZ, thereby splitting the load of the replicated packets. (The mrouted machine would not do any unicast forwarding.) Note that end user sites may participate with as little as one workstation that runs the packet audio and video software and has a tunnel to a network-provider node.

What skills are needed to participate and how much time might have to be devoted to this?

The person supporting a network's participation in the MBONE should have the skills of a network engineer, but a fairly small percentage of that person's time should be required. Activities requiring this skill level would be choosing a topology for multicast distribution within the provider's network and analyzing traffic flow when performance problems are identified.

To set up and run an mrouted machine will require the knowledge to build and install operating system kernels. If you would like to use a hardware platform other than those currently supported, then you might also contribute some software implementation skills!

We will depend on participants to read mail on the appropriate mbone mailing list and respond to requests from new networks that want to join and are "nearby" to coordinate the installation of new tunnel links. Similarly, when customers of the network provider make requests for their campus nets or end systems to be connected to the MBONE, new tunnel links will need to be added from the network provider's multicast routers to the end systems (unless the whole network runs MOSPF).

Part of the resources that should be committed to participate would be for operations staff to be aware of the role of the multicast routers and the nature of multicast traffic, and to be prepared to disable multicast forwarding if excessive traffic is found to be causing trouble. The potential problem is that any site hooked into the MBONE could transmit packets that cover the whole MBONE, so if it became popular as a "chat line," all available bandwidth could be consumed. Steve Deering plans to implement multicast route pruning so that packets only flow over those links necessary to reach active receivers; this will reduce the traffic level. This problem should be manageable through the same measures we already depend upon for stable operation of the Internet, but MBONE participants should be aware of it.

Which workstation platforms can support the mrouted program?

The most convenient platform is a Sun SPARCstation simply because that is the machine used for mrouted development. An older machine (such as a SPARC-1 or IPC) will provide satisfactory performance as long as the tunnel fanout is kept in the 5-10 range. Table C-1 shows the platforms for which software is available.

Table C-1 Platforms for Which mrouted Software is Available		
Machines	*Operating Systems*	*Network Interfaces*
Sun SPARC	SunOS 4.1.1,2,3	ie, le, lo
Vax or Microvax	4.3+ or 4.3-tahoe	de, qe, lo
Decstation 3100,5000	Ultrix 3.1c, 4.1, 4.2a	ln, se, lo
Silicon Graphics	All ship with multicast	

There is an interested group at DEC that may get the software running on newer DEC systems with Ultrix and OSF/1. Also, some people have asked about support for the RS-6000 and AIX or other platforms. Those interested could use the mbone list to coordinate collaboration on porting the software to these platforms!

An alternative to running mrouted is to run the experimental MOSPF software in a Proteon router (see MOSPF question that follows).

What documentation is available?

Documentation on the IP multicast software is included in the distribution on gregorio.stanford.edu, such as the README file (ftp://gregorio.stanford.edu/vmtp-ip/ipmulticast.README). A more up-to-date version is at http://www.research.att.com/ipmulticast.README. New RFC1112 specifies the "Host Extensions for IP Multicasting."

Multicast routing algorithms are described in the paper "Multicast Routing in Internetworks and Extended LANs" by S. Deering, in the Proceedings of the ACM SIGCOMM '88 Conference. His dissertation, "Multicast Routing in a Datagram Network," is available at ftp://gregorio.stanford.edu/vmtp-ip/.

There is an article in the June 1992 ConneXions about the first IETF audiocast from San Diego, and a later version of that article is in the July 1992 ACM SIGCOMM CCR. A reprint of the latter article is available by anonymous FTP from `ftp://venera.isi.edu/pub/ietf-audiocast-article.ps`.

Where can I get a map of the MBONE?

A small and large map are available at `ftp://parcftp.xerox.com/pub/net-research/mbone-map-small.ps` and `ftp://parcftp.xerox.com/pub/net-research/mbone-map-big.ps`, respectively. The small one fits on one page and the big one is four pages that have to be taped together for viewing. This map is produced from topology information collected automatically from all MBONE nodes running the up-to-date release of the mrouted program (some are not yet updated, so links beyond them cannot be seen). Pavel Curtis at Xerox PARC has added the mechanisms to automatically collect the map data and produce the map. (Thanks also to Paul Zawada of NCSA, who manually produced an earlier map of the MBONE.)

What is DVMRP?

DVMRP is the Distance Vector Multicast Routing Protocol; it is the routing protocol implemented by the mrouted program. An earlier version of DVMRP is specified in RFC-1075. However, the version implemented in mrouted is quite a bit different from what is specified in that RFC (different packet format, different tunnel format, additional packet types, and more). It maintains topological knowledge via a distance-vector routing protocol (like RIP, described in RFC-1058), upon which it implements a multicast forwarding algorithm called Truncated Reverse Path Broadcasting. DVMRP suffers from the well-known scaling problems of any distance-vector routing protocol.

What is MOSPF?

MOSPF is the IP multicast extension to the OSPF routing protocol, currently an Internet Draft. John Moy has implemented MOSPF for the Proteon router. A network of routers running MOSPF can forward IP multicast packets directly, sending no more than one copy over any link, and without the need for any tunnels. This is how IP multicasting within a domain is supposed to work.

Can MOSPF and DVMRP interoperate?

At the Boston IETF, John Moy agreed to add support for DVMRP to his MOSPF implementation. He hopes to have this completed "well in advance of the next IETF."

When it is finished, you will be able to set up a DVMRP tunnel from an mrouted to a Proteon router, glueing together the DVMRP with MOSPF domains (the MOSPF domains will look pretty much like ethernets to the multicast topology).

The advantages to linking DVMRP with MOSPF are fewer configured tunnels and less multicast traffic on the links inside the MOSPF domain. There are also a couple potential drawbacks: increasing the size of DVMRP routing messages and increasing the number of external routes in the OSPF systems. However, it should be possible to alleviate these drawbacks by configuring area address ranges and by judicious use of MOSPF default routing.

How is a tunnel configured?

mrouted automatically configures itself to forward on all multicast-capable interfaces, i.e., interfaces that have the IFF_MULTICAST flag set (excluding the loopback "interface"), and it finds other mrouteds directly reachable via those interfaces. To override the default configuration, or to add tunnel links to other mrouteds, configuration commands may be placed in /etc/mrouted.conf. There are two types of configuration command:

```
phyint    [disable]  [metric ] [threshold ]
tunnel    [metric ] [threshold ]
```

The phyint command can be used to disable multicast routing on the physical interface identified by local IP address, or to associate a non-default metric or threshold with the specified physical interface. phyint commands should precede tunnel commands.

The tunnel command can be used to establish a tunnel link between local IP address and remote IP address, and to associate a non-default metric or threshold with that tunnel. The tunnel must be set up in the mrouted.conf files of both ends before it will be used. The keyword "srcrt" can be added just before the keyword "metric" to choose source routing for the tunnel if necessary because the other end has not yet upgraded to use IP encapsulation. Upgrading is highly encouraged. If the methods don't match at the two ends, the tunnel will appear to be up according to mrouted typeouts, but no multicast packets will flow.

The metric is the "cost" associated with sending a datagram on the given interface or tunnel; it may be used to influence the choice of routes. The metric defaults to 1. Metrics should be kept as small as possible, because mrouted cannot route along paths with a sum of metrics greater than 31. When in doubt, the following metrics are recommended:

✦ LAN, or tunnel across a single LAN: 1

✦ Any subtree with only one connection point: 1

✦ Serial link, or tunnel across a single serial link: 1

✦ Multi-hop tunnel: 2 or 3

✦ Backup tunnels: sum of metrics on primary path + 1

The threshold is the minimum IP time-to-live required for a multicast datagram to be forwarded to the given interface or tunnel. It is used to control the scope of multicast datagrams. (The TTL of forwarded packets is only compared to the threshold, it is not decremented by the threshold. Every multicast router decrements the TTL by 1.) The default threshold is 1.

Since the multicast routing protocol implemented by mrouted does not yet prune the multicast delivery trees based on group membership (it does something called "truncated broadcast," in which it prunes only the leaf subnets off the broadcast trees), we instead use a kludge known as "TTL thresholds" to prevent multicasts from traveling along unwanted branches. This is NOT the way IP multicast is supposed to work; MOSPF does it right, and mrouted will do it right some day.

Before the November 1992 IETF, we established the following thresholds (see Table C-2). The "TTL" column specifies the originating IP time-to-live value to be used by each application. The "Thresh" column specifies the mrouted threshold required to permit passage of packets from the corresponding application, as well as packets from all applications above it in the table:

Table C-2 Time-to-live and Thresh Values for Various Applications		
	TTL	Thresh
IETF chan 1 low-rate GSM audio	255	224
IETF chan 2 low-rate GSM audio	223	192
IETF chan 1 PCM audio	191	160
IETF chan 2 PCM audio	159	128
IETF chan 1 video	127	96
IETF chan 2 video	95	64
local event audio	63	32
local event video	31	1

It is suggested that a threshold of 128 be used initially, and then raise it to 160 or 192 only if the 64 Kbps voice is excessive (GSM voice is about 18 Kbps), or lower it to 64 to allow video to be transmitted to the tunnel.

mrouted will not initiate execution if it has fewer than two enabled vifs, where a vif (virtual interface) is either a physical multicast-capable interface or a tunnel. It will log a warning if all of its vifs are tunnels, based on the reasoning that such an mrouted configuration would be better replaced by more direct tunnels (i.e., eliminate the middle man). However, to create a hierarchical fanout for the MBONE, we will have mrouted configurations that consist only of tunnels.

Once you have edited the mrouted.conf file, you must run mrouted as root. See ipmulticast.README for more information.

Are there security risks?

Security risks depend on the application. Most MBONE applications cannot be coaxed into writing to disk by arriving packets; they also do not run set-uid. One possible exception might be the LBL whiteboard, wb, since it contains a PostScript interpreter. As with any network application, it is possible for users to pick up an attractive-looking multicast application that acts as a Trojan horse or virus. Currently, all MBONE applications use UDP. While only machines that subscribe to a particular multicast address will receive multicast packets, multicast is at the IP layer and thus all UDP packets arriving with a given destination address will be accepted by the kernel. As an example, a host receiving audio on port 3456 at a certain multicast address will also unwittingly receive (possibly malicious) NFS packets sent to the same multicast address and different port.

Thus, any filtering routers have to inspect the UDP payload within the IP-over-IP packet for unwanted UDP ports or non-UDP protocols. If a tunnel crosses a protection boundary, IGMP packets (protocol 2) and IP-in-IP (protocol 4) traverse the tunnel. Since IGMP is separate from regular routing, external users cannot influence the internal routing of unicast packets. Sites that restrict incoming TCP and UDP traffic should be aware that MBONE traffic, without any action by internal users, may impose additional load on the network and thus impair the working of the internal network until the appropriate mrouted daemons are terminated.

How can I find out about teleconference events?

Many of the audio and video transmissions over the MBONE are advertised in "sd," the session directory tool developed by Van Jacobson at LBL. Session creators specify all the address parameters necessary to join the session, then sd multicasts the advertisement to be picked up by anyone else running sd. The audio and video programs can be invoked with the right parameters by clicking a button in sd. From `ftp.ee.lbl.gov`, get the file sd.tar.Z or sgi-sd.tar.Z or dec-sd.tar.Z.

Schedules for IETF audio/videocasts and some other events are announced on the IETF mailing list (send a message to `ietf-request@cnri.reston.va.us` to join). Some events are also announced on the rem-conf mailing list, along with discussions of protocols for remote conferencing (send a message to `rem-conf-request@es.net` to join).

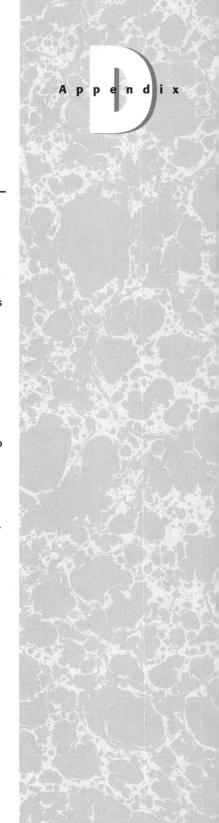

Getting the Software

In this appendix, you find where and how to get the software you need to participate in MBONE events. Some guidelines and recommendations are also presented. As a convention, I consider the default way of retrieving software to be anonymous FTP. Anonymous FTP is a way to exchange files on the Internet that doesn't require an account on the remote FTP site. You simply use your FTP software to connect to the remote site and log in as either ANONYMOUS or FTP.

Most filenames have a .Z ending. These have to be uncompressed with the UNIX uncompress utility that comes with every UNIX operating system.

Some of the files end with .gz. These files are gunzip files. Gunzip (or gzip used with the -c flag) is required to uncompress these package files. The gunzip (or gzip) software can be obtained from `prep.ai.mit.edu` in `/pub/gnu`. The file to get is gzip-1.2.4.tar.

Files with the extension .tar.z or .tar.gz need to be untarred after they have been uncompressed with gzip -c or the UNIX uncompress utlity. To untar these files, use the tar utility, which comes with all UNIX systems.

Multicast Router Software

UNIX platforms

If you choose to use your router (Cisco, Proteon, and so on) to route multicast traffic, I suggest you contact your vendor. It probably has a version of the router software that supports multicast routing.

As a rule of thumb, avoid versions of mrouted that are under version 3.3. Get the highest possible version number, the current version being 3.8. Currently, mrouted is available for UNIX platforms only. The software can be obtained from `parcftp.xerox.com` in the `/pub/net-research/ipmulti/` directory. The files in this directory have the form ipmulti*-*.tar.Z, where the first star represents a version of ipmulti and the second star represents an operating system version (example: sunos41x).

The ipmulti software comes in two parts, the kernel patches and the multicast router software. The kernel patches allow your machine to support the right level of multicast for doing multicast routing. If you are unsure how to install the patches, ask your favorite UNIX system administrator. The multicast router software in the ipmulti package is not the latest version, and I recommend that you also get the latest mrouted package from that same site and directory. The mrouted packages are named mrouted3.8-*.tar.Z, where the * represents an operating system name and version.

Note

You still may have to get this software if you plan to use a UNIX machine to run your MBONE desktop applications. For your UNIX machine to be able to use these applications, it must have the multicast host extensions. Currently, Solaris 2.*, Irix, FreeBSD, NeXTStep 3.3, and a number of other flavors of UNIX have these extensions already, and the ipmulti software is not needed.

Microsoft Windows

Microsoft has announced support for multicast in Windows NT and Windows 95. Multicast is also available in TCP/IP-32 for Windows for Workgroups, PC/TCP (TCP Software) 3.2, and more. Unfortunately, no MBONE applications that would use multicast are yet available for Windows, although some are under development in Singapore. However, using these applications in unicast mode may be possible.

The most certain way for Windows users to use the MBONE is to set a CU-SeeMe reflector and use the Cu-SeeMe application. The reflector and the application are available at `gated.cornell.edu` via FTP in the `/pub/video/` directory. The files are named PC.CU-SeeMe*, where the star represents a version number.

Macintosh

The Macintosh operating system 7.5.2 and more include OpenTransport TCP/IP, which supports multicast.

Again, like Windows systems, there is no real way for Macs to use multicast yet due to the lack of desktop applications. Maven (an audio tool) allows you to listen to some MBONE events but does not give you video. If you want to give it a try, Maven can be found at `k12.cnidr.org` under `/pub/Mac/Dir-Soundstuff/`. The files are named Maven-*.sea.bin, where the star represents a version number. Maven has some degree of interoperability with VAT.

The CU-SeeMe reflector and tool can be obtained from gated.cornell.edu in the /pub/video/ directory. The files are named MAC.CU-SeeMe*, where the star represents a version number.

MBONE Applications and Tools for UNIX

These tools and applications allow you to participate in MBONE events using UNIX platforms:

✦ **SD** (Session Directory). SD is getting obsolete but is production quality. I suggest that you get it in case you run into problems with the session directory tool I recommend (SDR).

SD can be obtained at ftp.ee.lbl.gov under /conferencing/sd/, and the files are named *.tar.Z, where the star represents an operating system name. Documentation relative to installation is included.

✦ **SDR** (Session Directory). This is the one I recommend, but it is only an alpha release and may have a few bugs.

SDR is available at bells.cs.ucl.ac.uk in /mice/sdr, and the file is named sdr.*.V2.1a8.gz, where the star represents an operating system name and number.

✦ **MMCC** (Session Directory, an alternate one). MMCC is stored at ftp.isi.edu in /confctrl/mmcc/, and the files are named mmcc-*.tar.Z, where the represents an operating system name.

✦ **VAT** (Audio Tool, I recommend this one). Vat can be obtained from ftp.ee.lbl.gov in /conferencing/vat/, and the files are named *.tar.Z, where the star represents an operating system name. The file contains documentation relative to installation.

✦ **NEVOT** (Audio tool, an alternate one). NEVOT can be obtained from gaia.cs.umass.edu in /pub/hgschulz/nevot/. The files are named nevot-3.32-*.tar.gz, where the star represents an operating system name.

✦ **NV** (Video tool, one of two that are mandatory). NV is available at parcftp.xerox.com in /pub/net-research/nv-3.3beta. The files are named nvbin-*, where the star represents an operating system name and version number. The file contains documentation relative to installation.

✦ **VIC** (Video tool, the second that is mandatory). VIC is available at ftp.ee.lbl.gov in /conferencing/vat/. The files are named *-vicbin-2.6.tar.Z, where the star represents an operating system name. The file contains documentation relative to installation.

✦ **IVS** (Video tool, an alternate one). IVS can be obtained from zenon.inria.fr in /rodeo/ivs/last_version/. The files are named Ivs3.5-*.Tar.Gz, where the star represents a version number, an operating system name.

✦ **WB** (Whiteboard, the only one that exists). WB is available at `ftp.ee.lbl.gov` `/conferencing/wb/`. The files are named *-wb-1.59.tar.Z, where the star represents an operating system version name.

✦ **IMM** (Image downloader). IMM is stored at `ftp.hawaii.edu` in `/paccom` `/imm-3.3/`. The files are named imm-*.tar.Z, where the star represents an operating system name.

✦ **RAT** (Audio tool, an alternate one). RAT is available at `bells.cs.ucl.ac.uk` in `/mice/rat`. The files are named rat-2.0a2.*.tar.gz where the star represents an operating system name.

✦ **MUMBLE** (Text tool). MUMBLE is available at these two sites in the same directory: `ftp.denet.dk` and `bells.cs.ucl.ac.uk` in `/pub/videoconference/` `mumble`. The files are named mumble_*.tar.gz, where the star represents an operating system name.

The following are MBONE management tools:

✦ **Traceroute.** Traceroute comes with most flavors of UNIX. You can get traceroute for Solaris 2.* from `opcom.sun.ca` in `/tars/`, and the file to get is traceroute.sol2.tar.gz.

Traceroute for Linux can be obtained from `ftp.funet.fi` in `/pub/Linux/` `kernel/src/`. The file to get is named traceroute.

✦ **Mtrace.** Mtrace comes with the mrouted 3.8 package. See the "Multicast Router Software" part of this appendix.

✦ **Netstat.** Netstat comes with every flavor of UNIX.

✦ **Mlisten and mprocess.** Mlisten and mprocess are two special cases. They can't be obtained from FTP, but they can be downloaded from a Web site. A Web browser is required, but it doesn't need to be a graphical one. Go to `http://` `www.cc.gatech.edu/computing/Telecomm/mbone/`.

You will be presented with the latest mlisten and mprocess news. The Web page contains a few more links to other documents, two of which contain mlisten and mprocess.

✦ **Mrinfo.** Mrinfo comes with the mrouted 3.8 package. See the "Multicast Router Software" part of this appendix.

For More Information

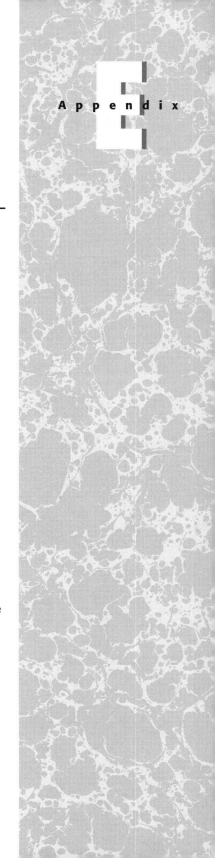

I f you want to get more information about the MBONE, here are some places to have a look at via FTP, the World Wide Web, and e-mail:

Via FTP

You can get the usenix-slides.ps.Z document from `ftp.isi.edu` in `/mbone`. This document is a collection of slides that Stephen Casner presented at USENIX and LISA conferences. There is a great deal of information in there.

From the same site and directory, you can get MBONE FAQs. This document answers the most common questions encountered by MBONE users.

RFC's 1112 (Hosts extensions for IP multicasting) and 1075 (DVMRP) can be obtained from the Internet. These are the technical explanations of how some parts of the MBONE work and can be found at `nic.ddn.mil` in `/pub/rfc/`. The filenames are rfc1112.txt and rfc1075.txt.

A nice article written by Stephen Casnet and Steve Deering can be obtained from `venera.isi.edu` in `/pub/`. The name of the file is ietf-audiocast-article.ps.

Via the World Wide Web

A very good starting point for learning more about the MBONE and easily retrieving MBONE software is `http://www.eit.com/techinfo/MBone/`. This page has many links to various MBONE resources.

Via E-Mail

Of course, sending mail to `mbone@isi.edu` and/or `rem-conf@es.net` is a very good source of information. People on these lists include those who develop the MBONE, and everyone on these lists is friendly.

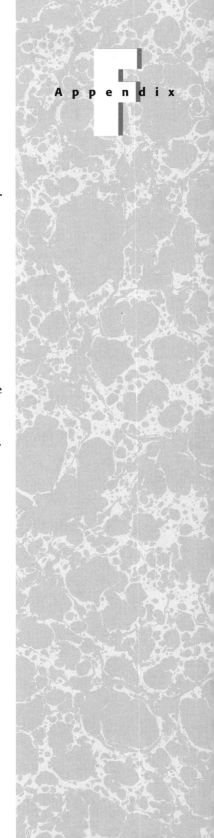
CU-SeeMe
Configuration File

This is the CU-SeeMe configuration file for the CU-SeeMe reflector that has been used for the Saint John String Quartet MBONE event (see Chapter 8). The CU-SeeMe reflector comes with an example configuration file that is very well explained and even if this example will help you, it doesn't explain everything.

For making this config file, the people at Cornell have proved to be very useful and friendly. The reflector also comes with a big README file that explains all the various parameters you can use in the config file.

The rest deals with just running the reflector itself, grabbing a CU-SeeMe client (see Appendix A) and connecting to it from your PC running Windows or your Mac. This is, in my opinion, the best and the easiest way for your PC and Mac users to enjoy the MBONE.

Thanks to Dwight Spencer from the University of New-Brunswick for providing me with this configuration file.

The following code is an example of a CU-SeeMe configuration file:

```
;  ADMIT-BCC-CLIENT ip-address
;       cause reflector to send a blind carbon
;       copy of all
;       streams to another reflector
ADMIT-BCC-CLIENT  131.202.70.81

;  NV-MC-PORT port-num   UDP port number to
;       communicate with nv via multicast
NV-MC-PORT 55842
```

```
;       ttl and multicast addr for sending CU-SeeMe video
;       to  nv via Mbone.  If NV-MC-IN and OUT are both
;       specified, multicast address must be identical.
NV-MC-OUT 127 224.2.158.58

; VAT-MC-PORT port UDP port number to communcicate with vat via
;       multicast
VAT-MC-PORT 43080

; VAT-MC-IN multicast-addr
;  multicast addr for receiving vat audio from mbone
VAT-MC-IN 224.2.158.58

; VAT-MC-OUT ttl multicast-addr
;        ttl and multicast addr for sending audio to vat via
;        Mbone.  If VAT-MC-IN and OUT are both
;        specified, multicast address must be identical.
VAT-MC-OUT 127 224.2.158.58

; VAT-CONF-ID id          conference id to use with vat
VAT-CONF-ID 4192


;
********************************************************************************
;                         START CONFIGURATION
;
********************************************************************************

MOTD
    CU-SeeMe for University of New Brunswick, Version 4.00B3
       Providing CUSM services to the UNB Community
//

; Specify your conference manager machine
CONF-MGR 131.202.3.18

; Name the machine where we can run refmon
REFMON 131.202.3.18

CONF-ID 0 We are using a conference ID of 0, please change your
       conference id.
//

CAP 80 1 Max transmission exceeds limit of 80 Kbits/sec. No
       reconnect for 1 minute.
//
;
;
```

```
MAX-PARTICIPANTS 20 Maximum participants. Please try your CUSM
      client on cspace.unb.ca
//

MAX-SENDERS 15 Maximum senders. Please try your CUSM client on
      cspace.unb.ca
//

; can keep this sort of low, to keep bandwidth down
MAX-LURKERS 20 Maximum lurkers. Please try your CUSM client on
      cspace.unb.ca
//
```

Index

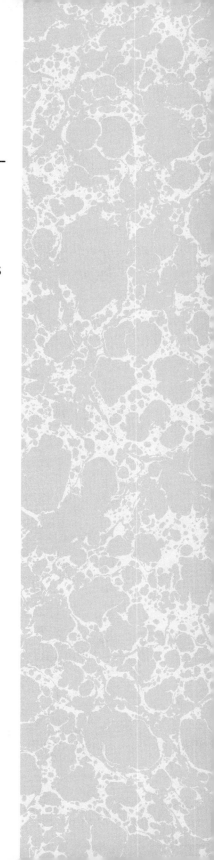

(continued)

(continued)

✦ S ✦

✦ T ✦

✦ U ✦

Title	Author	ISBN	Price
The Internet For Macs® For Dummies® 2nd Edition	by Charles Seiter	ISBN: 1-56884-371-2	$19.99 USA/$26.99 Canada
The Internet For Macs® For Dummies® Starter Kit	by Charles Seiter	ISBN: 1-56884-244-9	$29.99 USA/$39.99 Canada
The Internet For Macs® For Dummies® Starter Kit Bestseller Edition	by Charles Seiter	ISBN: 1-56884-245-7	$39.99 USA/$54.99 Canada
The Internet For Windows® For Dummies® Starter Kit	by John R. Levine & Margaret Levine Young	ISBN: 1-56884-237-6	$34.99 USA/$44.99 Canada
The Internet For Windows® For Dummies® Starter Kit, Bestseller Edition	by John R. Levine & Margaret Levine Young	ISBN: 1-56884-246-5	$39.99 USA/$54.99 Canada

MACINTOSH

Mac® Programming For Dummies®	by Dan Parks Sydow	ISBN: 1-56884-173-6	$19.95 USA/$26.95 Canada
Macintosh® System 7.5 For Dummies®	by Bob LeVitus	ISBN: 1-56884-197-3	$19.95 USA/$26.95 Canada
MORE Macs® For Dummies®	by David Pogue	ISBN: 1-56884-087-X	$19.95 USA/$26.95 Canada
PageMaker 5 For Macs® For Dummies®	by Galen Gruman & Deke McClelland	ISBN: 1-56884-178-7	$19.95 USA/$26.95 Canada
QuarkXPress 3.3 For Dummies®	by Galen Gruman & Barbara Assadi	ISBN: 1-56884-217-1	$19.99 USA/$26.99 Canada
Upgrading and Fixing Macs® For Dummies®	by Kearney Rietmann & Frank Higgins	ISBN: 1-56884-189-2	$19.95 USA/$26.95 Canada

MULTIMEDIA

Multimedia & CD-ROMs For Dummies® 2nd Edition	by Andy Rathbone	ISBN: 1-56884-907-9	$19.99 USA/$26.99 Canada
Multimedia & CD-ROMs For Dummies® Interactive Multimedia Value Pack, 2nd Edition	by Andy Rathbone	ISBN: 1-56884-909-5	$29.99 USA/$39.99 Canada

OPERATING SYSTEMS:

DOS

MORE DOS For Dummies®	by Dan Gookin	ISBN: 1-56884-046-2	$19.95 USA/$26.95 Canada
OS/2® Warp For Dummies® 2nd Edition	by Andy Rathbone	ISBN: 1-56884-205-8	$19.99 USA/$26.99 Canada

UNIX

MORE UNIX® For Dummies®	by John R. Levine & Margaret Levine Young	ISBN: 1-56884-361-5	$19.99 USA/$26.99 Canada
UNIX® For Dummies®	by John R. Levine & Margaret Levine Young	ISBN: 1-878058-58-4	$19.95 USA/$26.95 Canada

WINDOWS

MORE Windows® For Dummies® 2nd Edition	by Andy Rathbone	ISBN: 1-56884-048-9	$19.95 USA/$26.95 Canada
Windows® 95 For Dummies®	by Andy Rathbone	ISBN: 1-56884-240-6	$19.99 USA/$26.99 Canada

PCS/HARDWARE

Illustrated Computer Dictionary For Dummies® 2nd Edition	by Dan Gookin & Wallace Wang	ISBN: 1-56884-218-X	$12.95 USA/$16.95 Canada
Upgrading and Fixing PCs For Dummies® 2nd Edition	by Andy Rathbone	ISBN: 1-56884-903-6	$19.99 USA/$26.99 Canada

PRESENTATION/AUTOCAD

AutoCAD For Dummies®	by Bud Smith	ISBN: 1-56884-191-4	$19.95 USA/$26.95 Canada
PowerPoint 4 For Windows® For Dummies®	by Doug Lowe	ISBN: 1-56884-161-2	$16.99 USA/$22.99 Canada

PROGRAMMING

Borland C++ For Dummies®	by Michael Hyman	ISBN: 1-56884-162-0	$19.95 USA/$26.95 Canada
C For Dummies® Volume 1	by Dan Gookin	ISBN: 1-878058-78-9	$19.95 USA/$26.95 Canada
C++ For Dummies®	by Stephen R. Davis	ISBN: 1-56884-163-9	$19.95 USA/$26.95 Canada
Delphi Programming For Dummies®	by Neil Rubenking	ISBN: 1-56884-200-7	$19.99 USA/$26.99 Canada
Mac® Programming For Dummies®	by Dan Parks Sydow	ISBN: 1-56884-173-6	$19.95 USA/$26.95 Canada
PowerBuilder 4 Programming For Dummies®	by Ted Coombs & Jason Coombs	ISBN: 1-56884-325-9	$19.99 USA/$26.99 Canada
QBasic Programming For Dummies®	by Douglas Hergert	ISBN: 1-56884-093-4	$19.95 USA/$26.95 Canada
Visual Basic 3 For Dummies®	by Wallace Wang	ISBN: 1-56884-076-4	$19.95 USA/$26.95 Canada
Visual Basic "X" For Dummies®	by Wallace Wang	ISBN: 1-56884-230-9	$19.99 USA/$26.99 Canada
Visual C++ 2 For Dummies®	by Michael Hyman & Bob Arnson	ISBN: 1-56884-328-3	$19.99 USA/$26.99 Canada
Windows® 95 Programming For Dummies®	by S. Randy Davis	ISBN: 1-56884-327-5	$19.99 USA/$26.99 Canada

SPREADSHEET

1-2-3 For Dummies®	by Greg Harvey	ISBN: 1-878058-60-6	$16.95 USA/$22.95 Canada
1-2-3 For Windows® 5 For Dummies® 2nd Edition	by John Walkenbach	ISBN: 1-56884-216-3	$16.95 USA/$22.95 Canada
Excel 5 For Macs® For Dummies®	by Greg Harvey	ISBN: 1-56884-186-8	$19.95 USA/$26.95 Canada
Excel For Dummies® 2nd Edition	by Greg Harvey	ISBN: 1-56884-050-0	$16.95 USA/$22.95 Canada
MORE 1-2-3 For DOS For Dummies®	by John Weingarten	ISBN: 1-56884-224-4	$19.99 USA/$26.99 Canada
MORE Excel 5 For Windows® For Dummies®	by Greg Harvey	ISBN: 1-56884-207-4	$19.95 USA/$26.95 Canada
Quattro Pro 6 For Windows® For Dummies®	by John Walkenbach	ISBN: 1-56884-174-4	$19.95 USA/$26.95 Canada
Quattro Pro For DOS For Dummies®	by John Walkenbach	ISBN: 1-56884-023-3	$16.95 USA/$22.95 Canada

UTILITIES

Title	Author	ISBN	Price
Norton Utilities 8 For Dummies®	by Beth Slick	ISBN: 1-56884-166-3	$19.95 USA/$26.95 Canada

VCRS/CAMCORDERS

Title	Author	ISBN	Price
VCRs & Camcorders For Dummies™	by Gordon McComb & Andy Rathbone	ISBN: 1-56884-229-5	$14.99 USA/$20.99 Canada

WORD PROCESSING

Ami Pro For Dummies®	by Jim Meade	ISBN: 1-56884-049-7	$19.95 USA/$26.95 Canada
MORE Word For Windows® 6 For Dummies®	by Doug Lowe	ISBN: 1-56884-165-5	$19.95 USA/$26.95 Canada
MORE WordPerfect® 6 For Windows® For Dummies®	by Margaret Levine Young & David C. Kay	ISBN: 1-56884-206-6	$19.95 USA/$26.95 Canada
MORE WordPerfect® 6 For DOS For Dummies®	by Wallace Wang, edited by Dan Gookin	ISBN: 1-56884-047-0	$19.95 USA/$26.95 Canada
Word 6 For Macs® For Dummies®	by Dan Gookin	ISBN: 1-56884-190-6	$19.95 USA/$26.95 Canada
Word For Windows® 6 For Dummies®	by Dan Gookin	ISBN: 1-56884-075-6	$16.95 USA/$22.95 Canada
Word For Windows® For Dummies®	by Dan Gookin & Ray Werner	ISBN: 1-878058-86-X	$16.95 USA/$22.95 Canada
WordPerfect® 6 For DOS For Dummies®	by Dan Gookin	ISBN: 1-878058-77-0	$16.95 USA/$22.95 Canada
WordPerfect® 6.1 For Windows® For Dummies® 2nd Edition	by Margaret Levine Young & David Kay	ISBN: 1-56884-243-0	$16.95 USA/$22.95 Canada
WordPerfect® For Dummies®	by Dan Gookin	ISBN: 1-878058-52-5	$16.95 USA/$22.95 Canada

Fun, Fast, & Cheap!™

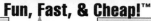

The Internet For Macs® For Dummies® Quick Reference
by Charles Seiter

ISBN:1-56884-967-2
$9.99 USA/$12.99 Canada

Windows® 95 For Dummies® Quick Reference
by Greg Harvey

ISBN: 1-56884-964-8
$9.99 USA/$12.99 Canada

Photoshop 3 For Macs® For Dummies® Quick Reference
by Deke McClelland

ISBN: 1-56884-968-0
$9.99 USA/$12.99 Canada

WordPerfect® For DOS For Dummies® Quick Reference
by Greg Harvey

ISBN: 1-56884-009-8
$8.95 USA/$12.95 Canada

Title	Author	ISBN	Price
DATABASE			
Access 2 For Dummies® Quick Reference	by Stuart J. Stuple	ISBN: 1-56884-167-1	$8.95 USA/$11.95 Canada
dBASE 5 For DOS For Dummies® Quick Reference	by Barrie Sosinsky	ISBN: 1-56884-954-0	$9.99 USA/$12.99 Canada
dBASE 5 For Windows® For Dummies® Quick Reference	by Stuart J. Stuple	ISBN: 1-56884-953-2	$9.99 USA/$12.99 Canada
Paradox 5 For Windows® For Dummies® Quick Reference	by Scott Palmer	ISBN: 1-56884-960-5	$9.99 USA/$12.99 Canada
DESKTOP PUBLISHING/ILLUSTRATION/GRAPHICS			
CorelDRAW! 5 For Dummies® Quick Reference	by Raymond E. Werner	ISBN: 1-56884-952-4	$9.99 USA/$12.99 Canada
Harvard Graphics For Windows® For Dummies® Quick Reference	by Raymond E. Werner	ISBN: 1-56884-962-1	$9.99 USA/$12.99 Canada
Photoshop 3 For Macs® For Dummies® Quick Reference	by Deke McClelland	ISBN: 1-56884-968-0	$9.99 USA/$12.99 Canada
FINANCE/PERSONAL FINANCE			
Quicken 4 For Windows® For Dummies® Quick Reference	by Stephen L. Nelson	ISBN: 1-56884-950-8	$9.95 USA/$12.95 Canada
GROUPWARE/INTEGRATED			
Microsoft® Office 4 For Windows® For Dummies® Quick Reference	by Doug Lowe	ISBN: 1-56884-958-3	$9.99 USA/$12.99 Canada
Microsoft® Works 3 For Windows® For Dummies® Quick Reference	by Michael Partington	ISBN: 1-56884-959-1	$9.99 USA/$12.99 Canada
INTERNET/COMMUNICATIONS/NETWORKING			
The Internet For Dummies® Quick Reference	by John R. Levine & Margaret Levine Young	ISBN: 1-56884-168-X	$8.95 USA/$11.95 Canada
MACINTOSH			
Macintosh® System 7.5 For Dummies® Quick Reference	by Stuart J. Stuple	ISBN: 1-56884-956-7	$9.99 USA/$12.99 Canada
OPERATING SYSTEMS:			
DOS			
DOS For Dummies® Quick Reference	by Greg Harvey	ISBN: 1-56884-007-1	$8.95 USA/$11.95 Canada
UNIX			
UNIX® For Dummies® Quick Reference	by John R. Levine & Margaret Levine Young	ISBN: 1-56884-094-2	$8.95 USA/$11.95 Canada
WINDOWS			
Windows® 3.1 For Dummies® Quick Reference, 2nd Edition	by Greg Harvey	ISBN: 1-56884-951-6	$8.95 USA/$11.95 Canada
PCs/HARDWARE			
Memory Management For Dummies® Quick Reference	by Doug Lowe	ISBN: 1-56884-362-3	$9.99 USA/$12.99 Canada
PRESENTATION/AUTOCAD			
AutoCAD For Dummies® Quick Reference	by Ellen Finkelstein	ISBN: 1-56884-198-1	$9.95 USA/$12.95 Canada
SPREADSHEET			
1-2-3 For Dummies® Quick Reference	by John Walkenbach	ISBN: 1-56884-027-6	$8.95 USA/$11.95 Canada
1-2-3 For Windows® 5 For Dummies® Quick Reference	by John Walkenbach	ISBN: 1-56884-957-5	$9.95 USA/$12.95 Canada
Excel For Windows® For Dummies® Quick Reference, 2nd Edition	by John Walkenbach	ISBN: 1-56884-096-9	$8.95 USA/$11.95 Canada
Quattro Pro 6 For Windows® For Dummies® Quick Reference	by Stuart J. Stuple	ISBN: 1-56884-172-8	$9.95 USA/$12.95 Canada
WORD PROCESSING			
Word For Windows® 6 For Dummies® Quick Reference	by George Lynch	ISBN: 1-56884-095-0	$8.95 USA/$11.95 Canada
Word For Windows® For Dummies® Quick Reference	by George Lynch	ISBN: 1-56884-029-2	$8.95 USA/$11.95 Canada
WordPerfect® 6.1 For Windows® For Dummies® Quick Reference, 2nd Edition	by Greg Harvey	ISBN: 1-56884-966-4	$9.99 USA/$12.99/Canada

"A lot easier to use than the book Excel gives you!"

Lisa Schmeckpeper, New Berlin, WI, on PC World Excel 5 For Windows Handbook

**Official Hayes Modem
Communications
Companion**
by Caroline M. Halliday

ISBN: 1-56884-072-1
$29.95 USA/$39.95 Canada
Includes software.

**1,001 Komputer Answers
from Kim Komando**
by Kim Komando

ISBN: 1-56884-460-3
$29.99 USA/$39.99 Canada
Includes software.

**PC World DOS 6
Handbook, 2nd Edition**
*by John Socha, Clint Hicks, &
Devra Hall*

ISBN: 1-878058-79-7
$34.95 USA/$44.95 Canada
Includes software.

BESTSELLER!

**PC World Word
For Windows® 6 Handbook**
*by Brent Heslop
& David Angell*

ISBN: 1-56884-054-3
$34.95 USA/$44.95 Canada
Includes software.

BESTSELLER!

**PC World Microsoft®
Access 2 Bible,
2nd Edition**
*by Cary N. Prague
& Michael R. Irwin*

ISBN: 1-56884-086-1
$39.95 USA/$52.95 Canada
Includes software.

**PC World Excel 5
For Windows® Handbook,
2nd Edition**
*by John Walkenbach
& Dave Maguiness*

ISBN: 1-56884-056-X
$34.95 USA/$44.95 Canada
Includes software.

**PC World WordPerfect® 6
Handbook**
by Greg Harvey

ISBN: 1-878058-80-0
$34.95 USA/$44.95 Canada
Includes software.

**QuarkXPress
For Windows® Designer
Handbook**
*by Barbara Assadi
& Galen Gruman*

ISBN: 1-878058-45-2
$29.95 USA/$39.95 Canada

NATIONAL
BESTSELLER!

**Official XTree
Companion, 3rd Edition**
by Beth Slick

ISBN: 1-878058-57-6
$19.95 USA/$26.95 Canada

NATIONAL
BESTSELLER!

**PC World DOS 6
Command Reference
and Problem Solver**
*by John Socha
& Devra Hall*

ISBN: 1-56884-055-1
$24.95 USA/$32.95 Canada

SUPER STAR

**Client/Server
Strategies™: A Survival
Guide for Corporate
Reengineers**
by David Vaskevitch

ISBN: 1-56884-064-0
$29.95 USA/$39.95 Canada

**"PC World Word
For Windows 6
Handbook is very
easy to follow with
lots of 'hands on'
examples. The
'Task at a Glance'
is very helpful!"**

Jacqueline Martens, Tacoma, WA

**"Thanks for publish-
ing this book! It's
the best money I've
spent this year!"**

*Robert D. Templeton,
Ft. Worth, TX, on* MORE
Windows 3.1 SECRETS

Microsoft and Windows are registered trademarks of Microsoft Corporation. WordPerfect is a registered trademark of Novell. ----STRATEGIES and the IDG Books Worldwide logos are trademarks under exclusive license to IDG Books Worldwide, Inc., from International Data Group, Inc.

r scholastic requests & educational orders please
l Educational Sales, at 1. 800. 434. 2086   **FOR MORE INFO OR TO ORDER, PLEASE CALL** ▶ **800 762 2974**   For volume discounts & special orders please call
Tony Real, Special Sales, at 415. 655. 3048

Unauthorized Windows® 95: A Developer's Guide to Exploring the Foundations of Windows "Chicago"
by Andrew Schulman

ISBN: 1-56884-169-8
$29.99 USA/$39.99 Canada

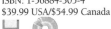

Unauthorized Windows® 95 Developer's Resource Kit
by Andrew Schulman

ISBN: 1-56884-305-4
$39.99 USA/$54.99 Canada

Best of the Net
by Seth Godin

ISBN: 1-56884-313-5
$22.99 USA/$32.99 Canada

Detour: The Truth About the Information Superhighway
by Michael Sullivan-Trainor

ISBN: 1-56884-307-0
$22.99 USA/$32.99 Canada

PowerPC Programming For Intel Programmers
by Kip McClanahan

ISBN: 1-56884-306-2
$49.99 USA/$64.99 Canada

Foundations™ of Visual C++ Programming For Windows® 95
by Paul Yao & Joseph Yao

ISBN: 1-56884-321-6
$39.99 USA/$54.99 Canada

Heavy Metal™ Visual C++ Programming
by Steve Holzner

ISBN: 1-56884-196-5
$39.95 USA/$54.95 Canada

Heavy Metal™ OLE 2.0 Programming
by Steve Holzner

ISBN: 1-56884-301-1
$39.95 USA/$54.95 Canada

Lotus Notes Application Development Handbook
by Erica Kerwien

ISBN: 1-56884-308-9
$39.99 USA/$54.99 Canada

The Internet Direct Connect Kit
by Peter John Harrison

ISBN: 1-56884-135-3
$29.95 USA/$39.95 Canada

Macworld® Ultimate Mac® Programming
by Dave Mark

ISBN: 1-56884-195-7
$39.95 USA/$54.95 Canada

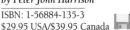

The UNIX®-Haters Handbook
by Simson Garfinkel, Daniel Weise, & Steven Strassmann

ISBN: 1-56884-203-1
$16.95 USA/$22.95 Canada

Learn C++ Today!
by Martin Rinehart

ISBN: 1-56884-310-0
34.99 USA/$44.99 Canada

Type & Learn™ C
by Tom Swan

ISBN: 1-56884-073-X
34.95 USA/$44.95 Canada

Type & Learn™ Windows® Programming
by Tom Swan

ISBN: 1-56884-071-3
34.95 USA/$44.95 Canada

IDG BOOKS WORLDWIDE REGISTRATION CARD

RETURN THIS REGISTRATION CARD FOR FREE CATALOG

Title of this book: **MBONE: Multicasting Tomorrow's Internet**

My overall rating of this book: ❑ Very good [1] ❑ Good [2] ❑ Satisfactory [3] ❑ Fair [4] ❑ Poor [5]

How I first heard about this book:

❑ Found in bookstore; name: [6]

❑ Advertisement: [8]

❑ Word of mouth; heard about book from friend, co-worker, etc.: [10]

❑ Book review: [7]

❑ Catalog: [9]

❑ Other: [11]

What I liked most about this book:

What I would change, add, delete, etc., in future editions of this book:

Other comments:

Number of computer books I purchase in a year: ❑ 1 [12] ❑ 2-5 [13] ❑ 6-10 [14] ❑ More than 10 [15]

I would characterize my computer skills as: ❑ Beginner [16] ❑ Intermediate [17] ❑ Advanced [18] ❑ Professional [19]

I use ❑ DOS [20] ❑ Windows [21] ❑ OS/2 [22] ❑ Unix [23] ❑ Macintosh [24] ❑ Other: [25]_____
(please specify)

I would be interested in new books on the following subjects:
(please check all that apply, and use the spaces provided to identify specific software)

❑ Word processing: [26]

❑ Data bases: [28]

❑ File Utilities: [30]

❑ Networking: [32]

❑ Other: [34]

❑ Spreadsheets: [27]

❑ Desktop publishing: [29]

❑ Money management: [31]

❑ Programming languages: [33]

I use a PC at (please check all that apply): ❑ home [35] ❑ work [36] ❑ school [37] ❑ other: [38] _____

The disks I prefer to use are ❑ 5.25 [39] ❑ 3.5 [40] ❑ other: [41]_____

I have a CD ROM: ❑ yes [42] ❑ no [43]

I plan to buy or upgrade computer hardware this year: ❑ yes [44] ❑ no [45]

I plan to buy or upgrade computer software this year: ❑ yes [46] ❑ no [47]

Name: _____ Business title: [48] _____ Type of Business: [49] _____

Address (❑ home [50] ❑ work [51]/Company name: _____)

Street/Suite#

City [52]/State [53]/Zipcode [54]: _____ Country [55] _____

❑ **I liked this book!** You may quote me by name in future
IDG Books Worldwide promotional materials.

My daytime phone number is _____

IDG BOOKS

THE WORLD OF COMPUTER KNOWLEDGE

❏ **YES!**

Please keep me informed about IDG's World of Computer Knowledge.
Send me the latest IDG Books catalog.